SO YOU THINK YOU'RE GOOD AT TRIVIA

PATRICK DOWNS
DEBRA WEISS

Avery Publishing Group
Garden City Park, New York

D1414102

To all the past and present members of the NTN family—
all the programmers, graphic artists, customer support folks,
shipping and receiving crew, editorial staff, marketing group,
sales force, accounting types and administrative support people
who make history every day by doing what they do
with so much dedication and enthusiasm.

And, to every single person who has participated in our products
over the years. Thanks for supporting us, we really appreciate it.

Cover Design: William Gonzalez
Typesetting: Bonnie Freid
In-House Editors: Rudy Shur and Evan Schwartz

Cataloging-in-Publication Data

Downs, Patrick
    So you think you're good at trivia : take the official NTN
trivia challenge / Patrick Downs, Debra Weiss
    p. cm.
    ISBN 0-89529-631-4

    1. Questions and answers.   I. Weiss, Debra.   II. Title.
AG195.D69 1995
                                                    793.73
                                                    QBI94-21256

Contents

Acknowledgments

Thanks go to Dan Downs for his leadership and courage in turning a vision into an industry.

Special thanks to Dan Purner, NTN's executive producer, who encourages us to do our best work. Thanks to Rudy Shur and Evan Schwartz at Avery Publishing Group for help with thrashing out the format of this book. Thanks to Barry Weiss for his technical assistance in putting our data through a virtual meat grinder to get it looking like it does in this book.

A note of thanks to team SYZYGY of New York—Selwin, Nelson, Shelly, Dennis, Gary, George, Sam, Marvin, Bernie, Evan and Rudy—for inspiring us to turn our questions into a book.

Finally, this book would not have been possible without the contributions of past and present members of the NTN writing staff, who sat in little dark rooms with reference books, ferreting out fascinating facts for your enjoyment: Abel Ramirez, Anne-Christine Walsh, Barbara Barnhill, Bill Lilley, Cambria Sherman, Charlotte Price, Currie Silver, Cynthia Long, Dean England, Denise Grace, Donna Harvey, Doug Desjardins, Elizabeth Henschel, Eric Magee, Ethan Wohl, Harry Fotinos, Ivan Harmon, Ivan Krim, Jack Smith, Janet Ratliff, Jim Yamanaka, Joan Lindroth, Joe Sprague, John Von Aspen, John Spies, Katy Benson, Keith Elsner, Ken Calhoun, Kent Harrill, Kerry O'Neal, Laura Trammel, Lee Littlewood, Louisiana Dalton, Mark Shapiro, Patricia Kittredge, Patrick Furlong, Patrick Johnston, Peggy Dean, Phil Rose, Rick Overmeer, Rob Triplett, Robert McNamara, Robert Ruffin, Scott Waszak, Sean Reilly, Stephen Johnson, Steve Waszak, Susan Wood, Ted Erdahl, Tina Houle, Tom Gentry, Tom Hall, and Tony Spies.

Preface

NTN Communications, Inc., started as a promotional idea back in the 1960's. Dan Downs, ticket manager of the Houston Oilers, and Don Klosterman, general manager, thought more folks would buy tickets to football games if all the seats in the stadium were wired so fans could call the plays on the field along with the quarterback. Investigating the feasibility of the idea proved that using then-current technology would be exorbitantly expensive, making the idea unworkable.

Good ideas have a way of sticking around, though, and the idea to develop an interactive football game began to take shape. The first version of the game, called QB1, was copyrighted in 1967.

Fast forward to the early 1980's. Dan's brother Pat Downs, former business manager of the San Diego Padres, saw advances in microelectronics and satellite technologies as the means to bring QB1 to the public. NTN Communications, Inc., was incorporated in 1983, and the founders envisioned an interactive television network beginning in the hospitality industry and then expanding into the home.

QB1 was a success right from the start. However, with seven months before the new football season started, NTN realized it needed to develop an entertainment system that could be used all year long. Enter game shows. Why not ask trivia questions and allow people to answer them?

My personal involvement with NTN begins at this point. In 1986, I was hired as a temporary word processor on a three-day assignment. In addition to doing everyone's typing, I was asked to type up trivia questions. Movie trivia. A writer by trade, a film major in college and a recent winner on a TV game show, I volunteered to do a little rewriting to "make the questions more fun." I brought in some reference books from home and got started. I had no idea that this little offer would extend my stay at NTN from three days to nine years.

All NTN players use a "handle" to identify themselves on the game scoreboards. Goofing around in the office one day, I signed on as TRVGODSS (player handles have since been shortened to six letters) and although my official title became "producer-game shows," that Triv

Goddess moniker, used in endless marketing permutations, has stuck to me ever since.

When I first started my journey at NTN, there were about fifteen subscribing locations. We were hard-pressed to broadcast three trivia games per day. Today, our network is a publicly held company trading on the American Stock Exchange (symbol: NTN) and has grown to over 2,000 subscribers across North America, Australia, and South Africa. More than eight million people participate in our products every month, and the numbers keep growing. Our programming can be found in over 250,000 hotel rooms, on cable services, in schools, and in homes via online services such as America Online, GEnie and the ImagiNation Network.

This book has been designed to be enjoyed by anyone who likes a real challenge. It includes some of the best material culled from our now vast collection of trivia questions created over the past decade, and we present it to you in a unique format. We've chosen material that will invite you to think, laugh, wonder, and learn.

We think of our product not as just a trivia game, but more of a general knowledge odyssey. We hope you'll have an interesting experience when you journey along with us. We're looking forward to sharing more of our collection in the future.

Introduction

So you think you're good at trivia? Well . . . what do humans have that clams don't? Who was king of England during World War II? How did they finally get rid of The Blob? And what the heck is Barbie's last name, anyway? Get ready to take the NTN Trivia Challenge.

You'll be playing against thousands of other people who have already taken the challenge, and you'll see their results after each question. See how you measure up!

A word of warning, though—these games can be addictive! Once you complete one game, it's nearly impossible to quit. If you finish going through this book and are craving more, help is on the way! There are over 2000 NTN locations throughout North America waiting for you to come on in and take the NTN Trivia Challenge in person. Every day, there are new questions, stiff competition and great prizes. Call **1-800-755-5459** to find the NTN location nearest you.

How to Use This Book

TYPES OF GAMES

There are three different game types. Each SHOWDOWN game is composed of thirty questions designed to test your general knowledge. The subject areas include pop culture, history, sports, nature, art, science, geography, and current events. Each TOPIX game contains 15 questions about one particular subject like dogs, cooking, or literature. Each BRAINBUSTER game contains ten real stumpers.

HOW TO PLAY

Each page is divided into five frames. Each frame is divided into two boxes. The box on the left is the question box, which includes five possible answers. The box on the right is an answer box. You'll notice that the answer has nothing to do with the question next to it. That would be too easy!!! You wanted a challenge, right?

You're going to play horizontally across pages, rather than vertically down the page. Huh? Okay, the first game begins on page 3. Start with the top frame, question 1. Ponder the question and choose your answer. Now, turn to the next odd-numbered page. This is page 5. Look at the answer box. You'll see the number of the correct answer, followed by some factual material that will either enlighten or infuriate you. You'll also be presented with a percentage. This percentage reflects the number of people who answered correctly when the question was presented on the NTN Network. How did you measure up?

Stay right where you are and play question 2 in that top frame. Turn to page 7. See if you got it right. Play question 3. Turn the page. Got it? Just keep playing and turning the page, staying in that top frame. Score one point for each question you get right. You'll play a SHOWDOWN game, then a TOPIX game, then a SHOWDOWN game, then a BRAINBUSTER game, and so on until you hit the back cover.

Now, switch to the first frame on the opposite page, and play in the top frame of all the even-numbered pages till you get back to the front of

SHOWDOWN

GAME NUMBER 1

Turn to page 3
top frame for
the first question.

SHOWDOWN

GAME NUMBER 19

Turn to page 3
second frame for
the first question.

SHOWDOWN

GAME NUMBER 37

Turn to page 3
middle frame for
the first question.

SHOWDOWN

GAME NUMBER 55

Turn to page 3
fourth frame for
the first question.

SHOWDOWN

GAME NUMBER 73

Turn to page 3
bottom frame for
the first question.

Turn to page 1 second frame and begin to play Game #19	ANSWER TO Q-30 **[5]** Crewel is a colorful type of embroidery often used for decorating clothing. 69%
Turn to page 1 middle frame and begin to play Game #37	ANSWER TO Q-30 **[5]** The last Iranian premier assassinated was Hassan Ali Mansour, who was killed in 1965. 78%
Turn to page 1 fourth frame and begin to play Game #55	ANSWER TO Q-30 **[3]** The final episode was aired in 1983. 87%
Turn to page 1 bottom frame and begin to play Game #73	ANSWER TO Q-30 **[2]** Archie Goodwin is the legman for the huge, cerebral detective. 45%
If you've enjoyed playing this book, why not go to an NTN location near you and play the Interactive version? To find the location nearest you, call 1-800-755-5459.	ANSWER TO Q-30 **[1]** A chinook describes a dry winter or spring wind that blows in the rocky mountains. 56%

1 Which is not the name of a Musketeer?	[1] D'Artagnan [2] Porthos [3] Aramis [4] Pathos [5] Athos	Turn to the top frame on the next right hand page for the correct answer and the next question.
1 Which game show features three contestants?	[1] Password [2] Joker's Wild [3] Match Game [4] Hollywood Squares [5] Wheel of Fortune	Turn to the second frame on the next right hand page for the correct answer and the next question.
1 Who was Fred Astaire's dancing and singing partner in "Easter Parade"?	[1] Ginger Rogers [2] Cyd Charisse [3] Judy Garland [4] Betty Hutton [5] Leslie Caron	Turn to the middle frame on the next right hand page for the correct answer and the next question.
1 Which battle was fought during the Korean War?	[1] Cold harbor [2] Yalu [3] Deerfield Massacre [4] Argonne-meuse [5] Bataan	Turn to the fourth frame on the next right hand page for the correct answer and the next question.
1 Which wine's name is not also the name of a type of grape?	[1] Cabernet Sauvignon [2] Chardonnay [3] Gamay [4] Chablis [5] Pinot noir	Turn to the bottom frame on the next right hand page for the correct answer and the next question.

30 What kind of tools are used in crewel work?	[1] Pen and ink [2] Metal plates [3] Acrylic crayons [4] Hammer and nails [5] Embroidery needles	ANSWER TO Q-29 [5] Capitoline is the highest of the cities seven hills. 78%
30 Which country did not have a premier assassinated in the 1980's?	[1] India [2] Sweden [3] Egypt [4] Lebanon [5] Iran	ANSWER TO Q-29 [3] They are long, narrow inlets along the coast; the name is derived from the Norse "fjord." 62%
30 What was the first TV show ever to be watched by over fifty million households?	[1] Last episode of Roots [2] Dallas's Who Shot J.R.? [3] Final M*A*S*H episode [4] PBS's Civil War series [5] Superbowl XX	ANSWER TO Q-29 [5] The modern adaptation, "Jedermann," was made by Austrian dramatist Hugo von Hofmansthal. 32%
30 Archie Goodwin is the sidekick to this Rex Stout detective:	[1] Perry Mason [2] Nero Wolfe [3] Lew Archer [4] Mike Hammer [5] Travis McGee	ANSWER TO Q-29 [1] DeLorean was acquitted on all counts because police had entrapped him, but his company was ruined. 56%
30 Which of these terms refers to a wind and a Native American tribe?	[1] Chinook [2] Mohawk [3] Pueblo [4] Apache [5] Choctaw	ANSWER TO Q-29 [2] The Native American church was founded by Navahos and 80 percent of them belong to it. 66%

4

2 Which type of beer is the darkest and strongest?

[1] Light
[2] Ale
[3] Pilsner
[4] Porter
[5] Stout

ANSWER TO Q-1

[4] Aramis, Porthos and Athos are the Three Musketeers; D'Artagnan joins them later.

57%

---

2 Dr. Faustus sells his soul to the devil in exchange for:

[1] Immortality
[2] Wealth
[3] Love
[4] Youth
[5] Knowledge and power

ANSWER TO Q-1

[5] Three contestants spin the big wheel for a chance to win cash and prizes.

81%

---

2 Comedian Paul Lynde was a regular panelist on this TV game show:

[1] Match Game
[2] Hollywood Squares
[3] What's My Line
[4] I've Got a Secret
[5] To Tell the Truth

ANSWER TO Q-1

[3] Irving Berlin composed the score for the annual favorite.

66%

---

2 Which is not a sailing tactic?

[1] Broaching
[2] Careening
[3] Reaching
[4] Tacking
[5] Trimming

ANSWER TO Q-1

[2] Macarthur's forces swept through North Korea to China, but were repulsed there by 33 divisions.

34%

---

2 In 1956, Imre Nagy led a revolt in this nation:

[1] Poland
[2] Estonia
[3] Lithuania
[4] Bulgaria
[5] Hungary

ANSWER TO Q-1

[4] French chablis is made from chardonnay grapes; California chablis is made from a blend.

45%

5

29 Capitoline Hill is the tallest hill of:	[1] Paris [2] London [3] Madrid [4] Washington, D.C. [5] Rome	ANSWER TO Q-28 **[3]** Abbreviated cwt., a hundred-weight is equal to 112 pounds in England. 45%
29 In what part of Scotland would you find natural land formations called "firths"?	[1] Mountains [2] Deserts [3] Seacoast [4] Plains [5] River beds	ANSWER TO Q-28 **[2]** Tapioca is made from the root of the manioc plant. 59%
29 The medieval morality play ___ is performed annually in the Salzburg Cathedral Square.	[1] Piers Plowman [2] Reynard the Fox [3] The Pilgrim's Progress [4] Parsifal [5] Everyman	ANSWER TO Q-28 **[4]** Lawrencium, mendelevium and rutherfordium are other elements named after individuals. 67%
29 What was gifted self-promoter and engineer John DeLorean convicted of in 1984?	[1] Nothing [2] Narcotics distribution [3] Tax evasion [4] Mail fraud [5] Embezzlement	ANSWER TO Q-28 **[5]** Agatha Christie used the rhyme with its gruesome murders in "And Then There Were None." 68%
29 Peyote is used as a sacramental food in the:	[1] Rastafarian ceremonies [2] Native American church [3] Santeria cult [4] Mormon church [5] Branch Davidian cult	ANSWER TO Q-28 **[5]** Only reproductives can mature sexually and grow into queen and king termites. 79%

3 The library at Alexandria was the most famous of antiquity. Who destroyed it?	[1] Christians [2] Greeks [3] Romans [4] Egyptians [5] Muslims	ANSWER TO Q-2 **[5]** Both stout and porter are brewed with roasted malt, but stout is darker and heavier. 67%
3 In the sentence "The fat sheriff held a smoking gun," which word is a participle?	[1] Sheriff [2] Fat [3] Smoking [4] Held [5] Gun	ANSWER TO Q-2 **[5]** The fact that he also got Helen of Troy, the world's greatest beauty, is immaterial. 45%
3 Which country is not considered a kingdom?	[1] Belgium [2] Denmark [3] Monaco [4] Saudi Arabia [5] Sweden	ANSWER TO Q-2 **[2]** Paul Lynde, who died in 1982, also appeared regularly on the 1960's comedy "Bewitched." 91%
3 Birds have two:	[1] Livers [2] Stomachs [3] Hearts [4] Brains [5] Bladders	ANSWER TO Q-2 **[2]** Boats are careened when they are turned on their side for cleaning and repairs. 45%
3 At the 1984 Olympics, Mary Lou Retton won the gold in the:	[1] Uneven bars [2] All-around gymnastics [3] Floor exercise [4] Vault [5] Balance beam	ANSWER TO Q-2 **[5]** He was later executed for his part in the revolt against Stalin. 45%

28 In the United States, a hundred-weight is equal to one hundred:

[1] Drams
[2] Ounces
[3] Pounds
[4] Tons
[5] Grams

ANSWER TO Q-27
[5] Albondigas is a popular Mexican meatball soup.
55%

---

28 All of these foods are seeds except:

[1] Rice
[2] Tapioca
[3] Corn
[4] Navy bean
[5] Peanut

ANSWER TO Q-27
[4] The novel is notorious for its sex scenes.
56%

---

28 All these famous people have elements named after them except:

[1] Alfred Nobel
[2] Pierre and Marie Curie
[3] Albert Einstein
[4] Max Planck
[5] Enrico Fermi

ANSWER TO Q-27
[3] A symphony orchestra has 22 to 26 violins, divided into two sections.
78%

---

28 In the classic rhyme "Ten Little Indians" none of the Indians:

[1] Gets shot
[2] Falls out of a canoe
[3] Kicks the bucket
[4] Breaks his neck
[5] Hangs himself

ANSWER TO Q-27
[4] Chicle, a base for making chewing gum, is actually a latex derived from this tree.
56%

---

28 Which type of insect is divided into groups of reproductives, soldiers and workers?

[1] Cricket
[2] Honeybee
[3] Praying mantis
[4] Cockroach
[5] Termite

ANSWER TO Q-27
[1] Admiral Chester Nimitz commanded the Pacific fleet throughout WWII.
54%

4 On which TV sitcom did Bob Denver play the lead role?	[1] Get Smart [2] Gilligan's Island [3] Hogan's Heroes [4] Green Acres [5] I Spy	ANSWER TO Q-3 **[5]** The caliph reasoned that all knowledge necessary to man was contained in the Koran. 34%
4 References to the occult can be found in the works of all these writers except:	[1] Rabelais [2] Shakespeare [3] Swift [4] Goethe [5] Dante	ANSWER TO Q-3 **[3]** A participle is a verb acting as an adjective. 24%
4 In which movie does Steve Martin have to share his body with Lily Tomlin?	[1] The Man with Two Brains [2] The Lonely Guy [3] L.A. Story [4] Inner Space [5] All of Me	ANSWER TO Q-3 **[3]** Monaco, like Andorra and Liechtenstein, is a principality, meaning it's ruled by a prince. 45%
4 Which verb does not mean to steal?	[1] Purloin [2] Proscribe [3] Plunder [4] Filch [5] Pilfer	ANSWER TO Q-3 **[2]** The gizzard grinds hard foods and the other stomach digests it. 67%
4 Goulash is a beef soup associated with this nation:	[1] Morocco [2] Greece [3] Israel [4] Hungary [5] Jamaica	ANSWER TO Q-3 **[2]** Mary Lou was also the first gymnast to be elected to the U.S. Olympic Hall of Fame. 66%

27 These are prepared Swedish style and are used in Mexico's albondigas soup:	[1] Cabbages [2] Sausages [3] Flounder [4] Noodles [5] Meatballs	ANSWER TO Q-26 [3] Chalcopyrite is called peacock pyrite because of its shiny iridescent qualities. 32%
27 Who wrote the novel "Fear of Flying"?	[1] Jacqueline Susann [2] Mary Gordon [3] Fay Weldon [4] Erica Jong [5] Jackie Collins	ANSWER TO Q-26 [1] The chain was founded in 1921, more than 30 years before McDonald's. 43%
27 A symphony orchestra uses more of these than any other instrument:	[1] Trumpets [2] Clarinets [3] Violins [4] Trombones [5] Cellos	ANSWER TO Q-26 [5] Among his hits are: "My Blue Heaven," "Making Whoopee" and "Yes Sir, That's My Baby." 43%
27 Which of these familiar products is derived from the Central American sapodilla tree?	[1] Chocolate [2] Pepper [3] Cinnamon [4] Chewing gum [5] Quinine	ANSWER TO Q-26 [1] This type of publication gets its name from the cheap paper which was used. 87%
27 The largest warship currently afloat is the U.S.S. Nimitz. It is named after a _____ hero.	[1] World War II [2] Revolutionary War [3] Civil War [4] Mexican War [5] Spanish-American war	ANSWER TO Q-26 [4] Often called the finest Greek sculpture, this marble piece is in the Louvre. 67%

5 He wrote such books as "The Stranger," "The Rebel" and "The Plague":	[1] Albert Camus [2] George Orwell [3] John Steinbeck [4] William Golding [5] Franz Kafka	ANSWER TO Q-4 **[2]** The name "Gilligan" was randomly chosen from the Los Angeles phone book. 91%
5 All these countries have coastline on the Arabian Sea except:	[1] Oman [2] Afghanistan [3] Pakistan [4] Iran [5] India	ANSWER TO Q-4 **[3]** It is known that Dante belonged to a secret order. Many believe the other three did as well. 23%
5 "Tin Men," "Always" and "Nuts" are films starring this actor:	[1] Robert Duvall [2] Alan Alda [3] Richard Dreyfuss [4] John Goodman [5] Danny Devito	ANSWER TO Q-4 **[5]** Lily Tomlin's character ends up in Steve Martin's body after an experiment goes awry. 92%
5 What French town was the scene of history's greatest military evacuation?	[1] Dunkirk [2] Bordeaux [3] Marseilles [4] Lyons [5] Nice	ANSWER TO Q-4 **[2]** To proscribe means to banish, outlaw or exile. 89%
5 The alcohol found in wine, beer and liquor is known as grain alcohol or:	[1] Methadone [2] Ethanol [3] Acetic acid [4] Phenol [5] Calomel	ANSWER TO Q-4 **[4]** The dish dates from the 9th century and is named after the nomadic tribes who kept oxen. 78%

26 Chalcopyrite is an important ore of:	[1] Iron [2] Steel [3] Copper [4] Silver [5] Gold	ANSWER TO Q-25 **[5]** Jeff King won in 1993, with a record time of 10 days, 15 hours and 38 minutes. 58%
26 Which fast food chain came first?	[1] White Castle [2] McDonald's [3] Dairy Queen [4] Burger King [5] Jack-in-the-Box	ANSWER TO Q-25 **[2]** Boris Pasternak wrote "Doctor Zhivago." 68%
26 Which Kahn was a songwriter for Broadway and Hollywood?	[1] Madeline [2] Kublai [3] Herman [4] Harry [5] Gustav	ANSWER TO Q-25 **[1]** Porticos are often located at the entrances of buildings. 42%
26 Conan the Barbarian, Doc Savage, and the Shadow are all heroes who first appeared in:	[1] Pulp magazines [2] Folk ballads [3] Silent movies [4] Dime novels [5] Puppet shows	ANSWER TO Q-25 **[4]** His revolutionary designs were aimed at deriving maximum output from minimum energy. 68%
26 Which famous statue is Greek?	[1] The Thinker [2] Saint Teresa [3] The Kiss [4] Victory of Samothrace [5] Adam and Eve	ANSWER TO Q-25 **[3]** The mountainous country is one of the world's leading exporters of copper. 42%

12

6 A country that is divided into 22 administrative regions and subdivided into 95 departments is:	[1] Canada [2] China [3] India [4] Brazil [5] France	ANSWER TO Q-5 **[1]** More of a humanist than most modern writers, Camus rejected the idea of the artist as rebel. 79%
6 Which book about totalitarianism is not a work of fiction?	[1] 1984 [2] The Gulag Archipelago [3] Darkness at Noon [4] Bend Sinister [5] Animal Farm	ANSWER TO Q-5 **[2]** Afghanistan is landlocked. 67%
6 Steven Bochco was a creator of both "L.A. Law" and:	[1] Simon and Simon [2] Hill Street Blues [3] Life Goes On [4] Cagney and Lacey [5] Law and Order	ANSWER TO Q-5 **[3]** Dreyfuss earned an Oscar for his role as a struggling actor in "The Goodbye Girl." 91%
6 "Sister of the Road" is the depression-era memoir of:	[1] Boxcar Bertha [2] Aimee Semple Macpherson [3] Rosie the Riveter [4] Ma Barker [5] Winnie Ruth Judd	ANSWER TO Q-5 **[1]** During World War II more than 300,000 troops were rescued by British boats. 67%
6 Who would use a creel?	[1] Writer [2] Fisherman [3] Native American mother [4] Customs agent [5] Factory worker	ANSWER TO Q-5 **[2]** The colorless liquid is produced by the fermentation of sugars or starches. 34%

25 The annual Iditarod Dogsled Championship is a 1,159-mile race from Anchorage to:	[1] Kodiak [2] Juneau [3] Fairbanks [4] Barrow [5] Nome	ANSWER TO Q-24 **[5]** The house of Bourbon was restored and Juan Carlos was made king in 1975. 67%
25 Which literary work was not written by Leo Tolstoy?	[1] War and Peace [2] Doctor Zhivago [3] Anna Karenina [4] Resurrection [5] The Power of Darkness	ANSWER TO Q-24 **[2]** To the Romans, Zeus was Jupiter, Dionysus was Bacchus, Hades was Pluto and Hermes was Mercury. 68%
25 A covered ambulatory or colonnade in classical architecture is a:	[1] Portico [2] Promissory [3] Pylon [4] Pediment [5] Parallax	ANSWER TO Q-24 **[2]** In later times, it was sacked by Alexander the Great and taken over by crusaders. 35%
25 Architect/engineer Richard Buckminster Fuller is famous for designing the:	[1] Louvre [2] Lincoln Memorial [3] Golden Gate Bridge [4] Geodesic Dome [5] Guggenheim Museum	ANSWER TO Q-24 **[2]** "Lost in Yonkers" is a play by Neil Simon. 54%
25 Chile's economy is largely based on its:	[1] Tourist industry [2] Local handicrafts [3] Mineral wealth [4] Wild animals [5] Cattle ranches	ANSWER TO Q-24 **[5]** The other writers listed here are Irish-born. 45%

7 Which city was once named York?	[1] Detroit [2] Toronto [3] Melbourne [4] Johannesburg [5] Seattle	ANSWER TO Q-6 **[5]** The traditional French division into provinces was replaced by a new system in the 1700's. 56%
7 Who would wear a sou'wester?	[1] A sailor [2] Someone in the tropics [3] A jockey [4] Palace guards [5] The pope	ANSWER TO Q-6 **[2]** Solzhenitsyn's book is a mixture of history, autobiography and analysis. 55%
7 Which performer received a gold single for the song "Daniel" in 1973?	[1] Billy Joel [2] Michael Jackson [3] Paul Simon [4] Neil Diamond [5] Elton John	ANSWER TO Q-6 **[2]** Several stylistic devices popularized on "Hill Street" were used on "L.A. Law." 78%
7 Who painted "The Garden of Earthly Delights"?	[1] Salvador Dali [2] Hieronymus Bosch [3] Francisco Goya [4] Rembrandt [5] El Greco	ANSWER TO Q-6 **[1]** Her book about her life as a female hobo turned her into an American folk heroine. 34%
7 Which Greek prefix is matched with a misleading translation?	[1] Omni - all [2] Mono - one [3] Pseudo - false [4] Proto - first [5] Para - distant	ANSWER TO Q-6 **[2]** A creel is that basket fishermen use to carry their fish. 78%

24 A fascist government ruled _____ from 1939 to 1975.

[1] Italy
[2] Austria
[3] Brazil
[4] Panama
[5] Spain

ANSWER TO Q-23

[3] Quilting is one of the most widely appreciated American folk arts.

49%

---

24 Which god has the same name in both Roman and Greek mythology?

[1] Zeus
[2] Apollo
[3] Dionysus
[4] Hades
[5] Hermes

ANSWER TO Q-23

[1] The tropical zone in the new world extends from northern Argentina to just north of Cuba.

56%

---

24 This ancient city is remembered for its purple dye and for founding Carthage:

[1] Jerusalem
[2] Tyre
[3] Jericho
[4] Damascus
[5] Babylon

ANSWER TO Q-23

[4] The Iranian mountains border Turkey, Iraq and the Persian Gulf.

52%

---

24 Which book listed is not a novel?

[1] The Maltese Falcon
[2] Lost in Yonkers
[3] Advise and Consent
[4] From the Terrace
[5] Catcher in the Rye

ANSWER TO Q-23

[5] This classic novel by F. Scott Fitzgerald was written in 1924.

67%

---

24 Which playwright was born in the United States?

[1] Samuel Beckett
[2] Oscar Wilde
[3] Brendan Behan
[4] Sean O'Casey
[5] Eugene O'Neill

ANSWER TO Q-23

[5] The classic Disney film stars Oscar winner Julie Andrews in her film debut.

65%

8 All these are utensils used by cooks except:	[1] Zester [2] Vitrine [3] Skimmer [4] Colander [5] Trussing needle	ANSWER TO Q-7 **[2]** The city was named York in 1793, by the British lieutenant governor. 67%
8 Which is not an example of a telecommunications satellite?	[1] Hermes [2] Symphony [3] Hovercraft [4] Anik [5] Intelsat	ANSWER TO Q-7 **[1]** The hat is named for a strong wind from the southwest. 78%
8 Flavored with almonds, raisins and orange peel, what is glogg?	[1] Chewy dessert [2] Duck sauce [3] Hot punch [4] Hangover antidote [5] Fish stew	ANSWER TO Q-7 **[5]** Elton John received his first gold single for "Crocodile Rock" earlier in the same year. 91%
8 All these writers are known for both their poetry and prose except:	[1] Henry James [2] Jorge Luis Borges [3] Rudyard Kipling [4] Thomas Hardy [5] Edgar A. Poe	ANSWER TO Q-7 **[2]** The 16th century artist is hailed as a forerunner of 20th century surrealism. 67%
8 "Play It Again, Sam" and "Don't Drink the Water" are hit plays by:	[1] Woody Allen [2] Neil Simon [3] John Guare [4] David Mamet [5] Harvey Fierstein	ANSWER TO Q-7 **[5]** The prefix "para" refers to something either approximate or a close substitute. 54%

23 The patchwork quilt originated in this part of the world:	[1] Australia [2] Ancient Greece [3] North America [4] Polynesia [5] Hungary	ANSWER TO Q-22 **[2]** The Mesopotamians and Egyptians were the greatest beer drinkers of the ancient world. 36%
23 The distance from the equator is measured in terms of:	[1] Latitude [2] Longitude [3] Meridian line [4] Equatorial departure [5] Range	ANSWER TO Q-22 **[5]** This verb originates from the old language phrase "e rogo," meaning from this direction. 79%
23 The Zagros mountains are found in this country:	[1] Greece [2] Israel [3] Poland [4] Iran [5] Australia	ANSWER TO Q-22 **[1]** Nikos Kanzantzakis, the celebrated modern Greek writer, also wrote a sequel to "The Odyssey." 43%
23 Which famous literary piece was written first?	[1] World According to Garp [2] The Grapes of Wrath [3] Naked and the Dead [4] Catcher in the Rye [5] The Great Gatsby	ANSWER TO Q-22 **[3]** The title isn't ironic. In ancient Greece, an idiot was a man without social ties and values. 43%
23 The tales of P.L. Travers were the basis for this 1964 screen musical:	[1] The Sound of Music [2] The King and I [3] Swiss Family Robinson [4] The Little Prince [5] Mary Poppins	ANSWER TO Q-22 **[2]** The war, which lasted from 1337-1453, began when Edward III invaded France. 45%

9 The Battle of the Bulge was a counter-offensive move of the ____ in World War II.	[1] Japanese [2] Australians [3] Germans [4] Soviet Russians [5] Italians	ANSWER TO Q-8 **[2]** A vitrine is a glass showcase for art objects or curios. 45%
9 Which hideous ailment is not correctly matched with the body part it affects?	[1] Pyorrhea - intestines [2] Bursitis - joints [3] Encephalitis - brain [4] Rhinitis - nose [5] Phlebitis - veins	ANSWER TO Q-8 **[3]** The hovercraft is a type of marine transportation. 68%
9 Which was the only major league baseball team to win two World Series in the 1980's?	[1] St. Louis Cardinals [2] KC Royals [3] NY Yankees [4] Oakland A's [5] Los Angelas Dodgers	ANSWER TO Q-8 **[3]** A Swedish Christmas dish, it consists mostly of wine, brandy and sherry. 78%
9 In Muslim society, what is a hajj?	[1] Koran expert [2] Holy pilgrimage [3] Virgin [4] Shrine in Mecca [5] Sacred building	ANSWER TO Q-8 **[1]** High accomplishment in both types of literature is relatively rare. 34%
9 On which food would you put remoulade?	[1] Barbecued meat [2] Ice cream [3] Cold cooked crab [4] Toasted bread [5] Pasta	ANSWER TO Q-8 **[1]** Apart from some revue sketches, these two comedies are Allen's entire dramatic output. 45%

22 This is the oldest alcoholic beverage in the world:	[1] Wine [2] Beer [3] Whiskey [4] Rum [5] Cognac	ANSWER TO Q-21 **[3]** Radium was discovered by Marie and Pierre Curie in 1898. 31%
22 What does the Latin term "ergo" mean?	[1] Totally [2] Because [3] Without [4] Why [5] Therefore	ANSWER TO Q-21 **[3]** It's Ethiopia's largest city and the center for communication and trade. 68%
22 "The Last Temptation of Christ" was written by the same writer who wrote:	[1] Zorba the Greek [2] The Magic Mountain [3] The Stranger [4] Of Human Bondage [5] Siddhartha	ANSWER TO Q-21 **[3]** Harry is a writer who goes on a safari to "work the fat off his mind." 42%
22 Which Dostoevsky novel attempts to portray a saintly man?	[1] The Double [2] The Possessed [3] The Idiot [4] Crime and Punishment [5] The Brothers Karamazov	ANSWER TO Q-21 **[4]** Desire for military independence led him to leave the alliance and develop the atom bomb. 56%
22 Which country was the aggressor in the Hundred Years War?	[1] France [2] England [3] Spain [4] Portugal [5] Scotland	ANSWER TO Q-21 **[4]** Beatrix Potter created "Peter Rabbit." Louisa May Alcott wrote "Little Women." 54%

10 Mount Godwin Austin is also known as:	[1] Pike's Peak [2] Ayers Rock [3] Snowdon [4] K2 [5] Sugar Loaf	ANSWER TO Q-9 **[3]** It occurred in December of 1944 and was the last major German onslaught. 89%
10 Name the reclusive author of "The Catcher in the Rye" and "Franny and Zooey":	[1] J.D. Salinger [2] Thomas Pynchon [3] John Cheever [4] Joyce Carol Oates [5] John Barth	ANSWER TO Q-9 **[1]** Pyorrhea has a gruesome effect on the gums but your intestines are safe from this scourge. 68%
10 In which country will you find the Dinaric Alps?	[1] Poland [2] Belgium [3] Croatia [4] Bulgaria [5] Slovakia	ANSWER TO Q-9 **[5]** The Dodgers beat the Yankees in 1981 and took the A's to win the 1988 title. 57%
10 Name the faithful wife of Ulysses in Homer's "Odyssey":	[1] Penelope [2] Antigone [3] Daphne [4] Eurydice [5] Hippolyta	ANSWER TO Q-9 **[2]** A person who has undertaken the pilgrimage is called a hajji. 55%
10 Someone known as a finagler is one who:	[1] Speaks several languages [2] Hunts game [3] Cheats [4] Fights fires [5] Performs high wire acts	ANSWER TO Q-9 **[3]** Remoulade is used to accompany cold meat, fish and shellfish. 45%

21 The element not discovered by 19th century scientist Humphry Davy:

[1] Potassium
[2] Magnesium
[3] Radium
[4] Sodium
[5] Titanium

ANSWER TO Q-20

[1] The pituitary gland produces hormones which regulate other glands in the body.

72%

21 Which of these is Addis Ababa?

[1] Olympian winner
[2] Shoe magnate
[3] Ethiopia's capital
[4] Greek god
[5] Arabian Nights hero

ANSWER TO Q-20

[2] Hawkins and Lester Young jointly brought the saxophone into its current prominence.

43%

21 Hemingway's "The Snows of Kilimanjaro" features this animal:

[1] Laughing hyena
[2] Charging elephant
[3] Frozen leopard
[4] Obnoxious baboon
[5] Dancing hippo

ANSWER TO Q-20

[3] David Lynch's bizarre film has not been and is not likely to become a TV series.

81%

21 Which of these French presidents pulled his country out of NATO?

[1] George Clemenceau
[2] Henri Petain
[3] Valery Giscard D'Estaing
[4] Charles de Gaulle
[5] Georges Pompidou

ANSWER TO Q-20

[2] Defoe's book was based on a real-life account and tries to be as realistic as possible.

69%

21 Each of these authors is matched with the character they created, except:

[1] Schultz - Charlie Brown
[2] Sewell - Black Beauty
[3] Milne - Winnie the Pooh
[4] Alcott - Peter Rabbit
[5] Barrie - Peter Pan

ANSWER TO Q-20

[3] Christiaan Huygens developed the wave theory of light and Herschel discovered infrared light.

34%

22

11 Who was making headlines in late summer and fall of 1888?	[1] Jack the Ripper [2] Lindbergh Baby Kidnaper [3] Boston Strangler [4] Charles Manson [5] Al Capone	ANSWER TO Q-10 [4] The world's second highest mountain, it was first climbed in 1954. 54%
11 The crocus and the gladiolus belong to this flower family:	[1] Daffodil [2] Rose [3] Daisy [4] Lilac [5] Iris	ANSWER TO Q-10 [1] Salinger went into hiding after the overwhelming success of his novels. 89%
11 In what form did G.I. Joe first appear?	[1] TV character [2] Doll [3] Action-book author [4] Comic strip [5] Comedy routine	ANSWER TO Q-10 [3] An extension of the Swiss Alps, they extend through several Balkan countries. 34%
11 Which word refers to something ominous?	[1] Apocryphal [2] Prodigious [3] Portentous [4] Abhorrent [5] Acrimonious	ANSWER TO Q-10 [1] When Ulysses arrived home in Ithaca, he cleaned house by killing Penelope's suitors. 56%
11 Which river flows from Mt. Hermon and empties into the Dead Sea?	[1] Tigris [2] Jordan [3] Ganges [4] Meander [5] Euphrates	ANSWER TO Q-10 [3] It is defined as someone who uses trickery and slyness in order to get what they want. 67%

20 Where are the pineal and pituitary glands located?

[1] Base of the brain
[2] In the throat
[3] Behind the torso
[4] Under the abdomen
[5] In the pelvis

ANSWER TO Q-19

[5] Exogenous factors are those introduced from or produced outside the organism.

32%

---

20 Coleman Hawkins is considered the first master of this jazz instrument:

[1] Clarinet
[2] Tenor saxophone
[3] Trumpet
[4] Cornet
[5] Piano

ANSWER TO Q-19

[5] These statisticians work primarily for insurance companies.

78%

---

20 There are both TV and movie versions of all these titles except:

[1] The Addams Family
[2] Peyton Place
[3] Blue Velvet
[4] M*A*S*H
[5] Dragnet

ANSWER TO Q-19

[2] In addition to being a jazz pianist, William Basie was also a band leader.

89%

---

20 Impossible things happen in all these works except:

[1] Gulliver's Travels
[2] Robinson Crusoe
[3] Alice in Wonderland
[4] The Arabian Nights
[5] The Wizard of Oz

ANSWER TO Q-19

[5] The Soviets subsequently invaded Finland in 1939, but it remained independent.

51%

---

20 William Herschel, Christiaan Huygens, and Johann Ritter all made discoveries regarding:

[1] Gravity
[2] Motion
[3] Light
[4] Sound
[5] Heat

ANSWER TO Q-19

[1] The 14,690-foot peak on the Swiss-Italian border is a favorite of many climbers.

42%

12 The Thar desert is also known by this name:

[1] Great Indian
[2] Death Valley
[3] Empty Quarter
[4] Great Sandy
[5] Painted Desert

ANSWER TO Q-11

[1] Jack the Ripper killed at least 7 prostitutes in Whitechapel between Aug. 7 and Nov. 10.
56%

---

12 Botanically speaking, the flower that develops into a banana is a:

[1] Berry
[2] Fungi
[3] Seed
[4] Pod
[5] Root

ANSWER TO Q-11

[5] This family is distributed worldwide except in the coldest regions.
34%

---

12 What sauce do you make by adding white wine, vinegar and tarragon to hollandaise?

[1] Lyonnaise
[2] Bordelaise
[3] Veloute
[4] Mornay
[5] Bernaise

ANSWER TO Q-11

[4] Cartoonist Dave Gerger first combined G.I. and Joe for his 1942 strip that appeared in "Yank."
45%

---

12 The Vistula, Oder and Narew are chief rivers found in this European nation:

[1] Russia
[2] Poland
[3] France
[4] Belgium
[5] Denmark

ANSWER TO Q-11

[3] A portent is an omen or a sign of things to come.
67%

---

12 The parathyroid glands govern _____ metabolism.

[1] Iron
[2] Carbon
[3] Calcium and phosphorus
[4] Protein
[5] Vitamin

ANSWER TO Q-11

[2] It flows through the Sea of Galilee.
45%

19 In biology, which is an example of an exogenous factor?	[1] Respiration [2] Genetic makeup [3] Body chemistry [4] Hormones [5] Humidity	ANSWER TO Q-18 **[3]** He won the Academy Award for best supporting actor for his role in the Neil Simon comedy. 79%
19 What is a person who calculates risks called?	[1] Cartographer [2] Philploger [3] Graphologist [4] Librettist [5] Actuary	ANSWER TO Q-18 **[1]** Liquid carbon dioxide, formed under pressure, is used in fire extinguishers. 79%
19 Which famous musician is not matched with the instrument he played?	[1] Louis Armstrong-trumpet [2] Count Basie-saxophone [3] Pablo Casals-cello [4] Benny Goodman-clarinet [5] Scott Joplin-piano	ANSWER TO Q-18 **[2]** This special breed of greyhound is used in racing. 65%
19 Finland declared itself independent of ____ in 1917.	[1] Sweden [2] Norway [3] Denmark [4] Germany [5] Russia	ANSWER TO Q-18 **[2]** Keith Gordon has made an acclaimed film based on this rather grim book. 66%
19 Europe's Mount Cervin is also known as:	[1] The Matterhorn [2] Mount Etna [3] Annapurna [4] Mont Blanc [5] Table Mountain	ANSWER TO Q-18 **[3]** Mead's most famous work is her 1928 study "Coming of Age in Samoa." 78%

13 "La Marseillaise" is the national _____ of France.

[1] Constitution
[2] Flower
[3] Anthem
[4] Dance
[5] Dish

ANSWER TO Q-12

[1] This vast desert that covers over 100,000 sq. miles is found in N.W. India and Pakistan.

23%

---

13 What word describes the tendency of alcohol to evaporate quickly?

[1] Conductivity
[2] Volatility
[3] Solubility
[4] Viscosity
[5] Polarity

ANSWER TO Q-12

[1] Only female flowers develop into the banana, and each plant bears fruit only once.

23%

---

13 Which "family" band has no members who are related to each other?

[1] Beach Boys
[2] Ramones
[3] Isley Brothers
[4] Bee Gees
[5] Cowsills

ANSWER TO Q-12

[5] Whipping cream is added to hollandaise to make mousseline sauce.

34%

---

13 Which is not a desert found in Africa?

[1] Sahara
[2] Somali
[3] Atacama
[4] Kalahari
[5] Namib

ANSWER TO Q-12

[2] Almost all of Poland is drained into the Baltic sea by way of the Vistula & Oder rivers.

35%

---

13 Tom Selleck, Steve Guttenberg and _____ were the three men in "Three Men and a Baby."

[1] Michael Keaton
[2] Sylvester Stallone
[3] Michael Douglas
[4] Chevy Chase
[5] Ted Danson

ANSWER TO Q-12

[3] This major endocrine gland is located on the thyroid gland found in the neck area.

12%

18 After a 36-year layoff, George Burns made his big screen return in:	[1] Two of a Kind [2] Oh God [3] The Sunshine Boys [4] Going in Style [5] Just You and Me Kid	ANSWER TO Q-17 **[2]** A quahog is a full-grown hard-shell clam. Younger clams are called cherry- stones or littlenecks. 56%
18 Dry ice is the solid form of:	[1] Carbon dioxide [2] Chloral hydrate [3] Magnesium sulphate [4] Hydrochloric acid [5] Carbon monoxide	ANSWER TO Q-17 **[1]** The foramen is a hole or passageway in the bone through which nerves pass. 64%
18 The fastest dog on flat ground is the:	[1] Doberman pinscher [2] Whippet [3] Dachshund [4] Standard poodle [5] Collie	ANSWER TO Q-17 **[1]** The earliest concordats were in the 11th and 12th centuries. 42%
18 A young adult story that deals with the pressure to conform in a Catholic school:	[1] Lord of the Flies [2] The Chocolate War [3] Dragon's Blood [4] The Outsiders [5] Interview with the Vampire	ANSWER TO Q-17 **[4]** The Jew's harp is still used as a folk instrument in Austria. 59%
18 Margaret Mead is best known for her contributions in the field of:	[1] Medicine [2] Physics [3] Anthropology [4] Athletics [5] Politics	ANSWER TO Q-17 **[2]** Green Lantern uses his magic ring to make whatever weapons he needs to battle evil. 87%

14 The drug lovastatin helps to:	[1] Regulate heart [2] Clean the blood [3] Lower cholesterol [4] Relieve insomnia [5] Strengthen bones	ANSWER TO Q-13 [3] The day it was first sung was also the first day a French guillotine was used. 91%
14 This country is in South America, not Africa:	[1] Gabon [2] Mauritania [3] Guinea [4] Suriname [5] Senegal	ANSWER TO Q-13 [2] A "volatile" person is one who moves quickly from one idea to another. 66%
14 The Hittite empire flourished in this area:	[1] Asia Minor [2] Saudi Arabia [3] Tibet [4] India [5] Iberian Peninsula	ANSWER TO Q-13 [2] Joey, Johnny, Dee Dee and Tommy adopted the name and the black hair, but not each other. 57%
14 Red Connors was which TV cowboy's sidekick?	[1] Hopalong Cassidy [2] Wild Bill Hickok [3] Roy Rogers [4] The Cisco Kid [5] Kit Carson	ANSWER TO Q-13 [3] The Atacama desert is in South America. 67%
14 Which herb seed can be either black or white, and yields an oil that resists turning rancid?	[1] Pepper [2] Sesame [3] Sunflower [4] Caraway [5] Cardamon	ANSWER TO Q-13 [5] Danson is best known as the character Sam Malone in the TV series "Cheers." 92%

17 If you caught a quahog at the seashore, what kind of creature would you have?

[1] Oyster
[2] Clam
[3] Scallop
[4] Baby shark
[5] Squid

ANSWER TO Q-16
[2] Vegetables, spices, salt-pork and roasted chicken are additional ingredients.
59%

17 Which is not a meteorological term?

[1] Foramen
[2] Jet stream
[3] Low
[4] Trough
[5] Warm front

ANSWER TO Q-16
[1] Although light, it is very flammable, which is why non-flammable helium is used in balloons.
78%

17 A ____ is a pact between a secular authority and the church.

[1] Concordat
[2] Treaty
[3] Bann
[4] Papal bull
[5] Codex

ANSWER TO Q-16
[5] Before the terms became synonymous, it referred to one of the hills on which the city was built.
79%

17 What musical instrument is held between the teeth and plucked with a finger?

[1] Dulcimer
[2] Recorder
[3] Blues harp
[4] Jew's harp
[5] Tambura

ANSWER TO Q-16
[3] The stories that ballads tell are usually tragic or supernatural.
76%

17 Which of these comic book heroes is deprived of his power by the color yellow?

[1] Flash
[2] Green Lantern
[3] Captain America
[4] Silver Surfer
[5] Captain Marvel

ANSWER TO Q-16
[3] Quint is the name of the salty captain in the 1975 film; Queeg is in "The Caine Mutiny."
79%

15 Stasi was the intelligence agency of the former:

[1] East Germany
[2] Yugoslavia
[3] Czechoslovakia
[4] Soviet Union
[5] South Vietnam

ANSWER TO Q-14

[3] The drug prevents the production of cholesterol in the liver.

23%

---

15 American Oscar de la Hoya is a world class athlete in this sport:

[1] Auto racing
[2] Cycling
[3] Boxing
[4] Horse racing
[5] Tennis

ANSWER TO Q-14

[4] Suriname was established by the Dutch in northern South America.

55%

---

15 "...A rose by any other name would smell as sweet" is said by which character?

[1] Juliet
[2] Lady Macbeth
[3] Hamlet
[4] Richard II
[5] Othello

ANSWER TO Q-14

[1] Hittite iron workers helped initiate the Iron Age.

56%

---

15 Because of its large size, this breed of dog is called "king of the terriers":

[1] Yorkshire
[2] West Highland
[3] Wire-Haired
[4] Airedale
[5] Silky

ANSWER TO Q-14

[1] Edgar Buchanan played Red in the popular series.

45%

---

15 This name is shared by a Mexican state, a river and a condiment:

[1] Worcestershire
[2] Caliente
[3] Heinz
[4] Tabasco
[5] Mustardo

ANSWER TO Q-14

[2] Sesame oil is used extensively in India for cooking, making soap and medicine.

45%

16 What is the main ingredient of mock turtle soup?	[1] Iguana meat [2] Calf's head [3] Smoked sausage [4] Abalone [5] Frog legs	ANSWER TO Q-15 [3] These French settlers came to what is now Nova Scotia in the early 17th century. 59%
16 What is the lightest known substance?	[1] Hydrogen [2] Oxygen [3] Helium [4] Neon [5] Nitrogen	ANSWER TO Q-15 [1] After being restored, he lost the throne again in 1922 due to disastrous policies. 32%
16 Which biblical term refers to the city of Jerusalem?	[1] Canaan [2] Beulah [3] Jericho [4] Eden [5] Zion	ANSWER TO Q-15 [5] This is a generic term that covers all plastic surgery whether serious or cosmetic. 51%
16 "The Wreck of the Hesperus" and "The Rime of the Ancient Mariner" are:	[1] Horror tales [2] Sonnets [3] Ballads [4] Novels [5] Epics	ANSWER TO Q-15 [2] Part of the Netherland Antilles, this island processes oil and is a popular tourist spot. 49%
16 Which is not true of the movie thriller "Jaws"?	[1] Chief Brody is the hero [2] Shark is a great white [3] Features Captain Queeg [4] Set aboard the Orca [5] Set at Amity Isl.	ANSWER TO Q-15 [4] The substance is favored by the health-food crowd and is produced in the salivary glands of bees. 69%

16 Which film about filmmaking is not set in Hollywood?

[1] The Player
[2] A Star Is Born (1937)
[3] Day for Night
[4] Sunset Boulevard
[5] The Big Knife

ANSWER TO Q-15

[1] The agency was dismantled in 1989, as part of Germany's reunification.

67%

---

16 This term describes the unswerving and unquench-able will to possess all knowledge:

[1] Darwinism
[2] Faustian
[3] Orwellian
[4] Bowdlerize
[5] Machiavellian

ANSWER TO Q-15

[3] De la Hoya earned a gold medal in the lightweight class at the 1992 games in Barcelona.

55%

---

16 In which type of restaurant would you order soba noodles?

[1] Italian
[2] Japanese
[3] Chinese
[4] French
[5] Cuban

ANSWER TO Q-15

[1] She's unhappily musing about her family's feud with Romeo's family.

78%

---

16 This actor portrayed a police detective in the television show, "Dan August":

[1] Hal Linden
[2] Robert Urich
[3] Dennis Weaver
[4] Burt Reynolds
[5] Gerald Mcraney

ANSWER TO Q-15

[4] They've been used as wartime dispatchers, police dogs, guards and big-game hunters.

67%

---

16 The first successful collaboration between George and Ira Gershwin was the musical:

[1] Porgy and Bess
[2] Oklahoma!
[3] Lady Be Good
[4] Kiss Me Kate
[5] Show Boat

ANSWER TO Q-15

[4] The condiment is made from chili peppers marinated in spirit vinegar with salt.

78%

15 Some 300,000 Acadians, distant cousins of Louisiana's Cajuns, reside here:	[1] West Indies [2] Brittany [3] Canada [4] Key West [5] Channel Islands	ANSWER TO Q-14 **[2]** The plague can then be transmitted to man by flea bites or airborne infection. 49%
15 Which monarch was deposed because of his pro-German sympathies during WWI?	[1] Constantine I of Greece [2] Leopold II of Belgium [3] Emperor Pu-Yi of China [4] Umberto II of Italy [5] Idris I of Libya	ANSWER TO Q-14 **[2]** Used for measuring column length, the agate is equal to 1/14 of an inch. 32%
15 Which operation would fall into the category of anaplasty?	[1] Kidney transplant [2] Cardiac bypass [3] Root canal [4] Vasectomy [5] Facelift	ANSWER TO Q-14 **[1]** It is derived from cellulose, the main element of the cell walls of plants. 32%
15 The island of Aruba is located off the coast of:	[1] Australia [2] Venezuela [3] Morocco [4] Portugal [5] Argentina	ANSWER TO Q-14 **[4]** The subject of many ballads and tall tales, he rode a horse named Black Bess. 43%
15 What produces the substance known as royal jelly?	[1] Magnolia trees [2] Brahman cows [3] Dandelion flowers [4] Honey bees [5] Salmon	ANSWER TO Q-14 **[2]** Many critics consider "Gravity's Rainbow" to be the greatest of recent American novels. 21%

17 All these technological terms are part of the same system except:

[1] Baffle
[2] Boom
[3] Feedback
[4] Microscope
[5] Diaphragm

ANSWER TO Q-16
[3] Francois Truffaut's film is set in Paris.
69%

---

17 All these words function as both nouns and verbs except:

[1] Support
[2] Advocate
[3] Fix
[4] Construct
[5] Describe

ANSWER TO Q-16
[2] The legend of Faust, who sold his soul to the devil for knowledge, comes from Germany.
44%

---

17 This is Evelyn Waugh's biting satire on American life and Hollywood mortuaries:

[1] Of Human Bondage
[2] Naked Lunch
[3] The Day of the Locust
[4] The Loved One
[5] The Silver Screen

ANSWER TO Q-16
[2] The noodle is made of buckwheat and is delicate but still firm.
89%

---

17 Which of these is not part of a flower?

[1] Stamen
[2] Sepal
[3] Calyx
[4] Spore
[5] Anther

ANSWER TO Q-16
[4] Robert Urich played detective Dan Tanna in the drama, "Vegas."
91%

---

17 Cilantro and _____ come from the same plant.

[1] Basil
[2] Fennel seeds
[3] Allspice
[4] Coriander
[5] Dill

ANSWER TO Q-16
[3] The show's two biggest hits were the title song and "Fascinating Rhythm."
57%

14 Bubonic plague is often carried by infected:	[1] Birds [2] Rodents [3] Fish [4] Livestock [5] Water	ANSWER TO Q-13 **[3]** Melville's sea story takes place aboard ship. 53%
14 Agate is a measurement used for:	[1] Space travel [2] Printing [3] Construction [4] Liquor [5] Sound	ANSWER TO Q-13 **[3]** George Reeves starred as the Man of Steel in the series which lasted from 1951-57. 45%
14 What was the first synthetic plastic?	[1] Celluloid [2] Polyurethane [3] Teflon [4] Vinyl [5] Cellophane	ANSWER TO Q-13 **[4]** It was an important channel for travelers until construction of the Panama Canal. 45%
14 Dick Turpin was a legendary English:	[1] Explorer [2] Spy [3] Labor agitator [4] Highwayman [5] Fashion plate	ANSWER TO Q-13 **[2]** Britt's father, Dan, was the Lone Ranger's nephew. 59%
14 Name the author of such books as "The Crying of Lot 49" and "Gravity's Rainbow":	[1] Tom Wolfe [2] Thomas Pynchon [3] John Cheever [4] Ken Kesey [5] Gore Vidal	ANSWER TO Q-13 **[2]** A "bon mot" is a clever saying or witticism. 54%

18 This green pigment in plants is responsible for producing the basic elements of food:

[1] Xylem
[2] Retinal
[3] Carotene
[4] Albumen
[5] Chlorophyll

ANSWER TO Q-17
[4] The other four terms are parts of a microphone system.
67%

---

18 Which writer is not known for his crime novels?

[1] Chester Himes
[2] Ed McBain
[3] Evelyn Waugh
[4] Elmore Leonard
[5] John D. MacDonald

ANSWER TO Q-17
[5] Describe is only used as a verb.
66%

---

18 Wilhelm Konrad von Roentgen is best known as the discoverer of:

[1] Pluto
[2] The atom
[3] X rays
[4] Quantum mechanics
[5] Vitamin D

ANSWER TO Q-17
[4] In the end, the hero cremates the heroine in a dog cemetery.
34%

---

18 American artist Grant Wood's most famous work of art was:

[1] Christina's World
[2] Blue Boy
[3] American Gothic
[4] Helga
[5] The Oxbow

ANSWER TO Q-17
[4] This is a single cell of a plant, such as algae, ferns, mosses or fungi, that reproduces itself.
45%

---

18 This tiny country is nestled between France and Spain:

[1] Liechtenstein
[2] Luxembourg
[3] Monaco
[4] Andorra
[5] Malta

ANSWER TO Q-17
[4] Cilantro comes from the leaves of the coriander plant while the seeds are known as coriander.
44%

13 Which famous literary work is not set primarily on an island?

[1] The Tempest
[2] Lord of the Flies
[3] Billy Budd
[4] Robinson Crusoe
[5] Ten Little Indians

ANSWER TO Q-12

[2] The current Aga Khan IV, Prince Karim, inherited the title in 1957.

54%

---

13 Which comic book hero was the first to spawn a television series?

[1] Spider-Man
[2] Batman
[3] Superman
[4] Wonder Woman
[5] Green Hornet

ANSWER TO Q-12

[4] The first Super Bowl was played between the Packers and Chiefs on January 15, 1967.

54%

---

13 Which strait separates the tip of South America from Tierra del Fuego?

[1] Kerch
[2] Cook
[3] Torres
[4] Magellan
[5] Gibraltar

ANSWER TO Q-12

[2] The portable windmill and the steel plow are the other two.

41%

---

13 The Green Hornet, Britt Reid, is related to:

[1] Aquaman
[2] The Lone Ranger
[3] Spiderman
[4] Captain Marvel
[5] Davy Crockett

ANSWER TO Q-12

[5] Scarlatti composed 600 sonatas and fugues for this ancestor of the piano.

31%

---

13 Which of these French expressions has nothing to do with trendiness or fashion?

[1] A la mode
[2] Bon mot
[3] De rigueur
[4] Haute couture
[5] Demode

ANSWER TO Q-12

[1] The hero first appeared in pulp novels and has since appeared in other media.

32%

19 All of these terms describe types of astronomical orbits except:	[1] Aphelion [2] Apogee [3] Eccentric [4] Perigee [5] Parallax	ANSWER TO Q-18 [5] The chlorophyll makes carbon, hydrogen and water. 91%
19 Technically termed lipids, they are more commonly referred to as:	[1] Enzymes [2] Calories [3] Narcotics [4] Fats [5] Vegetables	ANSWER TO Q-18 [3] Evelyn Waugh is known for books such as "Brideshead Revisited," a treatment of English aristocrats. 56%
19 Author George Sand had a notorious affair with which great composer?	[1] Brahms [2] Chopin [3] Stravinsky [4] Rachmaninoff [5] Schubert	ANSWER TO Q-18 [3] The German physicist won the 1901 Nobel Prize for physics with his discovery. 61%
19 All these mythological creatures are part human and part animal except:	[1] Minotaur [2] Harpy [3] Centaur [4] Leviathan [5] Sphinx	ANSWER TO Q-18 [3] "Christina's World" and the "Helga" series are by another American, Andrew Wyeth. 68%
19 All of these words describe a type of swamp except:	[1] Heath [2] Morass [3] Bayou [4] Slough [5] Quagmire	ANSWER TO Q-18 [4] Tourism and postage stamps are the main sources of income for the basque state. 68%

12 The Aga Khan is the spiritual leader of a sect of:	[1] Buddhism [2] Islam [3] Judaism [4] Hinduism [5] Taoism	ANSWER TO Q-11 [3] The surface of the lake lies at 1,312 feet below sea level. 68%
12 Which event did not occur during the 1950's?	[1] Castro takes over Cuba [2] Elvis debuts on TV [3] Korean War ends [4] First Super Bowl played [5] Rosa Parks jailed	ANSWER TO Q-11 [2] Unfortunately for Carmen, the soldier catches up with her and takes his revenge. 58%
12 Considered one of the 3 most important inventions that "won the west":	[1] Colt .45 [2] Barbed wire [3] Conestoga wagon [4] Bowie knife [5] Winchester rifle	ANSWER TO Q-11 [2] Margo Channing is the central character of the classic, "All About Eve." 67%
12 Which composer was chiefly known for his music for harpsichord?	[1] Franz Liszt [2] Frederic Chopin [3] Johannes Brahms [4] Claude Debussy [5] Domenico Scarlatti	ANSWER TO Q-11 [5] Jameson land is part of Greenland. 51%
12 Which of these popular characters was created by Robert E. Howard?	[1] Conan the Barbarian [2] The Terminator [3] Rambo [4] Tarzan [5] Friday the 13th's Jason	ANSWER TO Q-11 [3] Oxygen accounts for nearly 50% of the earth's crust. 58%

20 In the Old Testament, Caleb was a:

[1] High priest
[2] King of Israel
[3] Babylonian god
[4] Spy for Moses
[5] Jacob's son

ANSWER TO Q-19

[5] Parallax is the apparent change in an object's position due to the observer's movement.

43%

---

20 "The Last of the Wine" and "The King Must Die" are historical novels set in:

[1] Ancient Greece
[2] Victorian England
[3] Colonial America
[4] Czarist Russia
[5] Contemporary Israel

ANSWER TO Q-19

[4] Fats or lipids are the body's most concentrated source of energy.

78%

---

20 Which statement about the basking shark is false?

[1] A.K.A. "dogfish"
[2] 2nd largest fish
[3] Eats plankton
[4] Prefers temperate seas
[5] Prized for its liver oil

ANSWER TO Q-19

[2] The love letters of Chopin and Sand are classics of their kind.

55%

---

20 Princess Beatrix was installed as the queen of this country in 1980:

[1] Norway
[2] Belgium
[3] Sweden
[4] Netherlands
[5] Finland

ANSWER TO Q-19

[4] The Biblical sea monster is invariably pictured as a sea serpent or a whale.

58%

---

20 Arch-bishop Thomas à Becket was executed under the order of which English ruler?

[1] Elizabeth I
[2] William the Conqueror
[3] George III
[4] Henry II
[5] Richard the Lionhearted

ANSWER TO Q-19

[1] A heath is a tract of open land with uncultivated vegetation such as heather.

47%

11 Besides being extremely salty, the Dead Sea is unique in that it is:	[1] The sea Moses parted [2] Infested with sea snakes [3] Earth's lowest point [4] Not fed by any rivers [5] Bottomless	ANSWER TO Q-10 [2] Kazakhstan occupies nearly 1.1 million square miles. 57%
11 This famous character left her soldier lover for a bullfighter:	[1] Lady Chatterley [2] Carmen [3] Desdemona [4] Juliet [5] Charo	ANSWER TO Q-10 [2] The griffin was sacred to the sun and kept guard over hidden treasures. 51%
11 Which actress is a fictional character?	[1] Jeanne Eagles [2] Margo Channing [3] Gertrude Lawrence [4] Anna Neagle [5] Uta Hagen	ANSWER TO Q-10 [3] Tontine is a term in economics for a type of finance scheme. 43%
11 Which is not part of Canada's Northwest Territories?	[1] Great Slave Lake [2] Ellesmere Island [3] District of Mackenzie [4] Great Bear Lake [5] Jameson land	ANSWER TO Q-10 [2] Beardsley was the art editor of the influential "Yellow Book" magazine. 51%
11 What is the most abundant element on earth?	[1] Silicon [2] Carbon [3] Oxygen [4] Iron [5] Calcium	ANSWER TO Q-10 [3] A diadem is a royal headband signifying regal power and dignity. 54%

21 The French liqueur creme de cassis is made from this fruit:

[1] Cranberries
[2] Elderberries
[3] Passion fruit
[4] Strawberries
[5] Black currants

ANSWER TO Q-20

[4] He was one of the spies Moses sent ahead to the promised land of Canaan.

78%

---

21 Which Caribbean island has the greatest area?

[1] Jamaica
[2] Cuba
[3] Puerto Rico
[4] Hispaniola
[5] Trinidad

ANSWER TO Q-20

[1] English novelist Mary Renault wrote several such books dealing with history and mythology.

34%

---

21 Which biblical figure was not a king?

[1] David
[2] Ahab
[3] Samson
[4] Saul
[5] Solomon

ANSWER TO Q-20

[1] A completely different shark family, dogfishes are the smallest of sharks.

23%

---

21 Which musical group is not a quartet?

[1] Eurythmics
[2] The Beatles
[3] U2
[4] Van Halen
[5] The Bangles

ANSWER TO Q-20

[4] Beatrix replaced her mother, Juliana, who abdicated the throne on her 71st birthday.

89%

---

21 What is a sapote?

[1] Succulent
[2] Fruit
[3] Knife
[4] Nut
[5] Grain

ANSWER TO Q-20

[4] Becket's death was part of a larger struggle between church and state powers.

44%

10 After Russia, which is the largest former Soviet Republic in terms of square miles?	[1] Ukraine [2] Kazakhstan [3] Armenia [4] Georgia [5] Belarus	ANSWER TO Q-9 **[4]** Originally bred to hunt hares, like greyhounds, they are used in parimutuel betting. 76%
10 This mythical monster is said to be the offspring of the lion and eagle:	[1] Cyclops [2] Griffin [3] Medusa [4] Gorgon [5] Grendel	ANSWER TO Q-9 **[5]** That's why allergies and sinus problems make you feel wobbly as well as stuffed up. 68%
10 These are all geo-graphical formations except:	[1] Massif [2] Cay [3] Tontine [4] Isthmus [5] Reef	ANSWER TO Q-9 **[1]** Jean de Brunhoff created a series of books about this popular character. 61%
10 English artist Aubrey Beardsley was associated with all these except:	[1] Art Nouveau movement [2] Celebrity portraits [3] Book illustrations [4] Black and white drawings [5] The yellow book	ANSWER TO Q-9 **[3]** It is widely believed that field marshall Potemkin was her lover as well. 43%
10 Who would have worn a diadem?	[1] Monk [2] Squire [3] King [4] Nun [5] Merchant	ANSWER TO Q-9 **[2]** Philosopher Karl Marx wrote the treatise with fellow German Friedrich Engels. 52%

22 Which novel was not written by William Goldman?	[1] Marathon Man [2] Prizzi's Honor [3] Heat [4] The Princess Bride [5] Magic	ANSWER TO Q-21 [5] Black currants are not grown in many states due to agricultural diseases. 43%
22 Morgiana saves ____ by pouring boiling oil into the jars where thieves are hidden.	[1] Abraham [2] Mohammed [3] Peter Pan [4] Robin Hood [5] Ali Baba	ANSWER TO Q-21 [2] The 114,524 square mile island has three mountain regions, but is mostly gently rolling terrain. 78%
22 Which film does not end with an assassination attempt?	[1] Foul Play [2] The Dead Zone [3] The Bodyguard [4] To Live and Die in L.A. [5] In the Line of Fire	ANSWER TO Q-21 [3] A man of great strength, Samson was a Hebrew folk hero in the days before kings ruled the land. 79%
22 Which prefix signifies "all"?	[1] Para- [2] Pan- [3] Pen- [4] Poly- [5] Peri-	ANSWER TO Q-21 [1] This band, whose hits include "Sweet Dreams," was fronted by Annie Lennox and Dave Stewart. 81%
22 According to Mattel, her manufacturer, Barbie's last name is:	[1] Johnson [2] Roberts [3] Kelly [4] Stuart [5] Casey	ANSWER TO Q-21 [2] The tree of the tropical American fruit is sometimes called "marmalade tree." 55%

9 Whippets are small, slender dogs widely used as ____ dogs.	[1] Police [2] Seeing-eye [3] Watch [4] Racing [5] Fighting	ANSWER TO Q-8 **[3]** Michigan beat Stanford, 49-0, in the first Rose Bowl in 1902. 68%
9 Which part of the ear helps maintain balance?	[1] Outer ear [2] Eardrum [3] Ear canal [4] Ear lobe [5] Semi-circular canal	ANSWER TO Q-8 **[2]** The base is gelatin, meat broth, or other leftovers, often with a dash of wine added. 69%
9 Celesteville is a city ruled over by:	[1] Babar the Elephant [2] Baron Munchausen [3] The Queen of Hearts [4] Lemuel Gulliver [5] Peter Pan	ANSWER TO Q-8 **[4]** The largest nerve in the human body, the sciatic nerve runs from the pelvis to the thigh. 79%
9 Grigory Potemkin entered history as a soldier and advisor to this ruler:	[1] Stalin [2] Ivan the Terrible [3] Catherine the Great [4] Rurik [5] Lenin	ANSWER TO Q-8 **[3]** The duodenum is the first section of the small intestine in the digestive tract. 76%
9 In what language was the "Communist Manifesto" written?	[1] Latin [2] German [3] Russian [4] French [5] English	ANSWER TO Q-8 **[2]** The little-known movie "Rope" was filmed all in one shot, without any close-ups or cutaways. 78%

23 A gorget, a tasse and a gauntlet are articles that would have been worn by:

[1] Monks
[2] Coal miners
[3] Deep sea divers
[4] Knights
[5] Carpenters

ANSWER TO Q-22
[2] "Prizzi's Honor" is by William Condon.
42%

---

23 The Beatles played at the Cavern Club, which was located in which European city?

[1] London
[2] Liverpool
[3] Hamburg
[4] Glasgow
[5] Amsterdam

ANSWER TO Q-22
[5] Morgiana was Ali Baba's slave in "Ali Baba and the Forty Thieves."
68%

---

23 Stirlings, halifaxes and lancasters were all names of:

[1] Early autos
[2] Nuclear missiles
[3] WW II bombers
[4] 19th c. rifles
[5] German dirigibles

ANSWER TO Q-22
[4] This film centers on a government agent tracking down a murderous counterfeiter.
79%

---

23 The people who created the Hardy Boys and Nancy Drew also created:

[1] The Corsican Brothers
[2] Richie Rich
[3] Bobbsey Twins
[4] Archie
[5] Beavis and Butthead

ANSWER TO Q-22
[2] An example would be pantheism, which is the belief that God is in all things.
79%

---

23 An autopsy showed more than 10 drugs in his system, including morphine and quaaludes:

[1] Harry Houdini
[2] Jim Morrison
[3] Elvis Presley
[4] John Belushi
[5] Sigmund Freud

ANSWER TO Q-22
[2] Besides the dolls, Mattel sells 20 million Barbie outfits a year.
23%

8 Which is the oldest of the major college football bowl games?	[1] Orange [2] Sugar [3] Rose [4] Cotton [5] Gator	ANSWER TO Q-7 **[2]** All are 1 troy ounce of gold, but collectors pay the least for the krugerrand. 53%
8 In French cooking, what is an aspic?	[1] Cheese casserole [2] Molded gelatin salad [3] Oyster stew [4] Goose liver pate [5] Cold potato soup	ANSWER TO Q-7 **[4]** The middle class manner and dress of the constitutional monarch gave him his moniker. 65%
8 The sciatic nerve is found in the:	[1] Arm [2] Face [3] Chest [4] Leg [5] Neck	ANSWER TO Q-7 **[5]** Although Africa is home to the true vipers, it is entirely without pit vipers. 43%
8 In the body, the duodenum is part of the:	[1] Nervous system [2] Circulatory system [3] Digestive tract [4] Respiratory system [5] Skeleton	ANSWER TO Q-7 **[3]** This house ruled from 1154 to 1399, beginning with Henry II and ending with Richard II. 48%
8 Who directed the films "Family Plot," "Topaz," "Rope" and "Dial M for Murder"?	[1] Orson Welles [2] Alfred Hitchcock [3] John Huston [4] Walter Hill [5] Elia Kazan	ANSWER TO Q-7 **[4]** The tiny bone-dry nation lies to the south of Saudi Arabia, at the mouth of the Red Sea. 56%

24 Which ground bird is capable of killing a rattlesnake with little effort?	[1] Roadrunner [2] Pheasant [3] Grouse [4] Wild turkey [5] Partridge	ANSWER TO Q-23 **[4]** Other parts of a knight's armor included the pauldron, cuisse and the breastplate. 46%
24 Who collaborated with Karl Marx on "The Communist Manifesto"?	[1] Heinrich Heine [2] Friedrich Engels [3] Jean-Baptiste Fourier [4] John S. Mill [5] Immanuel Kant	ANSWER TO Q-23 **[2]** The Fab Four came from Liverpool and got their start at the local club. It is now closed. 92%
24 Mel Brooks does not act in this film:	[1] Blazing Saddles [2] Silent Movie [3] Young Frankenstein [4] High Anxiety [5] The Muppet Movie	ANSWER TO Q-23 **[3]** They carried out raids everywhere in Germany and were integral in the assault on Berlin. 61%
24 Which famous work was not published during the twenties?	[1] An American Tragedy [2] The Grapes of Wrath [3] The Waste Land [4] Babbitt [5] The Great Gatsby	ANSWER TO Q-23 **[3]** Separate pen names were used for each series of books for youngsters. 32%
24 Which Henry Fonda film is not a western?	[1] My Darling Clementine [2] Fort Apache [3] Return of Frank James [4] 12 Angry Men [5] Ox Bow Incident	ANSWER TO Q-23 **[3]** The amazing thing was that it wasn't the drugs but an irregular heart beat that killed him. 59%

7 The eagle, maple leaf, panda and krugerrand are all:	[1] Passenger trains [2] Gold coins [3] Volcanoes [4] European rock groups [5] International newspapers	ANSWER TO Q-6 **[4]** They proved the existence of a water passage from Canada to the Gulf of Mexico. 59%
7 Which French ruler was known as "The Citizen King"?	[1] Louis Napoleon [2] Charlemagne [3] Pepin the Short [4] Louis Philippe [5] Charles Martel	ANSWER TO Q-6 **[3]** The Romans identified her with the goddess Juno. 34%
7 There are no pit vipers native to this part of the world:	[1] North America [2] Southeastern Europe [3] South America [4] Eastern Asia [5] Africa	ANSWER TO Q-6 **[5]** The saxophone is in the woodwind family, as are the flute and the oboe. 69%
7 Which royal house of England ruled for over 200 years?	[1] Stuart [2] Godwin [3] Plantagenet [4] York [5] Tudor	ANSWER TO Q-6 **[4]** The "blue-eyed soul" duo consisted of singers Bill Medley and Bobby Hatfield. 69%
7 Which country did the queen of Sheba once rule?	[1] Turkey [2] Morocco [3] Ethiopia [4] South Yemen [5] Pakistan	ANSWER TO Q-6 **[2]** Released in 1960, "100 Rifles" starred Burt Reynolds, Raquel Welch and Jim Brown. 76%

25 These are composed of transistors, which function as switches in computers:

[1] Chips
[2] Quirks
[3] Curies
[4] Mites
[5] Bosons

ANSWER TO Q-24

[1] The nimble and swift roadrunner has been clocked at speeds of up to 15 miles per hour.

43%

25 All of these fabrics contain synthetic fibers except:

[1] Rayon
[2] Satin
[3] Poplin
[4] Mohair
[5] Polyester

ANSWER TO Q-24

[2] They formed a permanent partnership with the aim of promoting European socialism.

51%

25 What is kohlrabi?

[1] Fruit
[2] Cheese
[3] Organ meat
[4] Vegetable
[5] Herb

ANSWER TO Q-24

[3] He directs a cast including Gene Wilder, Madeline Kahn, Teri Garr and Gene Hackman.

61%

25 What is the material from which most micro-electronic chips are made?

[1] Teflon
[2] Silicon
[3] Carbon
[4] Celluloid
[5] Graphite

ANSWER TO Q-24

[2] John Steinbeck's novel was published in 1939.

61%

25 All of these cities are located in The Netherlands except:

[1] Amsterdam
[2] Haarlem
[3] Rotterdam
[4] Leerdam
[5] Potsdam

ANSWER TO Q-24

[4] Adapted from a play, the film focuses on jurists deliberating in a murder trial.

62%

6 Together with Louis Joliet, he discovered the upper Mississippi:	[1] Samuel de Champlain [2] Jacques Cartier [3] Sieur de la Salle [4] Jacques Marquette [5] Jean Nicolet	ANSWER TO Q-5 **[5]** The name comes from the curling angle in which polished stones are pushed toward tees. 78%
6 In Greek mythology, she was the protectress of women, marriage and childbirth:	[1] Venus [2] Persephone [3] Hera [4] Minerva [5] Aphrodite	ANSWER TO Q-5 **[4]** The folkways deemed best for the good of a society often form the basis of formal law. 67%
6 Which instrument is not in the brass family?	[1] French horn [2] Trumpet [3] Tuba [4] Cornet [5] Saxophone	ANSWER TO Q-5 **[1]** Australian currency is based on the dollar. 57%
6 Which group was not an actual family?	[1] Brothers Johnson [2] The Everly Brothers [3] The Staple Singers [4] The Righteous Brothers [5] The Jackson 5	ANSWER TO Q-5 **[4]** At sea, the letter "Q" is used in place of the yellow flag. 64%
6 Which western did not star John Wayne?	[1] The Shootist [2] 100 Rifles [3] Fort Apache [4] How the West Was Won [5] El Dorado	ANSWER TO Q-5 **[2]** Part of it was an area for political meetings; the remainder served as a marketplace. 56%

26 The final section of this novel consists of a famous stream of consciousness monologue:	[1] The World According to Garp [2] Ulysses [3] Slaughterhouse-5 [4] The Sound and the Fury [5] The Trial	ANSWER TO Q-25 **[1]** They've made everything from hand-held radios to satellite communications possible. 81%
26 Tandoori is a popular style of cooking that originated in:	[1] Vietnam [2] Saudi Arabia [3] Korea [4] Hungary [5] India	ANSWER TO Q-25 **[4]** The long, shiny hair of the angora goat is highly prized for sweaters. 82%
26 When unripe, this bright orange fruit is notoriously bitter:	[1] Passion fruit [2] Pomegranate [3] Quince [4] Persimmon [5] Gooseberry	ANSWER TO Q-25 **[4]** It is similar in taste to turnips and celery. 85%
26 This type of poem first became popular in the mid 19th century:	[1] Limerick [2] Epigram [3] Ballad [4] Sonnet [5] Couplet	ANSWER TO Q-25 **[2]** Silicon is the second most abundant element (28% by weight) in the earth's crust. 79%
26 Which of these historical events happened first?	[1] First Olympic games [2] Founding of Rome [3] Beginnings of Judaism [4] Han dynasty in China [5] Death of Buddha	ANSWER TO Q-25 **[5]** Although Dutch influence has given Potsdam its ambience, the city is in Germany. 68%

5 The team sport of curling takes place on this surface:

[1] Asphalt
[2] Wooden floor
[3] Dirt
[4] Grass
[5] Ice

ANSWER TO Q-4

[1] Your dentition is how many teeth you have, what kind, and how they are spaced.
67%

---

5 A society's mores are its:

[1] Minority populations
[2] Passing fads
[3] Economic infrastructures
[4] Values and customs
[5] Social classes

ANSWER TO Q-4

[1] Taft-Hartley refers to an act of Congress, aka the National Labor Relations Act.
56%

---

5 Which country is mismatched with its unit of currency?

[1] Australia - pound
[2] Israel - shekel
[3] Jordan - dinar
[4] Italy - lira
[5] Mexico - peso

ANSWER TO Q-4

[3] It took a Roman army of 15,000 two years to subdue 1,000 Jews hidden on the mountaintop.
78%

---

5 Waving a yellow flag is an international symbol for:

[1] Hostile group
[2] Cease fire
[3] Surrender
[4] Infectious disease
[5] Ally ahead

ANSWER TO Q-4

[3] Far from being a local product, petroleum is imported by Jordan, mostly from the Saudis.
45%

---

5 Agoraphobes are afraid of open spaces. In ancient Athens, what was the agora?

[1] Huge practice field
[2] Market & meeting area
[3] Mythical monster
[4] Battlefield
[5] Sacred mountain

ANSWER TO Q-4

[5] Jean-Paul Sartre rejected the Nobel Prize, believing homage undermines commitment.
56%

27 What city was captured during the Six-Day War?	[1] Mecca [2] Baghdad [3] Jerusalem [4] Tel Aviv [5] Beirut	ANSWER TO Q-26 **[2]** Molly Bloom's monologue is a single, uninterrupted sentence ending in "Yes." 69%
27 Which fictional captain is not a human?	[1] Ahab [2] Queeg [3] Bligh [4] Hook [5] Flint	ANSWER TO Q-26 **[5]** It refers to dishes cooked in a special clay oven. 69%
27 What type of fish is caught by the old man in Hemingway's "The Old Man and the Sea"?	[1] Shark [2] Marlin [3] Whale [4] Sawfish [5] Stingray	ANSWER TO Q-26 **[4]** It is a traditional late fall-early winter treat in many parts of North America. 54%
27 If lovers are said to be "star-crossed," their relationship is:	[1] Ideal [2] Stormy [3] Doomed [4] Platonic [5] Unorthodox	ANSWER TO Q-26 **[1]** Victorian writer Edward Lear popularized the form in his 1846 "Book of Nonsense." 42%
27 All raptorial birds have:	[1] Red heads [2] Singing ability [3] Sharp talons [4] Long swordlike beaks [5] Long legs	ANSWER TO Q-26 **[3]** The beginnings of Judaism occurred around 1200 B.C. 52%

4 If you talked about your dentition, you would be talking about your:

[1] Set of teeth
[2] Love life
[3] Religious convictions
[4] Eating habits
[5] Exercise program

ANSWER TO Q-3

[3] One would camber a road to allow for drainage off the sides.

45%

---

4 All of these terms designate U.S. political scandals except:

[1] Taft-Hartley
[2] Teapot Dome
[3] Watergate
[4] Abscam
[5] Iran-Contra

ANSWER TO Q-3

[5] The thymus is part of the immune system and it regulates lymphocytes in the body.

45%

---

4 The mountain called Masada played a major role in a heroic confrontation between:

[1] Jews and Arabs
[2] Egyptians and Romans
[3] Jews and Romans
[4] Greeks and Turks

ANSWER TO Q-3

[4] Both a duke and duchess are addressed as "Your Grace" and are only topped by king or queen.

53%

---

4 Which country does not have petroleum as its largest export product?

[1] Saudi Arabia
[2] Iran
[3] Jordan
[4] Iraq
[5] Kuwait

ANSWER TO Q-3

[2] Arugula is a form of loose-leafed cabbage that is often used as a salad green.

45%

---

4 While some claim "War is hell" or "Life is hell," a Sartre character says hell is:

[1] Television
[2] A muggy Parisian summer
[3] Lack of knowledge
[4] An absence from being
[5] Other people

ANSWER TO Q-3

[3] The others are either from the Grimm brothers or in Charles Perrault's "Mother Goose."

56%

28 The lamprey closely resembles this animal:	[1] Hyena [2] Whale [3] Eel [4] Antelope [5] Eagle	ANSWER TO Q-27 **[3]** Annexed by Jordan during the Arab-Israeli war, Jerusalem was captured by Israel in 1967. 69%
28 Which world leader "spoke softly and carried a big stick"?	[1] Winston Churchill [2] Theodore Roosevelt [3] Charles de Gaulle [4] Napoleon Bonaparte [5] Francisco Franco	ANSWER TO Q-27 **[5]** Cap'n Flint is the trusty parrot of Long John Silver in "Treasure Island." 58%
28 Which is not a fruit?	[1] Tomato [2] Rhubarb [3] Cucumber [4] Pumpkin [5] Pineapple	ANSWER TO Q-27 **[2]** Ernest Hemingway learned about marlin fishing during the 1930's in Key West and put it to good use. 52%
28 What is the relation of Genghis Khan to Kublai Khan?	[1] Father [2] Grandfather [3] Son [4] Nephew [5] Brothers	ANSWER TO Q-27 **[3]** The astrological metaphor comes from "Romeo and Juliet." 68%
28 When the solar wind collides with the earth's magnetic field, we observe this:	[1] Extremely high tides [2] Aurora Borealis [3] Sunspots [4] Volcanic eruptions [5] Tectonic plate shifts	ANSWER TO Q-27 **[3]** Raptors are birds of prey such as the eagle, hawk and owl. 55%

3 To camber something is to ____ it.	[1] Shock [2] Irritate [3] Curve [4] Melt [5] Smooth	ANSWER TO Q-2 **[5]** A repository of wisdom, he was the teacher of Jason, Achilles and Hercules. 54%
3 Which is not part of the hormonal system?	[1] Pancreas [2] Testes [3] Pineal [4] Pituitary [5] Thymus	ANSWER TO Q-2 **[3]** All the rest are ruminants, which chew their cud and have many stomachs. 45%
3 Which British title of nobility is "highest"?	[1] Baron [2] Viscount [3] Earl [4] Duke [5] Marquess	ANSWER TO Q-2 **[3]** Succulents have thick, fleshy tissues for storing water. 39%
3 All of these are fruits except:	[1] Kumquat [2] Arugula [3] Sapote [4] Persimmon [5] Citron	ANSWER TO Q-2 **[4]** First isolated in 1935, it is a product of the adrenal cortex. 68%
3 Which famous tale is found in Aesop's fables?	[1] Cinderella [2] Tom Thumb [3] The Boy Who Cried Wolf [4] Sleeping Beauty [5] Little Red Riding Hood	ANSWER TO Q-2 **[4]** Written by Dumas in the 1840's, they tell of an earlier, more romantic period. 23%

58

29 Lou Gehrig was the first major leaguer to:	[1] Pitch a no hitter [2] Hit 4 home runs in one game [3] Marry a movie star [4] Steal a base [5] Have his number retired	ANSWER TO Q-28 **[3]** Most lampreys are parasitic bloodsuckers, attaching themselves to other fish. 71%
29 Dachshunds, whippets and basenjis are all:	[1] Sporting dogs [2] Toy dogs [3] Hounds [4] Mongrels [5] Working dogs	ANSWER TO Q-28 **[2]** This famous line by Teddy Roosevelt emphasized his policy towards foreign affairs. 72%
29 Which Indian group is not from Central or South America?	[1] Aztecs [2] Arawaks [3] Mayas [4] Pueblo [5] Incas	ANSWER TO Q-28 **[2]** Fruits have seeds. Vegetables don't. Rhubarb is a member of the buckwheat family. 55%
29 Which bird's feathers turn white during the winter?	[1] Great Horned Owl [2] Woodcock [3] Roadrunner [4] Mourning dove [5] Ptarmigan	ANSWER TO Q-28 **[2]** During Kublai Khan's rule (1260-94), the great Khanate became the Yuan dynasty of China. 55%
29 A squall line is a term used to describe a:	[1] Fault pattern [2] Weather front [3] Desert horizon [4] Planet's rotation [5] Mountain formation	ANSWER TO Q-28 **[2]** The Eskimos believed the Northern Lights were spirits of the dead playing catch at night. 57%

2 What kind of creature is Greek mythology's Chiron?	[1] Three-headed dog [2] Fire-breathing dragon [3] Princess of Troy [4] God of war [5] Wise centaur	ANSWER TO Q-1 [4] To finish off the cash flow; $100s are yellow, $50s are blue, and $1s are white. 78%
2 Which animal does not have a multi-chambered stomach?	[1] Cow [2] Camel [3] Pig [4] Antelope [5] Goat	ANSWER TO Q-1 [5] A Bearnaise sauce includes onions, white wine, tarragon, egg yolks and parsley. 54%
2 What kind of plant is the agave?	[1] Ivy [2] Fern [3] Succulent [4] Flowering annual [5] Shrub	ANSWER TO Q-1 [1] In Italian, the opposite is "antipatico," or not such a nice guy. 67%
2 Cortisone is used especially in the treatment of:	[1] Epilepsy [2] Hepatitis [3] Shingles [4] Rheumatoid arthritis [5] Sciatica	ANSWER TO Q-1 [3] This major figure of the Italian Renaissance met his death in a military skirmish at age 31. 34%
2 "Twenty Years After" and "The Viscount of Bragelonne" are the sequels to this classic:	[1] Treasure Island [2] Robinson Crusoe [3] Moll Flanders [4] The Three Musketeers [5] Gulliver's Travels	ANSWER TO Q-1 [1] The formula is known as the law of equivalence of mass and energy. 56%

30 What is the main ingredient in the soup called gazpacho?	[1] Potatoes [2] Beets [3] Tomatoes [4] Veal [5] Onions	ANSWER TO Q-29 [5] On Lou Gehrig Day he said, "I consider myself the luckiest man on the face of the Earth." 53%
30 Which of these writers was an innovator of the stream of consciousness technique?	[1] Herman Melville [2] Ernest Hemingway [3] James Joyce [4] Alexander Dumas [5] Isaac Asimov	ANSWER TO Q-29 [3] Hounds were originally bred to hunt animals, mostly using their sense of smell. 54%
30 Which famous symbol was variously represented as a chalice, dish or stone?	[1] Holy grail [2] Zodiac [3] Mandala [4] Homunculus [5] Microcosm	ANSWER TO Q-29 [4] Inhabiting the southwestern U.S., the Pueblos are noted for fine craftsman-ship. 32%
30 Which ageless toy was originally made from the knuckle bones of dogs and sheep?	[1] Dice [2] Marbles [3] Jacks [4] Tops [5] Hoops	ANSWER TO Q-29 [5] Ptarmigans are members of the grouse family of game birds. 41%
30 This 1915 D.W. Griffith epic treats the Civil War and Re-construction:	[1] The Birth of a Nation [2] Red Dust [3] Glory [4] Of Human Bondage [5] The Red Badge of Courage	ANSWER TO Q-29 [2] It is a line that precedes a cold front, marked by wind gusts and often heavy rain. 63%

1 What color is the $20 dollar bill in the game of Monopoly?	[1] White [2] Red [3] Blue [4] Green [5] Orange	Turn to the top frame on the next left hand page for the correct answer and the next question.
1 This dish is a broiled beef tenderloin covered with a Bearnaise sauce:	[1] Coq au vin [2] Bouillabaisse [3] Vichyssoise [4] Martinet [5] Chateaubriand	Turn to the second frame on the next left hand page for the correct answer and the next question.
1 If someone is "molto simpatico," they are:	[1] A nice guy [2] Stupid [3] Religious [4] Foolish [5] A relative	Turn to the middle frame on the next left hand page for the correct answer and the next question.
1 Which statement about Cesare Borgia is untrue?	[1] Son of a churchman [2] Captain of papal army [3] Died an old man [4] Influenced Machiavelli [5] Spanish descent	Turn to the fourth frame on the next left hand page for the correct answer and the next question.
1 Einstein's mass-energy formula states that energy equals mass times the ____ squared.	[1] Velocity of light [2] Width [3] Distance [4] Volume [5] Height	Turn to the bottom frame on the next left hand page for the correct answer and the next question.

A Dog's Life

GAME NUMBER 2

ANSWER TO Q-30

[3] The Spanish delicacy is properly served ice cold.

65%

Dangerous

GAME NUMBER 20

ANSWER TO Q-30

[3] The technique, which mimics the inner thought process, is used widely in his novel "Ulysses."

71%

Fools

GAME NUMBER 38

ANSWER TO Q-30

[1] The object of a quest by the Knights of the Round Table, it could be found only by the pure.

81%

Fruits/Vegetables

GAME NUMBER 56

ANSWER TO Q-30

[2] The oldest marbles were found in an ancient Egyptian child's tomb dating back to 3000 B.C.

57%

General Science

GAME NUMBER 74

ANSWER TO Q-30

[1] The film is now thought to be racist in its glorification of the Ku Klux Klan.

58%

GAME NUMBER 18

ANSWER TO Q-10

[1] It is the heel stamping used in both flamenco music and dance.

21%

GAME NUMBER 36

ANSWER TO Q-10

[3] Disgusted with Ken Russell's film version, Chayefsky insisted his name not be used.

32%

GAME NUMBER 54

ANSWER TO Q-10

[3] It becomes final after a set interval, unless cause to the contrary can be shown.

21%

GAME NUMBER 72

ANSWER TO Q-10

[4] "Experiments on Plant Hybrids" dealt with traits passed between strains of garden peas.

56%

GAME NUMBER 90

ANSWER TO Q-10

[4] Mel Blanc, born in San Francisco, is the voice of many well-known cartoon characters.

61%

1 You should be most concerned about a dog attacking when it is:	[1] Barking loudly [2] Growling [3] Growling and barking [4] Snarling [5] Silently aggressive	Turn to the top frame on the next right hand page for the correct answer and the next question.
1 Which of these occupations has the highest mortality rate per 1000 workers?	[1] High-wire performer [2] Hydroplane driver [3] Power-line worker [4] Boxer [5] Lumberjack	Turn to the second frame on the next right hand page for the correct answer and the next question.
1 Which vaudeville comic billed himself as "The Perfect Fool"?	[1] Eddie Cantor [2] Jack Benny [3] W.C. Fields [4] Edgar Bergen [5] Ed Wynn	Turn to the middle frame on the next right hand page for the correct answer and the next question.
1 Which fruit has the least nutritional value?	[1] Apple [2] Apricot [3] Grapefruit [4] Cantaloupe [5] Strawberries	Turn to the fourth frame on the next right hand page for the correct answer and the next question.
1 You mix aluminum soap with gasoline in order to make:	[1] A molotov cocktail [2] Napalm [3] Asbestos [4] Lye [5] Fiberglass	Turn to the bottom frame on the next right hand page for the correct answer and the next question.

10 Zapateodo is a rhythmic device used in what kind of music?	[1] Flamenco [2] Bossa nova [3] Calypso [4] Jazz [5] Rock	ANSWER TO Q-9 **[3]** He won the Best Actor Award for work in "The Way of All Flesh" and "The Last Command." 41%
10 "Altered States" is credited to screenwriter Sydney Aaron, a pseudonym for:	[1] Oliver Stone [2] Kurt Vonnegut [3] Paddy Chayefsky [4] Stephen King [5] Judith Rossner	ANSWER TO Q-9 **[3]** The loom weaved its complex patterns using instructions coded on punched cards. 21%
10 In law, what is the result of a decree nisi?	[1] Contract is broken [2] Evidence is presented [3] Conditional divorce [4] Case is dismissed [5] Mistrial	ANSWER TO Q-9 **[3]** Used to constrict blood vessels, it is also found in the gastric mucosa of mammals. 31%
10 Austrian monk Gregor Mendel's 1866 book lay the foundation for this modern science:	[1] Geology [2] Psychology [3] Bible research [4] Genetics [5] Astronomy	ANSWER TO Q-9 **[3]** Hughes was known for his part in the Harlem Renaissance, and poems about Black experience. 42%
10 Pick the only American born celebrity out of this list:	[1] Richard Attenborough [2] Dan Aykroyd [3] George Balanchine [4] Mel Blanc [5] Saul Bellow	ANSWER TO Q-9 **[4]** Many Tupamaros were university-educated, but unable to find jobs in the stagnant economy. 21%

2 According to Ann Landers, how should you tell a neighbor his dog keeps you awake at nite?	[1] Write a polite note [2] Call the police [3] Get a louder dog [4] Call him at 2 a.m. [5] Throw rocks at her window	ANSWER TO Q-1 **[5]** As the dog's fear level rises, so do the noises, from a snarl to a growl to a bark. 79%
2 The film "Dangerous Liaisons" is a costume drama set in 18th-century:	[1] England [2] France [3] Spain [4] Germany [5] America	ANSWER TO Q-1 **[2]** At 25 deaths for every thousand drivers, they are second only to astronauts at 30/1000. 67%
2 "Running Out of Fools" and "Chain of Fools" are two bluesy hits recorded by:	[1] Etta James [2] Dinah Washington [3] Nancy Wilson [4] Aretha Franklin [5] Dionne Warwick	ANSWER TO Q-1 **[5]** Ed Wynn was known for his trademark lisping, outlandish costumes and fluttering hands. 34%
2 If we refer to some as freestone and others as clingstone, we are talking about:	[1] Potatoes [2] Boysenberries [3] Tomatoes [4] Peaches [5] Beets	ANSWER TO Q-1 **[1]** The others are excellent sources of vitamins A or C. Apple skins have a small dose of vitamin C. 57%
2 In order for oxidation to occur, this process must also take place:	[1] Electrolysis [2] Osmosis [3] Reduction [4] Fermentation [5] Distillation	ANSWER TO Q-1 **[2]** Used in flame throwers and bombs, it burns hot and slow, and sticks to its target. 68%

9 Emil Jannings was a winner of the first:	[1] Nobel Peace Prize [2] Time "Man of the Year" [3] Academy Award [4] Pulitzer Prize [5] Heisman Trophy	ANSWER TO Q-8 **[4]** She wrote "Frankenstein: the Modern Prometheus," and he penned "Prometheus Unbound." 32%
9 This product's technology played an important role in the invention of computers:	[1] Mccormick Reaper [2] Water wheel [3] Jacquard Loom [4] Gatling Gun [5] Pressure cooker	ANSWER TO Q-8 **[3]** Murderer's Row was the 1927 Yankees' trio of Hall-of-Famers: Ruth, Gehrig and Lazzeri. 59%
9 Serotonin is a powerful vasoconstrictor found in:	[1] Human saliva [2] Seaweed [3] Blood serum [4] Honey [5] Snake venom	ANSWER TO Q-8 **[2]** The "Academy" flourished for 800 years, until philosophic schools were suppressed in 529 AD. 31%
9 "What happens to a dream deferred? Does it dry up like a ____?" End Langston Hughes' line.	[1] Host of golden daffodils [2] Portrait of a lady [3] Raisin in the sun [4] Lonely desert herd [5] Old fool's heart	ANSWER TO Q-8 **[1]** The metaphor is most often used in reference to heaven and its actual proximity to God. 42%
9 A 1960's Marxist rebel group called the Tupamaros waged a guerrilla war here:	[1] Uganda [2] Thailand [3] United States [4] Uruguay [5] Chile	ANSWER TO Q-8 **[4]** A central location in the Bible, the city is now a part of Israeli-occupied Jordan. 32%

3 In which sport would you hear the term "Dogleg"?

[1] Golf
[2] Track and field
[3] Horseracing
[4] Swimming
[5] Yachting

ANSWER TO Q-2

[4] Ann Landers suggests keeping this up every night Fido barks, until the owner solves the problem.

51%

---

3 Who is the target of an assassination attempt in the film "In the Line of Fire"?

[1] Singing celebrity
[2] Black rights leader
[3] U.S. president
[4] Movie star
[5] Corporate executive

ANSWER TO Q-2

[2] Glenn Close and John Malkovich star as the villainous schemers in this 1988 film.

81%

---

3 Silent screen vamp Theda Bara had her biggest hit with:

[1] Foolish Wives
[2] Men are Fools
[3] A Fool There Was
[4] Fools for Love
[5] Coulda Fooled Me

ANSWER TO Q-2

[4] These recordings remain among her most popular.

77%

---

3 Which vegetable offers the highest source of calcium?

[1] Celery
[2] Spinach
[3] Corn
[4] Asparagus
[5] Mushrooms

ANSWER TO Q-2

[4] The reference is to the degree of ease with which the seed separates from the flesh.

81%

---

3 A harmful waste product produced when protein is broken down to provide energy is:

[1] Sodium pentathol
[2] Ammonia
[3] Analgesia
[4] Hydrochloride
[5] Borax

ANSWER TO Q-2

[3] The two reactions occur simultaneously and in chemically equivalent quantities.

43%

8 In separate works, Percy Bysshe and Mary Shelley made reference to ____.

[1] The Frankenstein myth
[2] Marquis De Sade
[3] Nightingales
[4] Prometheus
[5] King Arthur's Court

ANSWER TO Q-7

[1] Except for Finland, the only other place you'll hear anything similar is in western Siberia.

31%

---

8 Where would you have found the famed "Murderer's Row"?

[1] Alcatraz
[2] Devil's Island
[3] Yankee Stadium
[4] Athens
[5] The Bastille

ANSWER TO Q-7

[1] The Spanish peninsula juts from the European mainland past the British Isles.

52%

---

8 The philosopher Plato's famous school near Athens was called the:

[1] Seminar
[2] Academy
[3] Alma Mater
[4] Conservatory
[5] Colloquium

ANSWER TO Q-7

[3] He cleared misconception on the speed of light, and later took the first clear photo of the sun.

31%

---

8 "Abraham's Bosom," a Biblical figure of speech, signifies a state of:

[1] Paternal care
[2] Drunken bliss
[3] Eternal damnation
[4] Slavery
[5] Homelessness

ANSWER TO Q-7

[3] Stubborn and fearless, he was killed in an 1820 duel with James Barron.

31%

---

8 If you want to live in a place called "House of Bread," which city ought you move to?

[1] Stockholm
[2] Amsterdam
[3] Trois Rivieres
[4] Bethlehem
[5] Acapulco

ANSWER TO Q-7

[5] The play's deranged main character pokes the eyes out of six horses, then is sent to his analyst.

21%

6 Which of these was not a famous film dog?	[1] Ben [2] Old Yeller [3] Sounder [4] Rin Tin Tin [5] Lassie	ANSWER TO Q-5 [4] It is a loosely structured verse with comic effect. 43%
6 All of these terms refer to something dangerous or evil except:	[1] Hazardous [2] Perilous [3] Insidious [4] Pernicious [5] Fastidious	ANSWER TO Q-5 [2] Her boyfriend was too much in debt to marry her, so she stole $40,000 from her boss. 81%
6 Who gave us the quote, "Fools rush in where angels fear to tread"?	[1] Ben Jonson [2] Benjamin Franklin [3] Winston Churchill [4] Alexander Pope [5] Truman Capote	ANSWER TO Q-5 [2] His famous book advocating resistance to authority was titled "Civil Disobedience." 68%
6 Which fruit has edible seeds?	[1] Apricot [2] Cherry [3] Nectarine [4] Papaya [5] Peach	ANSWER TO Q-5 [5] Commonly considered a vegetable because of its use, it is actually a fruit. 56%
6 This substance is produced by the human body when a person is angry or frightened:	[1] Menalin [2] Fibrinogen [3] Adrenalin [4] Keratin [5] Gonadatropins	ANSWER TO Q-5 [1] Antigens are foreign proteins; antibodies are proteins that combat them. 61%

5 The English celebrate "Guy Fawkes Day" on Nov. 5th. What did he do to merit his own holiday?	[1] Start China opium trade [2] Plant bomb in Parliament [3] Cultivate many orchids [4] Repel a Viking invasion [5] Die at Waterloo	ANSWER TO Q-4 **[2]** He attacked mass culture as a machine that produces the forgetfulness of being. 43%
5 Napoleon, Genghis Khan, Mao Tse-Tung and modern military leaders used his war manual:	[1] Julius Caesar [2] Sun Tzu [3] Homer [4] Isaac Newton [5] Alexander the Great	ANSWER TO Q-4 **[4]** The Guernica oak, where the Diet of Vizcaya met, symbolizes the lost liberty of the Basques. 41%
5 Which Greek prefix means "bad"?	[1] Caco- [2] Hexa- [3] Necro- [4] Hagio- [5] Phago-	ANSWER TO Q-4 **[3]** Governor of the colony for most of his life, he was largely responsible for Plymouth's success. 42%
5 During a wine-induced frenzy, Agave tears her son Pentheus limb from limb in which play?	[1] Beowulf [2] The Taming of the Shrew [3] Prometheus Bound [4] The Bacchae [5] Oresteia	ANSWER TO Q-4 **[1]** The Gestalt school of psychology ignores all distinct parts, focusing on integrated wholes. 32%
5 The eohippus is the extinct ancestor of this animal:	[1] Camel [2] Giraffe [3] Elephant [4] Horse [5] Hippopotamus	ANSWER TO Q-4 **[3]** Founded by Alexander the Great, it's been central to Greek, Hebrew and Christian culture. 41%

7 Which film does not revolve around a dog?	[1] Benji [2] Old Yeller [3] Casey's Shadow [4] Where the Red Fern Grows [5] Big Red	ANSWER TO Q-6 **[1]** Ben was a movie rat, not a movie dog. 89%
7 Those training for this sport are traditionally bricklayers during their apprenticeship:	[1] Pole vaulting [2] Cliff diving [3] Rugby [4] Fencing [5] Bullfighting	ANSWER TO Q-6 **[5]** Fastidious means unnecessarily committed to small details. 81%
7 Novice prospectors were tricked by "Fool's Gold," which is properly known as:	[1] Obsidian [2] Magnetite [3] Lignite [4] Mica [5] Iron pyrite	ANSWER TO Q-6 **[4]** Pope is regarded as the greatest of all English verse satirists. 32%
7 The name of this fruit is also the name of a bird:	[1] Hyrax [2] Currant [3] Kiwi [4] Fig [5] Filbert	ANSWER TO Q-6 **[4]** The peppery seeds can be used whole as a garnish or ground as a seasoning. 55%
7 Produced by the brain, this natural painkiller is three times stronger than morphine:	[1] Serotonin [2] Endorphin [3] Dopamine [4] Cadmium [5] Synesthesia	ANSWER TO Q-6 **[3]** Doctor Bruce Banner was conducting adrenalin research when he was converted into the hulk. 91%

4 Considered one of its founders, this philosopher denied he was an existentialist:	[1] Jean Jacques Rousseau [2] Martin Heidegger [3] Friedrich Nietzsche [4] Jean-Paul Sartre [5] Carl Jung	ANSWER TO Q-3 **[5]** It is made up of two branched open curves, or a plane slicing two circular cones. 64%
4 Guernica, the subject of Picasso's painting, was a sacred city to these people:	[1] Spanish Moors [2] French Huguenots [3] Gypsies [4] Basques [5] The "black" Irish	ANSWER TO Q-3 **[2]** Developer of a strong nationalistic style, he founded the Norwegian Academy of Music. 32%
4 His "History of Plymouth Plantation" included an account of the voyage of the "Mayflower":	[1] Miles Standish [2] John Carver [3] William Bradford [4] Cotton Mather [5] John Alden	ANSWER TO Q-3 **[4]** Andrew Wyeth's neighbor, she was the subject of a secret series of works by the artist. 46%
4 Which phrase most accurately states the meaning of the German word "gestalt"?	[1] Whole is more than parts [2] Your personal double [3] Mind over matter [4] Sign of the times [5] Shattered myth	ANSWER TO Q-3 **[3]** A proper magician's wand is cut from a hazelwood tree at sunrise, to draw on yet untouched solar power. 32%
4 This city is located where the Nile River empties into the Mediterranean Sea:	[1] Cairo [2] Algiers [3] Alexandria [4] Tel Aviv [5] Bombay	ANSWER TO Q-3 **[2]** Rod Laver was a major force in men's tennis throughout the decade. 51%

8 This is known as the world's longest dogsled race:	[1] Anchorage [2] Nome Express [3] Cicely Course [4] Iditarod [5] Sitka Sprint	ANSWER TO Q-7 [3] This film, which stars Walter Matthau, centers on a thoroughbred race horse. 61%
8 Who was the first explorer to reach the North Pole?	[1] James Cook [2] Robert E. Peary [3] Francis Drake [4] George Vancouver [5] Edmund Hillary	ANSWER TO Q-7 [5] Training begins at the age of 12, leading to a career at the age of 20. 43%
8 Which Beatles album features the song "The Fool on the Hill"?	[1] A Hard Day's Night [2] Yellow Submarine [3] Magical Mystery Tour [4] Revolver [5] Help!	ANSWER TO Q-7 [5] This substance has a gold-like luster and is found in large nugget-like lumps. 68%
8 Which plant bears fruit a mere 15 months after planting?	[1] Avocado [2] Orange [3] Apple [4] Banana [5] Apricot	ANSWER TO Q-7 [3] The rare, flightless kiwi, native to New Zealand, occupies an order all by itself. 91%
8 What chemical will burn violently when mixed with water, but not at all in kerosene?	[1] Germanium [2] Tellurium [3] Sodium [4] Chlorine [5] Manganese	ANSWER TO Q-7 [2] This drug is released during laughter, which is why laughing feels so good. 79%

9 In sailing, how long is a dog watch?	[1] Sixty seconds [2] Ten minutes [3] Two hours [4] Eight hours [5] All night	ANSWER TO Q-8 [4] This dogsled race crosses from Anchorage to Nome. 89%
9 Members of this group were originally mercenaries hired to guard western settlers:	[1] Minutemen [2] Texas Rangers [3] Hessians [4] Janissaries [5] Pinkerton Detectives	ANSWER TO Q-8 [2] His accomplishment was recognized by the U.S. Congress in 1911. 89%
9 April Fools' Day came from _____ when the Gregorian calendar was adopted.	[1] Spain [2] Italy [3] China [4] Brazil [5] France	ANSWER TO Q-8 [3] The "Magical Mystery Tour" album also features "Penny Lane" and "Strawberry Fields Forever." 71%
9 While on a low-fat diet, you would do well to avoid eating any foods prepared with:	[1] Safflower oil [2] Palm kernel oil [3] Sesame oil [4] Soybean oil [5] Olive oil	ANSWER TO Q-8 [4] The banana plant is the largest of the herbs. 65%
9 What keeps a drowning man from breathing the oxygen in water?	[1] Panic [2] Hydrogen [3] Poor planning [4] Hyperthermia [5] Pulmonary blockage	ANSWER TO Q-8 [3] Sodium metal burns explosively in water and is stored in kerosene for safety. 32%

2 English-woman Mary Kingsley is known for her exploration and study of which land?	[1] Canada [2] South America [3] Africa [4] Australia [5] New Zealand	ANSWER TO Q-1 **[4]** In many cases, it is caused by a fear of intimacy or responsibility. 65%
2 Francisco de Orellana is remembered in history for his explorations of the:	[1] Aztec Empire [2] Antarctic [3] Amazon Basin [4] Andes Mountains [5] Southwestern U.S.A.	ANSWER TO Q-1 **[1]** This popular Mexican song is about a dove. 72%
2 In 1978, Daniel Arap Moi became president of this nation:	[1] Thailand [2] Finland [3] Australia [4] Kenya [5] Bulgaria	ANSWER TO Q-1 **[2]** 395-345 million years ago, armored fish and lungfish were the dominant species. 42%
2 From a place in this country, you can spot both the Atlantic and Pacific Oceans:	[1] Costa Rica [2] Alaska [3] Brazil [4] Cuba [5] Greenland	ANSWER TO Q-1 **[3]** Dividing Europe and Turkey, it was the Soviet Navy's sole access to open ocean. 41%
2 During the War of 1812, he and his Shawnee tribe fought with the British against the U.S.:	[1] Tecumseh [2] Sitting Bull [3] Geronimo [4] Crazy Horse [5] Pocahontas	ANSWER TO Q-1 **[4]** Kurtz is an ivory trader who sets up a violent, despotic republic of African natives. 53%

10 The Lhasa apso was originally bred in Tibet to be used as a:	[1] Hunter [2] Watchdog [3] Food source [4] Herder [5] Retriever	ANSWER TO Q-9 [3] It is a two-hour spell of watch duty from four to six, or from six to eight p.m. 44%
10 Which of these animals is dangerous even before it is born?	[1] Sand tiger shark [2] Tarantula [3] Portuguese man-of-war [4] Oyster [5] Chuckwalla lizard	ANSWER TO Q-9 [2] They evolved into an elite force that fought crime in the vast fringes of Texan lands. 54%
10 Which word is not a term for a type of fool?	[1] Dolt [2] Blockhead [3] Nincompoop [4] Newt [5] Numskull	ANSWER TO Q-9 [5] The new calendar changed New Year's Day from April 1 to January 1. 23%
10 Which famous person listed was not a vegetarian?	[1] Henry Thoreau [2] Pythagoras [3] Adolf Hitler [4] Diamond Jim Brady [5] George Bernard Shaw	ANSWER TO Q-9 [2] Palm and coconut oils are exceedingly high in saturated fats–each is over 80% saturated fat. 91%
10 According to the FDA, how does a food flavor enhancer work?	[1] Produces flavor bursts [2] Forms scents [3] Swells tastebuds [4] Deadens certain nerves [5] Advertising	ANSWER TO Q-9 [2] Actually, it would take an electric current to release the oxygen from its 2 hydrogen captors. 57%

1 Misogamy is:	[1] Hatred of males [2] Aversion to money [3] Suspicion of people [4] Hatred of marriage [5] Dislike of privacy	Turn to the top frame on the next left hand page for the correct answer and the next question.
1 All these songs are national anthems except:	[1] La Paloma [2] God Save the King [3] The Star-Spangled Banner [4] La Marseillaise [5] O Canada	Turn to the second frame on the next left hand page for the correct answer and the next question.
1 Which of these geological eras was dominated by fish?	[1] Precambrian [2] Devonian [3] Ordovician [4] Pleistocene [5] Triassic	Turn to the middle frame on the next left hand page for the correct answer and the next question.
1 This narrow strait is the only link between the Black Sea and the Mediterranean Ocean:	[1] Suez Canal [2] Strait of Gibraltar [3] Dardanelles [4] Mozambique Channel [5] Firth of Forth	Turn to the fourth frame on the next left hand page for the correct answer and the next question.
1 In this novel, Kurtz's last words are "The horror! The horror!":	[1] Billy Budd [2] Cask of Amontillado [3] War of the Worlds [4] Heart of Darkness [5] The Shining	Turn to the bottom frame on the next left hand page for the correct answer and the next question.

11 All of these are dog breeds except:	[1] Welsh corgi [2] Basenji [3] Whippet [4] Hungarian Puli [5] Tonkinese	ANSWER TO Q-10 **[2]** Lhasa apsos were also thought to bring good luck to their owners. 79%
11 In the business world, "shark repellent" is needed to combat:	[1] Government intervention [2] Foreign competition [3] Takeover attempts [4] Labor organizers [5] Environmentalists	ANSWER TO Q-10 **[1]** It is possible to be bitten by a sand tiger embryo when examining its pregnant mother. 68%
11 A Shakespearian king attended by his fool who comments sardonically on mankind is:	[1] King Lear [2] King Claudius [3] King Theseus [4] King Duncan [5] King Timon of Athens	ANSWER TO Q-10 **[4]** A newt is a type of amphibian. 88%
11 The only animal listed that is a vegetarian is the:	[1] Baboon [2] Gorilla [3] Weasel [4] Monkey [5] Hyena	ANSWER TO Q-10 **[4]** Diamond Jim was a fat, turn-of-the-century millionaire who was a legendary carnivore. 22%
11 Neutrons, gamma rays, alpha and beta particles make up:	[1] Cathode ray tubes [2] Cat scans [3] Liquid crystals [4] Concrete [5] Neutron bombs	ANSWER TO Q-10 **[4]** Certain taste buds are deadened, thereby increasing perception of other taste buds. 24%

BRAIN BUSTER

GAME NUMBER 17

ANSWER TO Q-30

[1] The thymus gland assists in the development of the immune system.

51%

BRAIN BUSTER

GAME NUMBER 35

ANSWER TO Q-30

[2] He painted his famous series of water lily landscapes when he was 80 years old.

42%

BRAIN BUSTER

GAME NUMBER 53

ANSWER TO Q-30

[2] Most pressure conduits are usually made of cast iron, steel and asbestos cement.

69%

BRAIN BUSTER

GAME NUMBER 71

ANSWER TO Q-30

[1] Also called the Seven Sisters, only seven of these hundreds of stars are visible to the eye.

49%

BRAIN BUSTER

GAME NUMBER 89

ANSWER TO Q-30

[5] Dylan Thomas recreated the holiday celebrations in the small seaside village of Swansea.

51%

12 The phrase "dog days" dates from:	[1] Ancient Greece [2] Medieval Europe [3] Colonial America [4] Turn of 19th century [5] Ancient Rome	ANSWER TO Q-11 [5] Tonkinese is a cat breed. 67%
12 Which artist released a 1991 album entitled "Dangerous"?	[1] Guns 'n Roses [2] Michael Bolton [3] Michael Jackson [4] Prince [5] Mariah Carey	ANSWER TO Q-11 [3] It's the term for an entire array of tactics used to prevent hostile takeovers. 71%
12 The medieval Feast of Fools was designed to honor this unlikely biblical figure:	[1] Drunken Noah [2] Old Methuselah [3] Jesus' donkey [4] Queen Jezebel [5] Lot's wife	ANSWER TO Q-11 [1] The fools of ancient courts were allowed liberties denied to all other subjects. 65%
12 These fruits have a fleshy outer layer and a hard inner layer:	[1] Pomes [2] Berries [3] Drupes [4] Sapwoods [5] Brambles	ANSWER TO Q-11 [2] The big ape eats leaves, stalks and bamboo shoots. 53%
12 A protein which catalyses one specific chemical reaction is a/an:	[1] Amino acid [2] Enzyme [3] Hormone [4] Prostaglandin [5] Collagen	ANSWER TO Q-11 [5] Nuclear explosions are a cocktail of these different types of radiation. 54%

30 This gland is located behind the breastbone:	[1] Thymus [2] Pituitary [3] Thyroid [4] Adrenal [5] Pancreas	ANSWER TO Q-29 **[4]** "The Band Wagon" and "An American in Paris" are two of his best. 56%
30 He is one of the foremost figures in the history of landscape painting:	[1] Pablo Picasso [2] Claude Monet [3] George Braque [4] Marcel Duchamp [5] Salvador Dali	ANSWER TO Q-29 **[2]** These well-sealed Greek vases are found occasionally in wrecks, still stopped-up tight. 43%
30 This is a pipe or channel for conveying water or protecting electric cables:	[1] Girder [2] Conduit [3] Abutment [4] Gasket [5] Camber	ANSWER TO Q-29 **[1]** It's a form of logic consisting of a major and minor premise and a conclusion. 49%
30 The cluster of stars known as the Pleiades is in which constellation?	[1] Taurus [2] Orion [3] Big Dipper [4] Southern Cross [5] Little Dipper	ANSWER TO Q-29 **[2]** The 18 trans-uranium or synthetic elements are made by bombardment with radioactive particles. 69%
30 Which Welshman wrote "A Child's Christmas in Wales"?	[1] Richard Burton [2] Tom Jones [3] Lord Byron [4] Thomas Carlyle [5] Dylan Thomas	ANSWER TO Q-29 **[4]** Of course, it also tells the classic tales of man's fall from grace, and of Cain and Abel. 83%

13 The dogfish is a type of:	[1] Shark [2] Mackerel [3] Starfish [4] Sturgeon [5] Catfish	ANSWER TO Q-12 **[5]** Romans believed that Sirius, the Dog Star, added its heat to the sun during this time. 51%
13 This frontier job was so unsafe, its recruiting posters read "Orphans Preferred":	[1] Yukon gold miners [2] Sailor on square-rigger [3] U.S. Cavalryman [4] Pony Express rider [5] Circuit judge	ANSWER TO Q-12 **[3]** Jackson received a $15 million cash advance and a royalty deal for $2 per album sold. 79%
13 Who wore motley on his body and a coxcomb on his head?	[1] Court jester [2] Office clown [3] Class cretin [4] Team duffer [5] Town dunce	ANSWER TO Q-12 **[3]** On this day, the people indulged in all sorts of tomfoolery, making asses of themselves. 32%
13 Which is not a fruit?	[1] Quince [2] Marengo [3] Pomegranate [4] Loquat [5] Persimmon	ANSWER TO Q-12 **[3]** Fruits such as peaches hold their seeds within a hardened casing called a stone. 42%
13 In chemistry, the melting point and the freezing point are:	[1] 32° apart [2] Flash points [3] The same temperature [4] 100° apart [5] Where explosions occur	ANSWER TO Q-12 **[2]** The enzyme is not permanently modified by its role in the chemical reaction. 46%

29 Vincent Minelli made more of this type of film than any other director:	[1] Westerns [2] Horror [3] Romantic comedy [4] Musicals [5] Silent films	ANSWER TO Q-28 **[2]** The amount of blood pumped by the heart is reduced by 5 between age 20 and age 90. 87%
29 An amphora is an ancient greek:	[1] Ship [2] Vase [3] Garment [4] Dwelling [5] Beverage	ANSWER TO Q-28 **[4]** The father of the "beat generation" died a virtual recluse in 1969 at age 47. 68%
29 Syllogism is a form of:	[1] Logic [2] Computer language [3] Practical joke [4] Disease [5] Philosophy	ANSWER TO Q-28 **[5]** Dean was killed in his car outside the small California town of Paso Robles. 69%
29 Elements with an atomic number greater than 92 are called:	[1] Rare earth elements [2] Transuranium elements [3] Metals [4] Gases [5] Nonmetals	ANSWER TO Q-28 **[5]** Cholesterol sometimes crystallizes in the gall bladder to form gallstones. 43%
29 Which biblical book contains the stories of Jacob, Abraham, and the sacrifice of Isaac?	[1] Revelations [2] Proverbs [3] Corinthians [4] Genesis [5] Judges	ANSWER TO Q-28 **[5]** Riots greeted his "The Plough and the Stars" because it was perceived as anti-Irish. 51%

#	Question	Answers	Answer to Previous

14 The Westminster Show is the most prestigious dog show in:

[1] Canada
[2] The USA
[3] England
[4] Mexico
[5] France

ANSWER TO Q-13
[1] These small sharks are valued as food fish in Europe.
46%

---

14 Which of these movies does not star Rodney Dangerfield?

[1] Easy Money
[2] Caddyshack
[3] Stripes
[4] Back to School
[5] It's Not Easy Being Me

ANSWER TO Q-13
[4] Riders braved 75-mile stretches of wild desert, facing hostile Indians and weather.
61%

---

14 Which "fool" title is a play by Sam Shepard?

[1] Foolish Heart
[2] Fool for Love
[3] Fools Hall of Fame
[4] Fool for You
[5] Fool Such as I

ANSWER TO Q-13
[1] The multicolored uniform was called motley. The red cap was a coxcomb.
43%

---

14 The main function of a tree's fruit is to:

[1] Store energy
[2] Protect the seed
[3] Fertilize the seed
[4] Absorb sunlight
[5] Build carbohydrates

ANSWER TO Q-13
[2] Marengo is a chicken dish named after one of Napoleon's battles.
53%

---

14 Litmus paper turns blue in alkaline solutions and ____ in acids.

[1] Red
[2] Yellow
[3] Green
[4] Purple
[5] White

ANSWER TO Q-13
[3] The temperature that a substance freezes is also the temperature that it melts.
62%

28 Gerontology is the study of:	[1] War [2] Aging [3] Dialects [4] Prehistory [5] Glaciers	ANSWER TO Q-27 **[4]** Gable won his Oscar for "It Happened One Night"; "The Misfits" was his last film as well as Marilyn Monroe's. 51%
28 Which writer lived to celebrate his 45th birthday?	[1] John Keats [2] Jack London [3] Franz Kafka [4] Jack Kerouac [5] Lord Byron	ANSWER TO Q-27 **[3]** The river rises in the Lesotho and flows westward to the Atlantic. 43%
28 Each of these famous people is matched with the city where he was killed except:	[1] John Kennedy - Dallas [2] Malcolm X - NYC [3] John Lennon - NYC [4] John Dillinger- Chicago [5] James Dean - San Francisco	ANSWER TO Q-27 **[3]** Two people speak the same language if they understand each other without instruction. 32%
28 Which gland is the main site of cholesterol biosynthesis?	[1] Pancreas [2] Heart [3] Kidney [4] Stomach [5] Liver	ANSWER TO Q-27 **[4]** Father Karras is in "The Exorcist" and William of Baskerville is in "The Name of the Rose." 32%
28 Which Irish writer is celebrated for his controversial plays?	[1] James Joyce [2] Conor Cruise O'Brien [3] Desmond O'Grady [4] Frank O'Hara [5] Sean O'Casey	ANSWER TO Q-27 **[4]** It is a poem lamenting a passing, usually of a person. 44%

15 Rin-tin-tin and Jim Belushi's dog in the film "K9" were both:	[1] Golden retrievers [2] Bulldogs [3] German shepherds [4] St. Bernards [5] Dobermans	ANSWER TO Q-14 [2] Held every year since 1877, it is one of the oldest annual sporting events in the country. 65%
15 The Michael Keaton film "Johnny Dangerously" is a spoof of this popular movie genre:	[1] Western [2] Gangster [3] Disaster [4] Science fiction [5] Sports	ANSWER TO Q-14 [3] "Stripes" starred Bill Murray and Harold Ramis as two unorthodox army recruits. 81%
15 Which "Peanuts" character pulls out the football from under Charlie Brown?	[1] Peppermint Patty [2] Snoopy [3] Sally [4] Lucy [5] Schroeder	ANSWER TO Q-14 [2] The title is taken from an Ike Turner song. 68%
15 In botany, which does not belong to the nightshade family?	[1] Potato [2] Tomato [3] Turnip [4] Tobacco [5] Eggplant	ANSWER TO Q-14 [2] When ripe, the fruit disperses the seed. 68%
15 Which element listed has the highest melting point?	[1] Carbon [2] Hydrogen [3] Uranium [4] Tungsten [5] Magnesium	ANSWER TO Q-14 [1] Litmus is an organic dye that is naturally pink in color. 91%

27 Which actor and the film for which he won his only Oscar are mismatched?	[1] Bogart - African Queen [2] Wayne - True Grit [3] Holden -Stalag 17 [4] Gable - The Misfits [5] Olivier - Hamlet	ANSWER TO Q-26 [4] The human body's largest tendon, it connects the muscles to the heel bone. 91%
27 South Africa's principal river is the:	[1] Tay [2] Po [3] Orange [4] Tweed [5] Severn	ANSWER TO Q-26 [2] Latvia gained its independence from the Soviet Union in August of 1991. 55%
27 "Mutual intelligibility" is a criterion applied by these professionals:	[1] Physicists [2] Historians [3] Linguists [4] Chefs [5] Stockbrokers	ANSWER TO Q-26 [2] Sashimi is raw fish, sliced paper thin, and served with wasabi paste. 44%
27 Which detective-priest was created by Catholic writer G.K. Chesterton?	[1] William of Baskerville [2] Father Karras [3] Brother Cadfael [4] Father Brown [5] Father Dowling	ANSWER TO Q-26 [1] It is derived from the word "silvanus," meaning belonging to or pertaining to the woods. 52%
27 An elegy can also be called a:	[1] Palinode [2] Saga [3] Fable [4] Dirge [5] Colloquy	ANSWER TO Q-26 [4] Guilty and shamed over the decay of his family, Quentin drowns himself while away at college. 42%

GAME NUMBER 3

ANSWER TO Q-15

[3] They became a popular breed when WWI soldiers witnessed their heroics during the war.

91%

GAME NUMBER 21

ANSWER TO Q-15

[2] Joe Piscopo and Danny Devito costar in this Prohibition-era satire.

89%

GAME NUMBER 39

ANSWER TO Q-15

[4] The loud-mouthed sister of Linus enjoyed making a fool of good ol' Charlie Brown.

95%

GAME NUMBER 57

ANSWER TO Q-15

[3] The turnip, along with cabbage and wallflower, belongs to the mustard family.

24%

GAME NUMBER 75

ANSWER TO Q-15

[1] Carbon melts at 3550° celsius. Tungsten is next at 3410° celsius.

35%

26 The Achilles tendon is located in the:

[1] Back
[2] Neck
[3] Shoulders
[4] Legs
[5] Elbow

ANSWER TO Q-25
[5] Wilder was born in Austria, Hitchcock and Attenborough in England and Polanski in Poland.

51%

---

26 Riga is the capital and largest city of:

[1] Romania
[2] Latvia
[3] Ukraine
[4] Slovenia
[5] Moldova

ANSWER TO Q-25
[3] In the slalom event, skiers must race down hill, dodging between a series of marked flags.

98%

---

26 Served early while the palate is clear, _____ is always part of a formal Japanese meal.

[1] Dim sum
[2] Sashimi
[3] Sukiyaki
[4] Sesame balls
[5] A Pu Pu platter

ANSWER TO Q-25
[2] The king's musketeers get involved in the queen's love affair with an English duke.

33%

---

26 Which environment is characterized by the word "sylvan"?

[1] Woodsy
[2] Oceanic
[3] Medical
[4] Theatrical
[5] Urban

ANSWER TO Q-25
[3] This is an international defense group made up of Europe, Canada and the United States.

52%

---

26 Which is a principal character in Faulkner's "The Sound and the Fury"?

[1] Ralph Nickleby
[2] George Thurstwood
[3] Willy Loman
[4] Quentin Compson
[5] Smerdyakov

ANSWER TO Q-25
[5] The body of someone in a trance will give off a kind of light known as the ectoplasm.

42%

1 The theoretical study of beauty and taste is called:	[1] Symmetrics [2] Art criticism [3] Aesthetics [4] Perspective [5] Formalism	Turn to the top frame on the next right hand page for the correct answer and the next question.
1 All of these containers were designed to hold a dead body except:	[1] Coffin [2] Bier [3] Casket [4] Sarcophagus [5] Monstrance	Turn to the second frame on the next right hand page for the correct answer and the next question.
1 Which French explorer of the New World was murdered by his own men?	[1] Joliet [2] Marquette [3] Champlain [4] La Salle [5] Cartier	Turn to the middle frame on the next right hand page for the correct answer and the next question.
1 Which geographical name is not used by a major pop music group?	[1] Ohio [2] Boston [3] Asia [4] Kansas [5] Chicago	Turn to the fourth frame on the next right hand page for the correct answer and the next question.
1 Illustrator Sydney Paget created the trademark cloak and deerstalker hat of:	[1] Dr. Frankenstein [2] Winnie-the-Pooh [3] Scrooge [4] Sherlock Holmes [5] Peter Pan	Turn to the bottom frame on the next right hand page for the correct answer and the next question.

25 Which of these famous directors was born in the United States?	[1] Billy Wilder [2] Alfred Hitchcock [3] Roman Polanski [4] Richard Attenborough [5] William Friedkin	ANSWER TO Q-24 [5] Dicots are plants with two seed leaves and monocots are those with a single seed leaf. 43%
25 Which sport uses the term "slalom"?	[1] Hockey [2] Tennis [3] Skiing [4] Soccer [5] Bowling	ANSWER TO Q-24 [4] Krypton is also used to fill electric lamp bulbs. 43%
25 The famous Three Musketeers fought for this king:	[1] Peter the Great [2] Louis XIII of France [3] Ludwig of Bavaria [4] George III of England [5] Philip I of Spain	ANSWER TO Q-24 [2] This snowcapped, extinct volcano is 17,058 feet high. 34%
25 Where are the NATO headquarters located?	[1] London [2] Stockholm [3] Brussels [4] Geneva [5] Oslo	ANSWER TO Q-24 [3] Blair won her fifth gold medal while competing in her fourth Olympic games in 1994. 69%
25 Ectoplasm is a term used by those interested in the:	[1] Earth's ecosystems [2] Fine arts [3] Aviation industry [4] Hard sciences [5] Occult	ANSWER TO Q-24 [1] It's been said that money is the real central character in Balzac's novels. 43%

2 Physicists & poets once referred to this as something similar to atmosphere:	[1] Ephemera [2] Cosmic mists [3] Ether [4] Vapors [5] Phantasmagora	ANSWER TO Q-1 **[3]** The term "aesthetics" is derived from the Greek word for perception– "aisthesis." 89%
2 Hiring your daughter as vice-president is called:	[1] Favoritism [2] Patronage [3] Familialism [4] Nepotism [5] Relativism	ANSWER TO Q-1 **[5]** A monstrance is a receptacle used by Catholics to hold the consecrated host. 79%
2 Which is not one of the women's colleges known as the "Seven Sisters"?	[1] Radcliffe [2] Smith [3] Wellesley [4] Brown [5] Vassar	ANSWER TO Q-1 **[4]** This was the same fate of another explorer, Henry Hudson. 57%
2 Who said "Genius is 99% perspiration and 1% inspiration"?	[1] Albert Einstein [2] Winston Churchill [3] Thomas Edison [4] Henry Ford [5] Benjamin Franklin	ANSWER TO Q-1 **[1]** Most of these bands were prominent in the 70's. 91%
2 Which witch on "Bewitched" was known for her forgetfulness?	[1] Endora [2] Serena [3] Aunt Clara [4] Uncle Arthur [5] Dr. Bombay	ANSWER TO Q-1 **[4]** Nothing in the stories of A. Conan Doyle really suggests the sleuth wore them. 68%

24 Monocots and dicots refer to different classifications of:	[1] Teas [2] Mammals [3] Birds [4] Insects [5] Plants	ANSWER TO Q-23 **[4]** Widely used at first in Arabian armies, they used their military skill to take over. 43%
24 Which of these noble gases is used to detect heart defects and fill electronic devices?	[1] Neon [2] Argon [3] Radon [4] Krypton [5] Helium	ANSWER TO Q-23 **[3]** However, sloe gin is flavored with the fruit of the blackthorn plant. 59%
24 What is the second highest mountain in Africa?	[1] Kilimanjaro [2] Mt. Kenya [3] Mt. Tahat [4] Ras Dashan [5] Drakensberg	ANSWER TO Q-23 **[5]** "Red Rover" is a children's game. 69%
24 Which of these American women athletes has won five Olympic gold medals?	[1] Evelyn Ashford [2] Pat McCormick [3] Bonnie Blair [4] Janet Evans [5] Peggy Fleming	ANSWER TO Q-23 **[4]** Lily Tomlin played Edith Ann and the love-starved operator Ernestine on "Laugh-In." 79%
24 "Pere Goriot" and "Cousin Bette" are two novels by the French writer:	[1] Balzac [2] Rabelais [3] Hugo [4] Dumas [5] Moliere	ANSWER TO Q-23 **[1]** Some fruits contain enough natural pectin and don't need any added in processing. 52%

3 Agronomy is a branch of this science:	[1] Physics [2] Archaeology [3] Paleontology [4] Psychology [5] Agriculture	ANSWER TO Q-2 [3] The "ethereal substance" was thought to permeate the universe so as to carry light. 68%
3 Which is not a novel by Stephen King?	[1] The Tommyknockers [2] Misery [3] The Stand [4] The Andromeda Strain [5] Pet Sematary	ANSWER TO Q-2 [4] Despots are often accused of this, but what do they care? 89%
3 Which type of shoe is not matched with the right style?	[1] Chukka - boot [2] Sabot - clog [3] Mule - slipper [4] Loafer - casual [5] Mukluk - sandal	ANSWER TO Q-2 [4] Brown University is a member of the Ivy League Eight. 78%
3 Romance languages like French and Spanish developed primarily from this source:	[1] Spoken Latin [2] Ancient Greek [3] Hebrew [4] Arabic [5] Anglo-Saxon	ANSWER TO Q-2 [3] He is arguably the greatest inventor of all time, with over 100 patents to his name. 78%
3 Which major league baseball team's last World Series title came in 1908?	[1] Cleveland Indians [2] Chicago Cubs [3] Boston Red Sox [4] Philadelphia Phillies [5] Chicago White Sox	ANSWER TO Q-2 [3] Elizabeth Montgomery tried to keep a normal household despite the magical surroundings. 91%

23 These former slaves ruled Egypt and Palestine during the late Middle Ages:	[1] Maccabees [2] Moabites [3] Minoans [4] Mamelukes [5] Montagnards	ANSWER TO Q-22 **[1]** Khrushchev's handling of the crisis led to his eventual ouster as Soviet premier in 1964. 58%
23 Juniper berries are often used to provide the flavor in this alcoholic beverage:	[1] Vodka [2] Rum [3] Gin [4] Whiskey [5] Beer	ANSWER TO Q-22 **[5]** This is the 3rd largest lake entirely in Canada, with a surface area of 3,064 square miles. 45%
23 Which title is not that of a traditional fairy tale?	[1] Briar Rose [2] Red Riding Hood [3] Snow White and Rose Red [4] The Pink [5] Red Rover	ANSWER TO Q-22 **[1]** Goteborg is a Swedish port. 59%
23 The "Saturday Night Live" role not played by Gilda Radner:	[1] Lisa Lupner [2] Emily Latella [3] Baba Wawa [4] Edith Ann [5] Roseanne Roseannadanna	ANSWER TO Q-22 **[1]** He won Pulitzer Prizes for both these works about U.S. Presidents. 23%
23 Ingredient that gives jams, preserves, and jellies their smooth semi-solid consistency:	[1] Pectin [2] Sugar [3] Gelatin [4] Cornstarch [5] Agar agar	ANSWER TO Q-22 **[5]** A kepi is a cap with a circular, flat top and horizontal visor, worn by French soldiers. 49%

4 The "Lady in Red" figured in the downfall of this criminal:	[1] Al Capone [2] Billy the Kid [3] Jesse James [4] Doc Holliday [5] John Dillinger	ANSWER TO Q-3 **[5]** Agronomists concern themselves with the big crops essential to human survival. 79%
4 Something said to be extant is:	[1] Lost [2] Destroyed [3] In existence [4] Valuable [5] Extinct	ANSWER TO Q-3 **[4]** "The Andromeda Strain" was written by Michael Crichton. 88%
4 He helped develop vector analysis and formulated the concept of chemical potential:	[1] Luigi Galvani [2] Josiah Willard Gibbs [3] John Metcalf [4] T.H. Huxley [5] Paul Kammerer	ANSWER TO Q-3 **[5]** Mukluks are eskimo boots made from seal or reindeer skin. 82%
4 Who was Jacob Marley?	[1] One of the wise men [2] Wrote Silent Night [3] Toymaker [4] Scrooge's late partner [5] Tiny Tim's dad	ANSWER TO Q-3 **[1]** Vulgar Latin was the everyday speech of the Roman people. 58%
4 Which term refers to breeds of both dog and cat?	[1] Borzoi [2] Maltese [3] Siamese [4] Merino [5] Peregrine	ANSWER TO Q-3 **[2]** The 80-odd years since winning the series is the longest drought in major league baseball. 58%

22 Which event in Soviet Union history occurred while Khrushchev was in power?	[1] Cuban missile crisis [2] Boycott/Moscow Olympics [3] Nixon's China visit [4] Afghanistan invasion [5] Trotsky's death	ANSWER TO Q-21 [1] Jezebel was the wife of King Ahab, who lived several centuries after King David. 59%
22 Which Canadian lake lies within both Alberta & Saskatchewan provinces?	[1] Dubawnt [2] Great Bear [3] Reindeer [4] Great Slave [5] Athabasca	ANSWER TO Q-21 [3] Dennis Quaid starred in this film about the sadness and confusion of growing up. 89%
22 Which city is not in Germany?	[1] Goteborg [2] Mannheim [3] Stuttgart [4] Hamburg [5] Wiesbaden	ANSWER TO Q-21 [2] There is both a real Devil's Island and an imaginary one in an old novel, "Amadis of Gaul." 76%
22 "The Age of Jackson" and "A Thousand Days" are works of this noted historian:	[1] Arthur Schlesinger, Jr. [2] Arnold Toynbee [3] Theodore White [4] Bruce Catton [5] Joseph Needham	ANSWER TO Q-21 [1] Shoemaker won the race at the age of 54. 62%
22 Which is not a type of Asian currency?	[1] Won [2] Baht [3] Yen [4] Dong [5] Kepi	ANSWER TO Q-21 [1] During a nova's explosion, light from the star becomes 10,000 times brighter. 51%

5 Which fruit ripens after picking?

[1] Grapes
[2] Bananas
[3] Oranges
[4] Pineapples
[5] Plums

ANSWER TO Q-4

[5] His end came in a trap set by the FBI and his "friend," Anna Sage, a brothel madam.

68%

---

5 Rosalind and Orlando fall in love while tromping through the forest of Arden in:

[1] Midsummer Night's Dream
[2] Oedipus Rex
[3] As You Like It
[4] The Alchemist
[5] Barefoot in the Park

ANSWER TO Q-4

[3] The term is often used in conjunction with literary manuscripts.

69%

---

5 "The Preserver," "The Destroyer" and "The Creator" constitute the main triad of:

[1] Buddhism
[2] Shinto
[3] Islam
[4] Hinduism
[5] Zoroastrianism

ANSWER TO Q-4

[2] His studies had a profound effect on industry, notably in the production of ammonia.

34%

---

5 Which was not a ruling house of England?

[1] Tudor
[2] Plantagenet
[3] Romanov
[4] Wessex
[5] Hanover

ANSWER TO Q-4

[4] He's the voice of Christmas past who awakens Scrooge's consciousness.

71%

---

5 _____ is the only heavyweight champion Muhammad Ali knocked out in the first round.

[1] Jerry Quarry
[2] Sonny Liston
[3] Ernie Shavers
[4] Joe Frazier
[5] Jimmy Young

ANSWER TO Q-4

[2] The small toy dogs originated from Malta. The cats are bluish-gray short-haired cats.

62%

21 Which biblical figure did not play a role in the life of King David?	[1] Queen Jezebel [2] Prince Absalom [3] Goliath the Giant [4] Samuel, Judge of Israel [5] King Saul	ANSWER TO Q-20 [4] The bed is named after its maker, W.L. Murphy. 78%
21 This 1979 Oscar-winning film portrayed the lives of four bike-racing friends in Indiana:	[1] American Flyers [2] Hoosiers [3] Breaking Away [4] Stand by Me [5] Mrs. Robinson	ANSWER TO Q-20 [1] Chekhov depicts the slow spiritual death of 3 educated women forced to live in a rural village. 34%
21 Which imaginary place is not in the stories of the Arabian Nights?	[1] Ape Mountain [2] Devil's Island [3] Sea of Karkar [4] City of Brass [5] Camphor Island	ANSWER TO Q-20 [4] The large fly sucks blood and transmits a one-celled parasite that causes the disease. 45%
21 While riding Ferdinand in 1986, Bill Shoemaker became the oldest jockey to win the:	[1] Kentucky Derby [2] Preakness Stakes [3] Belmont Stakes [4] National Steeplechase [5] Breeder's Cup	ANSWER TO Q-20 [3] Quixotic comes from Don Quixote, the central character of the Cervantes classic. 67%
21 In astronomy, what is a nova?	[1] Brilliant star explosion [2] Heat-producing comet [3] Edges of a black hole [4] Inhabitable planet [5] Asteroid belt	ANSWER TO Q-20 [4] Strokes result in the destruction of brain tissue due to impaired blood flow. 67%

6 This kind of music is written in 3/4 time, and is meant to be danced to:	[1] Fugue [2] Waltz [3] Scherzo [4] Sonata [5] Overture	ANSWER TO Q-5 **[2]** Peaches and pears are also expected to ripen after picking. 69%
6 A "hirsute" person is very:	[1] Tall [2] Obese [3] Skinny [4] Short [5] Hairy	ANSWER TO Q-5 **[3]** It's the usual comedic Shakespeare: woman poses as man to trick the feeble-minded males. 42%
6 What gives the drink "Black Cow" its dark color?	[1] Chocolate syrup [2] Coffee [3] Kahlua [4] Root beer [5] Myers rum	ANSWER TO Q-5 **[4]** Brahma, Vishnu and Shiva are the divine names given to these three functions. 54%
6 In India, many men wear a dhoti. What is it?	[1] Long white loin cloth [2] Jeweled turban [3] Spot on the forehead [4] Pith helmet [5] Magic amulet	ANSWER TO Q-5 **[3]** The Romanovs were the ruling house of Russia for over 300 years, ending in 1917. 61%
6 Which country was never a colony of Britain?	[1] Ghana [2] Venezuela [3] Singapore [4] India [5] Kenya	ANSWER TO Q-5 **[2]** Ali knocked out Sonny Liston in the first round of his title defense in 1965. 61%

20 A murphy bed is one which:	[1] Has double bunks [2] Converts to a couch [3] Has four posters [4] Folds into wall [5] Is canopied	ANSWER TO Q-19 **[4]** "The Lone Ranger" made its highly successful transition from radio to TV in 1949. 62%
20 Masha, Olga, and Irina are the central characters in this Anton Chekov play:	[1] Three Sisters [2] Three Comrades [3] The Threepenny opera [4] Three Strangers [5] Three Secrets	ANSWER TO Q-19 **[1]** Considered Joseph Conrad's greatest novel, this political story is set in Latin America. 43%
20 Africa's tse-tse fly is greatly feared because it carries this disease:	[1] Aids [2] Bubonic plague [3] Malaria [4] Sleeping sickness [5] Cholera	ANSWER TO Q-19 **[3]** A staple of the tropics, it belongs to the mulberry family of trees. 51%
20 Which adjective is not derived from an author?	[1] Byronic [2] Dantesque [3] Quixotic [4] Kafkaesque [5] Rabelesian	ANSWER TO Q-19 **[2]** Unlike Maine lobsters, spiny and rock lobsters don't have big claws, but large antennas. 45%
20 A cerebrovascular accident is commonly known as a/an:	[1] Appendicitis [2] Ulcer [3] Heart attack [4] Stroke [5] Epileptic seizure	ANSWER TO Q-19 **[5]** The 35th U.S. president is now known to have been a master bluffer as well as a negotiator. 59%

7 What do you obtain by fermenting molasses?

[1] Bitters
[2] Gin
[3] Rum
[4] Port
[5] Absinthe

ANSWER TO Q-6

[2] The waltz is derived from popular peasant dances of Austria and Bavaria. 88%

---

7 Which ailment results from kidney failure?

[1] Cirrhosis
[2] Jaundice
[3] Uremia
[4] Myocarditis
[5] Goiter

ANSWER TO Q-6

[5] Someone with hirsutism has an abnormally heavy growth of body hair. 69%

---

7 The magnificent rifle bird and the trumpeter manucode are members of this family:

[1] Pheasants and peacocks
[2] Hawks and falcons
[3] Geese and swans
[4] Herons and bitterns
[5] Birds of paradise

ANSWER TO Q-6

[4] It is another name for a root beer float. 46%

---

7 Francisco de Coronado searched for _____ in the southwestern United States.

[1] El Dorado
[2] The Fountain of Youth
[3] The Seven Cities of Cibola
[4] Timbuktu
[5] Shangri-La

ANSWER TO Q-6

[1] It is the garment westerners particularly associate with Mahatma Gandhi. 47%

---

7 Which was not a 1970's best seller?

[1] Love Story
[2] Jaws
[3] The Exorcist
[4] Lake Wobegon Days
[5] The Thorn Birds

ANSWER TO Q-6

[2] Venezuela, which means "little Venice," was originally a colony of Spain. 58%

19 "Return with us now to those thrilling days of yester-year" is the introduction to:

[1] The Green Hornet
[2] The Rifleman
[3] The Twilight Zone
[4] The Lone Ranger
[5] The Shadow

ANSWER TO Q-18
[1] Rudyard Kipling's "Captains Courageous" was made into a 1937 movie starring Spencer Tracy.
45%

---

19 Which classic novel is subtitled, "A Tale of the Seaboard"?

[1] Nostromo
[2] Kidnapped
[3] Billy Budd
[4] Moby Dick
[5] Robinson Crusoe

ANSWER TO Q-18
[2] In this condition, all of the liver cells are destroyed by hepatitis.
43%

---

19 Breadfruit belongs to the same plant family as the:

[1] Cherry
[2] Plum
[3] Fig
[4] Date
[5] Lime

ANSWER TO Q-18
[4] The original title of this famous ballad was "Scrambled Eggs."
74%

---

19 This seafood has claws, a tail, legs and a body, all edible. What is it?

[1] Crab
[2] Maine lobster
[3] Rock lobster
[4] Prawns
[5] Spiny lobster

ANSWER TO Q-18
[3] Equivocal statements may serve to deliberately confuse an issue.
62%

---

19 "Let us never negotiate out of fear, but let us never fear to negotiate." Who said it?

[1] Winston Churchill
[2] Malcolm X
[3] Jimmy Hoffa
[4] Norman Schwartzkopf
[5] John Kennedy

ANSWER TO Q-18
[2] Bonnie Franklin played a divorced mother raising two teenage daughters.
89%

8 The long-suffering wife, Flo, is a principal character in this comic strip:	[1] Beetle Bailey [2] Andy Capp [3] Cathy [4] Born Loser [5] Blondie	ANSWER TO Q-7 [3] Naturally colorless, it acquires a brown color from added caramel or burnt sugar. 69%
8 The aubergine or guinea squash is better known as the:	[1] Zucchini [2] Eggplant [3] Okra [4] Leek [5] Turnip	ANSWER TO Q-7 [3] A rise in blood urea is the most basic symptom. 69%
8 All of these are kinds of neckties except:	[1] Ascot [2] Foulard [3] Cravat [4] Jabot [5] Lorgnette	ANSWER TO Q-7 [5] These fabulous birds were introduced to westerners after Magellan's voyage. 24%
8 Poet Carl Sandburg won a Pulitzer Prize for "Complete Poems," and another Pulitzer for:	[1] Cornhuskers [2] Hoosiers [3] The Crimson Tide [4] Razorbacks [5] Sooners	ANSWER TO Q-7 [3] He found the cities, but they were not made of gold as anticipated. 47%
8 Identify Nick Adams:	[1] Pro hockey scoring king [2] Batman's brother [3] Historical Santa Claus [4] A Hemingway character [5] Invented freeway	ANSWER TO Q-7 [4] Written in the 1980's, Garrison Keillor's book sold almost 1.5 million copies. 79%

111

18 The author of "Captains Courageous" also wrote:	[1] Kim [2] Silas Marner [3] Of Human Bondage [4] War and Peace [5] The Idiot	ANSWER TO Q-17 **[2]** This popular tune reached number one in May 1966. 79%
18 Acute yellow atrophy is a term for a condition caused by:	[1] Sarcoma [2] Hepatitis [3] Glaucoma [4] Herpes [5] Heart disease	ANSWER TO Q-17 **[3]** The phoebe is a songbird native to North America. 34%
18 Name the most recorded song of all time:	[1] Ave Maria [2] White Christmas [3] New York, New York [4] Yesterday [5] Happy Birthday	ANSWER TO Q-17 **[5]** Other varieties of black grapes are cardinal, barlinka and napoleon. 23%
18 Define equivocal:	[1] Honest [2] Angry [3] Vague [4] Friendly [5] Noble	ANSWER TO Q-17 **[3]** The thin sheets are lightly buttered and used to make pastries or top casseroles. 92%
18 Which of these TV shows did not feature a single father raising children?	[1] My Three Sons [2] One Day at a Time [3] Benson [4] Andy Griffith Show [5] Gidget	ANSWER TO Q-17 **[4]** Gluten is found in the flour of wheat and gives the dough its tough, elastic quality. 62%

9 Which country is incorrectly matched with its capital city?	[1] Denmark - Copenhagen [2] Portugal - Lisbon [3] Greece - Athens [4] Bulgaria - Sofia [5] Belgium - Vienna	ANSWER TO Q-8 **[2]** Her husband Andy often frequents his local pub with pal Chalkie, just to avoid her. 91%
9 Which statement about asthma is untrue?	[1] Unaffected by stress [2] Usually allergy-related [3] Respiratory ailment [4] Treated with epinephrine [5] Chronic disorder	ANSWER TO Q-8 **[2]** The eggplant is a member of the nightshade family and is a close relation of the potato. 79%
9 What did the Balfour Declaration support?	[1] Freedom for Ireland [2] Death penalty [3] Women's rights [4] Abolition of slavery [5] Creation of Jewish state	ANSWER TO Q-8 **[5]** A lorgnette is a pair of glasses attached to a handle. 25%
9 Which insurance company claims you're in good hands with them?	[1] Met Life [2] Prudential [3] State Farm [4] Allstate [5] Kemper	ANSWER TO Q-8 **[1]** It brought him his first Pulitzer in 1919. 27%
9 Which comic strip character lives in Okefenokee swamp?	[1] Broom Hilda [2] Pogo [3] Hagar the Horrible [4] Zippy [5] Shoe	ANSWER TO Q-8 **[4]** Adams appears in many Hemingway stories and is thought to represent the author's alter ego. 58%

17 Which group had the #1 hit "Monday, Monday"?	[1] The Byrds [2] Mamas and the Papas [3] Crosby, Stills and Nash [4] The Grateful Dead [5] Three Dog Night	ANSWER TO Q-16 [1] This novel is about a primitive man who confronts an ominous futuristic society. 67%
17 Which of these animals is not an African antelope?	[1] Common eland [2] Greater kudu [3] Phoebe [4] Bongo [5] Nyala	ANSWER TO Q-16 [1] In allegories, the characters represent types, not individuals. 56%
17 A hamburg muscat is a:	[1] Stewing chicken [2] Squirrel stew [3] Fancy pastry [4] Freshwater fish [5] Black grape	ANSWER TO Q-16 [4] Taylor won in 1960 for "Butterfield 8." Fonda won in 1971 for "Klute." 56%
17 Phyllo, fila, or fillo are various spellings for a type of:	[1] Vegetable [2] Slab of meat [3] Pastry dough [4] Noodle [5] Custard pie	ANSWER TO Q-16 [2] Shakespeare's Polonius is a classic example of a tiresomely sententious character. 64%
17 Gluten is a nutritious substance found in this crop:	[1] Potatoes [2] Corn [3] Tomatoes [4] Wheat [5] Citrus fruits	ANSWER TO Q-16 [2] Bernaise is similar to hollandaise sauce but has tarragon, shallots and chervil added. 34%

10 What rock band has a skull and roses logo?	[1] Guns n' Roses [2] Grateful Dead [3] Black Sabbath [4] Fleetwood Mac [5] Led Zeppelin	ANSWER TO Q-9 [5] The capital of Belgium is Brussels; Vienna is the capital of Austria. 69%
10 A green film forming naturally on copper or bronze by long exposure is called a:	[1] Panacea [2] Patina [3] Panache [4] Papyrus [5] Paregoric	ANSWER TO Q-9 [1] Both illness and stress may precipitate asthma attacks. 65%
10 Plants using anemo-phily are pollinated by:	[1] Rodents [2] Winds [3] Birds [4] Insects [5] Humans	ANSWER TO Q-9 [5] The British government issued the declaration in 1917. 71%
10 All these words except _____ relate to knowledge, wisdom or understanding.	[1] Sagacious [2] Cursory [3] Discerning [4] Erudite [5] Oracular	ANSWER TO Q-9 [4] State Farm claims it's "like a good neighbor." Prudential gives you "a piece of the rock." 89%
10 "Deep Throat" is the source of inside inform-ation in this book:	[1] Mayflower Madam [2] The Hunt for Red October [3] All the President's Men [4] Helter Skelter [5] In Cold Blood	ANSWER TO Q-9 [2] An annual "Pogofest" is staged in Waycross, Georgia, near the famous swamp grounds. 89%

16 Which of these novels is not set around one character exploring a new land?	[1] Brave New World [2] Robinson Crusoe [3] Gulliver's Travels [4] Utopia [5] The New Atlantis	ANSWER TO Q-15 [2] An over-the-counter stock is traded between two individuals rather than on an exchange. 79%
16 All of these works are considered allegories except:	[1] Gone with the Wind [2] The Pilgrim's Progress [3] Animal Farm [4] The Lord of the Flies [5] Everyman	ANSWER TO Q-15 [5] The moral of the story is: any fool can despise what he cannot get. 67%
16 Both Elizabeth Taylor and Jane Fonda won their first Oscars playing:	[1] Precocious young girls [2] Divorced mothers [3] Space aliens [4] Prostitutes [5] Southern belles	ANSWER TO Q-15 [2] Wolves are social animals, traveling in packs while all members care for the young. 65%
16 Someone who is sententious tends to:	[1] Hurt feelings [2] Moralize [3] Seem prudish [4] Tell untruths [5] Inflame the masses	ANSWER TO Q-15 [1] Jamie Lee Curtis and Richard Lewis starred in this series set in Chicago. 89%
16 Which popular French sauce is seasoned with tarragon?	[1] Lyonnaise [2] Bernaise [3] Bordelaise [4] Espagnole [5] Hollandaise	ANSWER TO Q-15 [4] He took his oath of office April 20th, 1789. 45%

11 What emotion is an apoplectic person displaying?	[1] Remorse [2] Envy [3] Lust [4] Depression [5] Rage	ANSWER TO Q-10 [2] The logo was designed by rock poster artist "Mouse." 89%
11 Which tool is used for cutting an uneven edge on a piece of fabric?	[1] Bodkin [2] Spring scissors [3] Puncheon [4] Church key [5] Pinking shears	ANSWER TO Q-10 [2] By extension, the term has come to mean an aura or appearance that grows with age. 87%
11 What literary character was the victim of intense jealousy over his good looks?	[1] Cyrano de Bergerac [2] Bartleby the Scrivener [3] Bigger Thomas [4] Oliver Twist [5] Billy Budd	ANSWER TO Q-10 [2] This method is most common in conifers and cycads. 32%
11 The Cote D'Azur is better known to English-speaking people as the:	[1] Outback [2] Chateau country [3] French Riviera [4] Black Forest [5] Basque country	ANSWER TO Q-10 [2] Cursory means hasty. 79%
11 The name Daniel means:	[1] God's gift [2] Wise advisor [3] Ruler of the people [4] God will judge [5] Steadfast	ANSWER TO Q-10 [3] Bob Woodward and Carl Bernstein created this fictional composite to camouflage their source. 91%

15 In business terms, an O.T.C. is a type of:

[1] Option
[2] Stock
[3] Firm
[4] Bond
[5] Pension fund

ANSWER TO Q-14

[5] Winston Smith is tortured with the things he fears most for being disloyal to the party.
54%

---

15 The phrase "sour grapes" comes from an Aesop fable called "The ___ and The ___."

[1] Drunkard - Wine
[2] Wolf - Grapes
[3] Hare - Wine
[4] Horse - Cart
[5] Fox - Grapes

ANSWER TO Q-14

[5] Cerulean is the same as azure, a sky-blue color.
67%

---

15 Which of these animals mates for life?

[1] Chimpanzee
[2] Wolf
[3] Dolphin
[4] Cheetah
[5] Hippopotamus

ANSWER TO Q-14

[5] The hot springs in southern England have attracted visitors for thousands of years.
45%

---

15 Which of these TV shows featured the couple Hannah Miller and Marty Gold?

[1] Anything but Love
[2] Seinfeld
[3] Step by Step
[4] Hearts Afire
[5] Two of a Kind

ANSWER TO Q-14

[1] This 3-time Olympic gold medalist later gained success in Hollywood films.
59%

---

15 He was the first vice president of the United States:

[1] Thomas Jefferson
[2] George Washington
[3] Benjamin Franklin
[4] John Adams
[5] James Madison

ANSWER TO Q-14

[2] Yogi Berra threatened to sue for defamation of character, thinking he was Yogi's inspiration.
78%

12 Which TV show was not based on true events?	[1] Dragnet [2] Little House on Prairie [3] The FBI [4] Rockford Files [5] The Waltons	ANSWER TO Q-11 **[5]** It describes someone who looks like they have apoplexy, a disease that makes the face red. 76%
12 Which country does not border the Eastern European Republic of Georgia?	[1] Russia [2] Turkey [3] Armenia [4] Belarus [5] Azerbaijan	ANSWER TO Q-11 **[5]** The notched blades make a serrated edge, which is slower to unravel than a straight one. 69%
12 The "Henry" and the "Spencer" were the earliest successful:	[1] Steamships [2] Passenger trains [3] Electric stoves [4] Automobiles [5] Repeating rifles	ANSWER TO Q-11 **[5]** In Herman Melville's story, he was framed for a false mutiny charge by a jealous master-at-arms. 43%
12 Which baseball Hall of Famer did not begin his major league career with the New York Yankees?	[1] Babe Ruth [2] Joe DiMaggio [3] Mickey Mantle [4] Lou Gehrig [5] Yogi Berra	ANSWER TO Q-11 **[3]** The Riviera is a narrow coastal strip on the Mediterranean sea that includes Monaco. 89%
12 Liz Taylor has played in screen adaptions of all these classics except:	[1] The Taming of the Shrew [2] A Doll's House [3] Cat on a Hot Tin Roof [4] Little Women [5] Ivanhoe	ANSWER TO Q-11 **[4]** Daniel is a popular Hebrew name. 57%

14 A book whose character is tortured by fastening a cage of rats around his head:	[1] Anna Karenina [2] Heart of Darkness [3] Count of Monte Cristo [4] Crime and Punishment [5] 1984	ANSWER TO Q-13 **[3]** The strychnose tree is native to Sri Lanka, Australia and India. 53%
14 All of these words are associated with the color green except:	[1] Emerald [2] Verdigris [3] Pistachio [4] Malachite [5] Cerulean	ANSWER TO Q-13 **[1]** P.T. Barnum was a celebrated showman. 89%
14 The elaborate baths that give England's town of Bath its name were built by the:	[1] Druids [2] Puritans [3] Welsh [4] Normans [5] Romans	ANSWER TO Q-13 **[3]** If you beat the rap, you avoid getting punished. 57%
14 What nationality was Olympic figure skating champion Sonja Henie?	[1] Norwegian [2] French [3] German [4] Belgian [5] American	ANSWER TO Q-13 **[5]** Burns and Allen spent many years on radio and TV as partners; they were also married. 91%
14 Which cartoon cutup was inspired by Ed Norton of the TV series "The Honeymooners"?	[1] Dudley Doright [2] Yogi Bear [3] Huckleberry Hound [4] Bugs Bunny [5] Underdog	ANSWER TO Q-13 **[1]** Yeager broke the sound barrier in the experimental rocket plane in 1947. 56%

13 Who was the king of England during World War II?	[1] James II [2] George VI [3] William IV [4] Edward VIII [5] Charles I	ANSWER TO Q-12 **[4]** "The Rockford Files" dealt with the exploits of fictional detective Jim Rockford. 91%
13 The "Pentagon Papers" concerned the U.S. involvement in:	[1] Somalia [2] Grenada [3] Vietnam [4] Panama [5] Iran	ANSWER TO Q-12 **[4]** Belarus is surrounded by Lithuania, Latvia, Russia, Poland and Ukraine. 68%
13 Which literary female is a whore who accidentally marries her own brother?	[1] Madame Bovary [2] Moll Flanders [3] Becky Sharp [4] Mademoiselle Fifi [5] Lady Chatterley	ANSWER TO Q-12 **[5]** Abraham Lincoln tested the Spencer himself before approving it for service use. 57%
13 The first book of the New Testament is "The gospel according to _____."	[1] St. John [2] St. Luke [3] St. Matthew [4] St. Mark [5] St. Andrew	ANSWER TO Q-12 **[1]** Ruth began his career as a pitcher for the Boston Red Sox and was traded to N.Y. in 1920. 53%
13 This room is not on the board of the popular murder mystery game, "Clue":	[1] Billiard room [2] Ballroom [3] Lounge [4] Chamber room [5] Conservatory	ANSWER TO Q-12 **[2]** Jane Fonda and Claire Bloom have played Ibsen's heroine, but not Elizabeth Taylor. 67%

13 From what is the potent stimulant and poison strychnine derived from?

[1] Sulfur
[2] Wine grapes
[3] Seeds of a tree
[4] King cobra venom
[5] A mushroom

ANSWER TO Q-12
[2] It is about a scandal brewing in Edwardian high society.
46%

---

13 All these men are known primarily as writers of song lyrics except:

[1] P.T. Barnum
[2] Ira Gershwin
[3] Alan J. Lerner
[4] Oscar Hammerstein II
[5] Sammy Cahn

ANSWER TO Q-12
[3] The Swiss immigrant later founded a famous New York City museum that bears his name.
34%

---

13 The word "rap" can have all these meanings except:

[1] Talk
[2] Music form
[3] Filled with ecstasy
[4] Punishment
[5] Quick knock

ANSWER TO Q-12
[3] Skewbald, for example, refers to a horse with large patches of brown and white.
56%

---

13 Desi Arnaz is to Lucille Ball as George Burns is to:

[1] Dorothy Lamour
[2] Dale Evans
[3] Vivian Vance
[4] Audrey Meadows
[5] Gracie Allen

ANSWER TO Q-12
[1] Toronto has roughly 3.9 million, Montreal has 3.1 million and Vancouver has 1.6 million.
67%

---

13 The Bell X-1 is the plane flown by this important aviator:

[1] Chuck Yeager
[2] Charles Lindbergh
[3] Baron von Richthofen
[4] Amelia Earhart
[5] Orville Wright

ANSWER TO Q-12
[1] The Maori suffered the loss of most of their land and the disruption of their society.
54%

14 The study of the relationships between words and their meanings is called:	[1] Structuralism [2] Semiotics [3] Syntax [4] Syllogism [5] Semantics	ANSWER TO Q-13 [2] His visits to bombed areas, war plants and theaters of war helped keep up British morale. 61%
14 Where are the "Thousand Islands" located?	[1] English Channel [2] Red Sea [3] Panama Canal [4] St. Lawrence River [5] Florida Straits	ANSWER TO Q-13 [3] Classified at the time, "The New York Times" began publishing them June 13, 1971. 81%
14 What type of animal is the walrus?	[1] Mollusk [2] Pinniped [3] Ruminant [4] Monotreme [5] Echinoderm	ANSWER TO Q-13 [2] Defoe's criminal heroine ends up a wealthy, devout and perfectly respectable lady. 46%
14 Which California writer is the author of such books as "The White Album" & "Salvador"?	[1] John Steinbeck [2] Jack London [3] Susan Sontag [4] Ken Kesey [5] Joan Didion	ANSWER TO Q-13 [3] Although all four Gospels tell the same story, there are slight differences among them. 68%
14 The scientific term "half-life" is applied to:	[1] Inert gases [2] Natural fuel [3] Radioactive substances [4] Genetic material [5] Single-celled animals	ANSWER TO Q-13 [4] Possible murder sites also include the study, dining room, kitchen and hall. 88%

12 Which title is a play by Oscar Wilde?	[1] The Lady With a Dog [2] Lady Winde-mere's Fan [3] Lady Chatterley's Lover [4] The Lady and the Knight [5] The Lady Eve	ANSWER TO Q-11 [2] It is a telescope designed for observing the corona of the sun. 45%
12 He made his fortune smelting metal-lic ores in New Mexico and Colorado:	[1] John D. Rockefeller [2] J.P. Morgan [3] Meyer Guggenheim [4] Charles Crocker [5] William Hearst	ANSWER TO Q-11 [4] Lignite burns with a long, smoky flame but produces little heat. 46%
12 Skewbald and piebald are terms one would apply to:	[1] Maps [2] Beverages [3] Horse hides [4] Written texts [5] Stocks and bonds	ANSWER TO Q-11 [1] Oxygen is the most common nonmetallic element in the earth's crust. 67%
12 Other than Toronto and Montreal, which other Canadian city has over one million people?	[1] Vancouver [2] Quebec [3] Calgary [4] Edmonton [5] Ottawa	ANSWER TO Q-11 [3] The character Kane is loosely based on the life of William Randolph Hearst. 89%
12 The Maori war took place between European colonists and the natives of:	[1] New Zealand [2] Hawaii [3] Australia [4] India [5] Mexico	ANSWER TO Q-11 [5] A well-preserved specimen was recently uncovered in Colorado. 34%

15 Which is considered a spice rather than an herb?

[1] Thyme
[2] Rosemary
[3] Sage
[4] Cinnamon
[5] Dill

ANSWER TO Q-14

[5] By extension, semantics explores the influence words have on behavior.

81%

---

15 Which flowering plant is the source for the heart stimulant, digitalis?

[1] Poppy
[2] Foxglove
[3] Lily of the Valley
[4] Rose
[5] Nasturtium

ANSWER TO Q-14

[4] They are a popular resort area between New York and Ontario, east of Lake Ontario.

53%

---

15 Who wrote the poem "The Road Not Taken"?

[1] Rudyard Kipling
[2] Robert Frost
[3] E.E. Cummings
[4] Robert Lowell
[5] T.S. Eliot

ANSWER TO Q-14

[2] This type of mammal has all four limbs modified into flippers.

51%

---

15 This anonymous diary of a troubled teenager is favored reading among today's teens:

[1] My Boyfriend's Back
[2] My So-Called Life
[3] Twisted Sister
[4] Go Ask Alice
[5] I Been In Love Too Long

ANSWER TO Q-14

[5] She is known for her explorations of the emptiness of contemporary life.

35%

---

15 There are at least six different kinds of football. Which of these is not included?

[1] Soccer
[2] Rugby
[3] Canadian
[4] Australian
[5] Celtic

ANSWER TO Q-14

[3] It is the period needed for disintegration of half the atoms in a radioactive sample.

68%

11 Where would you find a coronagraph?

[1] Ophthalmology office
[2] Observatory
[3] Chemistry lab
[4] Map room
[5] Cardiology wing

ANSWER TO Q-10

[1] Lady Macbeth later kills herself because the blood of murder never washes off.

69%

11 Lignite is a cheap form of this fuel:

[1] Petroleum
[2] Wood pulp
[3] Kerosene
[4] Coal
[5] Natural gas

ANSWER TO Q-10

[4] Although the historical Hiawatha was an Onondaga Indian, Longfellow's hero is a Chippewa.

34%

11 What is the most common metallic element on earth?

[1] Aluminum
[2] Magnesium
[3] Potassium
[4] Oxygen
[5] Calcium

ANSWER TO Q-10

[4] Abjure means to deny or forbid.

49%

11 In Orson Welles' "Citizen Kane," Charles Foster Kane is a:

[1] Movie producer
[2] Texas oil magnate
[3] Newspaper tycoon
[4] Television executive
[5] U.S. senator

ANSWER TO Q-10

[3] Muscle tissue is classified according to structure and/or function.

54%

11 The ankylosaurus was a dinosaur that looked as if it were:

[1] Amphibious
[2] Capable of flight
[3] Mammalian
[4] Domesticated
[5] Armor-plated

ANSWER TO Q-10

[4] The word comes from "dendron," the Greek word for tree.

23%

16 Which Eastern European nation is farthest north?	[1] Latvia [2] Lithuania [3] Ukraine [4] Belarus [5] Estonia	ANSWER TO Q-15 **[4]** Herbs come from non-woody plants and spices from trees. Cinnamon is taken from bark. 75%
16 Who would you most likely see wearing a chevron?	[1] Soldier [2] Priest [3] Doctor [4] Scuba diver [5] Painter	ANSWER TO Q-15 **[2]** It is extracted from the dried leaves of the purple foxglove. 68%
16 "Ginnie Mae" is a term you could expect to hear from a:	[1] Performance artist [2] Used car salesman [3] Banker [4] Civil rights activist [5] Bartender	ANSWER TO Q-15 **[2]** The road in question is the "one less traveled," or the individualist's way. 69%
16 This green stone is used as a marble substitute:	[1] Topaz [2] Jasper [3] Agate [4] Tourmaline [5] Serpentine	ANSWER TO Q-15 **[4]** The popularity of this book signaled a change in reading trends among teenagers. 81%
16 Chinese Communists took over this country in 1950:	[1] Mongolia [2] Afghanistan [3] Burma [4] Tibet [5] Pakistan	ANSWER TO Q-15 **[5]** The other two are Gaelic and American and these teams range in size from 11 to 18 players. 57%

10 What does Lady Macbeth attempt to do as she sleepwalks?	[1] Wash her hands of blood [2] Beg God's forgiveness [3] Walk across a bridge [4] Leap from a castle wall [5] Speak to a ghost	ANSWER TO Q-9 [2] Rachel was his real love but his father-in-law made him marry Leah as well. 69%
10 Located north of Mexico, the Ojibwa Indians are better known as the:	[1] Comanche [2] Navajo [3] Sioux [4] Chippewa [5] Apache	ANSWER TO Q-9 [3] Pertussis, or whooping cough, is caused by bacteria. 65%
10 Which term does not mean criticize in some fashion?	[1] Impugn [2] Excoriate [3] Censure [4] Abjure [5] Castigate	ANSWER TO Q-9 [4] Tippi Hedren played the title character in this psychological thriller by Alfred Hitchcock. 87%
10 Which of these terms is not used to classify muscle?	[1] Skeletal [2] Smooth [3] Dynamic [4] Cardiac [5] Striated	ANSWER TO Q-9 [4] The levels of systolic and diastolic pressure can give doctors a good idea of your heart's health. 65%
10 Dendrology is a branch of botany which specializes in:	[1] Ferns [2] Flowers [3] Grasses [4] Trees [5] Sea plants	ANSWER TO Q-9 [2] Petroleum and natural gas make up two of Indonesia's exports. 52%

17 Like the leopard, this great cat has a melanistic or black form:

[1] Lion
[2] Tiger
[3] Lynx
[4] Cheetah
[5] Jaguar

ANSWER TO Q-16

[5] Estonia borders on the Baltic Sea, the gulfs of Riga and Finland. Latvia is to the south.

57%

---

17 Which river forms the border between Myanmar and Laos?

[1] Yenisei
[2] Mekong
[3] Irrawaddy
[4] Yellow
[5] Orinocco

ANSWER TO Q-16

[1] It is a sleeve badge consisting of one or more stripes indicating rank in the service.

79%

---

17 All of these were foreseen by Jules Verne except:

[1] Space travel
[2] The submarine
[3] Microwave cooking
[4] The aqualung
[5] Television

ANSWER TO Q-16

[3] The term "Ginnie Mae" is used by lenders to describe the government's national mortgage association.

81%

---

17 Author Antoine de Saint-Exupery is best known for writing:

[1] Little Women
[2] Little Red Riding Hood
[3] Little Bo Peep
[4] The Little Prince
[5] Little Drummer Boy

ANSWER TO Q-16

[5] Serpentine is sometimes used as a gemstone.

46%

---

17 The adult male of this species is called a reynard:

[1] Gorilla
[2] Frog
[3] Hippopotamus
[4] Fox
[5] Flamingo

ANSWER TO Q-16

[4] The Dalai Lama, Tibet's spiritual leader, fled to India after a failed 1959 uprising.

81%

9 Leah and Rachel were the two wives of this biblical figure:	[1] Isaac [2] Jacob [3] Abraham [4] Joseph [5] Moses	ANSWER TO Q-8 **[1]** "Diary of a Madman" is Guy de Maupassant's story about a murderous judge. 45%
9 All but which common childhood illness is caused by a virus?	[1] Chicken pox [2] Measles [3] Whooping cough [4] Mumps [5] Rubella	ANSWER TO Q-8 **[1]** Bromeliads retain water in their central cups, allowing them to survive dry spells. 34%
9 Which of these actresses is mismatched with one of her famous starring roles?	[1] Mahogany - Diana Ross [2] Jezebel - Bette Davis [3] Salome - Rita Hayworth [4] Marnie - Julie Andrews [5] Camille - Garbo	ANSWER TO Q-8 **[1]** The 1960 film is a fictionalized account of the famous Scopes "Monkey Trial" of 1925. 57%
9 A sphyg-momanometer measures:	[1] Dandruff concentration [2] Drugs in the body [3] Distance between stars [4] Blood pressure [5] Fur density	ANSWER TO Q-8 **[2]** Starboard is the term for right and port is the term for left. 89%
9 Which is the largest export of Indonesia?	[1] Timber [2] Petroleum [3] Textiles [4] Sugar [5] Cotton	ANSWER TO Q-8 **[1]** Peach, cherry, plum, apple and pear trees are all members of the rose family. 69%

18 Which story is not by Ernest Hemingway?	[1] Paul's Case [2] The Killers [3] Fifty Grand [4] My Old Man [5] The Snows of Kilimanjaro	ANSWER TO Q-17 **[5]** Black jaguars are less common than black leopards, which are also called black panthers. 69%
18 The coriolis force mainly affects:	[1] Agriculture [2] Air flow [3] Tides [4] Continental drift [5] Volcanic eruptions	ANSWER TO Q-17 **[2]** This 2600-mile river begins in the Tibetan plateau and flows into the South China Sea. 51%
18 The maxixe and the habanera are Latin American:	[1] Monkeys [2] Dances [3] Crime organizations [4] Martial arts [5] Indian tribes	ANSWER TO Q-17 **[3]** The French author (1828–1905) laid much of the foundation for modern science fiction. 58%
18 Before independence, Djibouti was known as:	[1] French Somaliland [2] Belgian Congo [3] Anglo-Egyptian Sudan [4] Portuguese East Africa [5] French Guiana	ANSWER TO Q-17 **[4]** The movie version cast Gene Wilder as the fox who teaches the prince about love. 47%
18 19th century Englishman Sir Robert Peel is remembered for his reorganization of:	[1] The colonies [2] Parliament [3] The national theater [4] Northern Ireland [5] London's police force	ANSWER TO Q-17 **[4]** The name comes from a French poem of the Middle ages, "Reynard the Fox." 69%

8 Which of these stories is not by Edgar Allan Poe?	[1] Diary of a Madman [2] The Oval Portrait [3] The Tell Tale Heart [4] The Black Cat [5] William Wilson	ANSWER TO Q-7 **[2]** She played the elderly, rich women Groucho courted for their money. 65%
8 The fruit of the ananas comosus plant of the bromeliad family is better known as the:	[1] Pineapple [2] Tangerine [3] Banana [4] Papaya [5] Fig	ANSWER TO Q-7 **[4]** This lively sort of music usually formed the third movement of a classical symphony. 45%
8 Which actor played Clarence Darrow in the film version of "Inherit the Wind"?	[1] Spencer Tracy [2] James Cagney [3] Jimmy Stewart [4] Humphrey Bogart [5] Marlon Brando	ANSWER TO Q-7 **[4]** Seven members of the "Bugs" Moran gang were killed over control of the Chicago bootleg trade. 68%
8 In seagoing terminology, which is the opposite of "port"?	[1] Keelhaul [2] Starboard [3] Halyard [4] Ensign [5] Scuttle	ANSWER TO Q-7 **[2]** Found only off New Zealand, they are the only survivors of the sphenodontida order. 34%
8 Onion, garlic and asparagus are in the same family as what flower?	[1] Lily [2] Rose [3] Violet [4] Hibiscus [5] Daffodil	ANSWER TO Q-7 **[2]** Audrey Hepburn played the country girl-turned-Manhattan escort in Blake Edwards' movie. 64%

19 Who would use a hammer and tongs?

[1] Blacksmith
[2] Cooper
[3] Haberdasher
[4] Catholic priest
[5] Teacher

ANSWER TO Q-18
[1] "Paul's Case" is a Willa Cather story.
55%

---

19 Which mountain peak is not in the Cascades?

[1] Mt. St. Helens
[2] Lassen Peak
[3] Mt. Egmont
[4] Mt. Rainier
[5] Mt. Shasta

ANSWER TO Q-18
[2] The coriolis effect causes objects going from north to south to veer west.
46%

---

19 What happens to Oedipus in the Greek tragedy "Oedipus Rex" by Sophocles?

[1] Slays minotaur
[2] Finds golden fleece
[3] Marries his mother
[4] Goes on an odyssey
[5] Wounds his heel

ANSWER TO Q-18
[2] Brazil's maxixe evolved into the tango while the habanera comes from Cuba.
23%

---

19 Which fictional pirate commanded a ship named "The Jolly Roger"?

[1] Captain Cook
[2] Captain Bligh
[3] Captain Blood
[4] Captain Kidd
[5] Captain Hook

ANSWER TO Q-18
[1] The name of the capital city became the name of the country upon independence in 1977.
46%

---

19 This term is loosely applied to limestone or dolomite which can be polished:

[1] Marble
[2] Obsidian
[3] Jade
[4] Quartz
[5] Basalt

ANSWER TO Q-18
[5] London police officers are called "bobbies" in honor of the man who re-organized the force.
42%

7 Margaret Dumont appeared regularly in the films of:	[1] Charlie Chaplin [2] The Marx Brothers [3] Shirley Temple [4] W.C. Fields [5] The Three Stooges	ANSWER TO Q-6 **[1]** His prominent family consisted of generations of poets and statesmen. 34%
7 The musical term "scherzo" comes from an Italian word for:	[1] Booklet [2] Song [3] Dance [4] Joke [5] Sound	ANSWER TO Q-6 **[3]** The Antarctic Peninsula separates the two seas. 45%
7 Mobster Al "Scarface" Capone is considered responsible for this criminal act:	[1] Luciano killing [2] Fixing the World Series [3] McKinley's death [4] Valentine's Day Massacre [5] Lindbergh baby kidnapping	ANSWER TO Q-6 **[3]** The word also describes something as weak, spiritless, thoughtless or ineffectual. 49%
7 The tuatara is an animal that is most like a:	[1] Penguin [2] Lizard [3] Cat [4] Heron [5] Beaver	ANSWER TO Q-6 **[5]** Husband of Queen Jezebel, King Ahab's name became a byword for wickedness. 45%
7 The central character of Truman Capote's "Breakfast at Tiffany's" is:	[1] Daisy Buchanan [2] Holly Golightly [3] Hester Prynne [4] Eliza Doolittle [5] Lara Antipova	ANSWER TO Q-6 **[5]** She appeared in Volume I, Number 1, Hugh Hefner's December, 1953, issue. 68%

20 Which explorer headed Darien, the first stable European settlement in South America?	[1] Vasco Balboa [2] Ponce de Leon [3] Hernando Cortes [4] Francisco Pizarro [5] Francisco Coronado	ANSWER TO Q-19 [1] "Strike while the iron is hot" is an old saying derived from blacksmithing practices. 51%
20 Which explorer took possession of the Mississippi Valley and named it Louisiana?	[1] Ponce de Leon [2] Walter Raleigh [3] John Cabot [4] Francis Drake [5] Robert LaSalle	ANSWER TO Q-19 [3] Egmont is a mountain on New Zealand's North Island. 58%
20 Which film featured "Dueling Banjos"?	[1] Nashville [2] Coal Miner's Daughter [3] Deliverance [4] Honkytonk Man [5] Southern Comfort	ANSWER TO Q-19 [3] Oedipus was a victim of fate. Fate also possessed him to kill his father. 79%
20 All these Latin American countries except ____ have sizable black populations.	[1] Venezuela [2] Argentina [3] Brazil [4] Ecuador [5] Dominican Republic	ANSWER TO Q-19 [5] In J.M. Barrie's classic "Peter Pan," Hook is the danger lurking in Never Never Land. 57%
20 The word "lucid" means:	[1] Erotic [2] Clear [3] Heavy [4] Difficult [5] Wicked	ANSWER TO Q-19 [1] The discovery of marble quarries in Italy helped give rise to an ancient architectural tradition. 58%

6 Considered a pioneer of confessional poetry, he wrote much about his family history:	[1] Robert Lowell [2] Robert Bly [3] Robert Frost [4] Robert Penn Warren [5] Robert Browning	ANSWER TO Q-5 [5] "The Champ" and the sports journal grew from contenders to kingpins together. 58%
6 The Bellingshausen and Weddell seas are located here:	[1] Mars [2] Middle East [3] Antarctica [4] Gulf of Mexico [5] Moon	ANSWER TO Q-5 [2] Because it contains the poisonous hydrocyanic acid, cassava must be processed carefully. 55%
6 Which more familiar word would describe a feckless person?	[1] Detailed [2] Vulnerable [3] Irresponsible [4] Curious [5] Relaxed	ANSWER TO Q-5 [5] The coming of spring symbolizes the rebirth of hope. 65%
6 Melville's Ahab, an obsessed captain who hunted Moby-Dick, was named after:	[1] A Spanish inquisitor [2] The flying dutchman [3] A Greek demi-god [4] A Persian monarch [5] A biblical king	ANSWER TO Q-5 [3] Set in Mexico, "The Plumed Serpent" is about an attempt to revive the ancient Aztec religion. 45%
6 The first nude "Playboy" centerfold was:	[1] Jayne Mansfield [2] Gypsy Rose Lee [3] Brigitte Bardot [4] Jane Russell [5] Marilyn Monroe	ANSWER TO Q-5 [4] "The 1001 Nights" is the more accurate title of this incomparable story collection. 78%

21 What type of galaxy is the Milky Way?

[1] Elliptical
[2] Irregular
[3] Circumflex
[4] Spiral
[5] Active nuclei

ANSWER TO Q-20
[1] Darien Province is now divided between Panama and Colombia.
23%

---

21 In the early 19th century, Tammany Hall controlled politics here:

[1] Chicago
[2] Los Angeles
[3] Miami
[4] New York
[5] New Orleans

ANSWER TO Q-20
[5] LaSalle was killed by his men after failing to find the mouth of the Mississippi.
34%

---

21 Which of these American writers is not a noted poet?

[1] Henry James
[2] Carl Sandburg
[3] Hart Crane
[4] Wallace Stevens
[5] Walt Whitman

ANSWER TO Q-20
[3] It's a suspenseful tale of four men whose weekend river trip turns into an adventure in terror.
91%

---

21 Which author is not noted for writing science fiction?

[1] Frank Herbert
[2] Eudora Welty
[3] Robert Heinlein
[4] Ray Bradbury
[5] Isaac Asimov

ANSWER TO Q-20
[2] 95% of Argentines are of European origin. Indians, Mestizos and Arabs make up the rest.
56%

---

21 Which is an example of a portmanteau word?

[1] Bat
[2] Noon
[3] Brunch
[4] Knee
[5] Radar

ANSWER TO Q-20
[2] The term derives from the Latin word for shining.
91%

5 Which athlete has been on the cover of "Sports Illustrated" a record 31 times?	[1] Hank Aaron [2] Jimmy Connors [3] Willie Shoemaker [4] Jack Nicklaus [5] Muhammad Ali	ANSWER TO Q-4 **[4]** He was given the name by those little guys, the Lilliputians. 78%
5 The cassava vegetable is the source of:	[1] Vanilla [2] Tapioca [3] Paprika [4] Cocoa [5] Farina	ANSWER TO Q-4 **[1]** This particular moral comes from "The Tortoise and the Hare." 89%
5 On goddess Persephone's return to Earth from Hades, what did she bring with her?	[1] Love [2] Health [3] Fire [4] Treasure [5] Spring	ANSWER TO Q-4 **[5]** It is agreed that a single author created "Beowulf," but his name is lost to history. 45%
5 Which D.H. Lawrence novel has not been the basis of a film?	[1] Women in Love [2] The Rainbow [3] The Plumed Serpent [4] Lady Chatterley's Lover [5] Sons and Lovers	ANSWER TO Q-4 **[4]** "In Search of Lost Time" is the revealing title of his multivolume masterpiece. 43%
5 Sinbad and Aladdin are two of the most famous characters from:	[1] Greek mythology [2] Marvel comics [3] American folklore [4] The Arabian Nights [5] Dante's "Inferno"	ANSWER TO Q-4 **[2]** The king of hearts is gruesomely depicted running a sword through his head. 62%

22 Each is a major world oil-producing area except:	[1] North Sea [2] Prudhoe Bay [3] Bahrain [4] Witwatersrand [5] Indonesia	ANSWER TO Q-21 **[4]** The classifications of galaxies were established by Edwin Hubble. 81%
22 Ripley is the unusual name of the heroine of this action saga:	[1] Romancing the Stone [2] Raiders of the Lost Ark [3] Alien [4] The Abyss [5] Blade Runner	ANSWER TO Q-21 **[4]** Often corrupt, it did bring political and economic opportunity to the immigrant poor. 55%
22 Which is not associated with the 1920's?	[1] Lindbergh's flight [2] Dance marathons [3] Sinking of Titanic [4] King Tut's tomb found [5] The charleston	ANSWER TO Q-21 **[1]** James is celebrated as one of America's great novelists. 57%
22 The dybbuk is a creature in ____ folklore.	[1] Chinese [2] Celtic [3] Viking [4] Hindu [5] Jewish	ANSWER TO Q-21 **[2]** Eudora Welty's stories are about the American South. 61%
22 What purpose does synovial fluid serve in the body?	[1] Carries waste matter [2] Secretes saliva [3] Collects mucus [4] Lubricates joints [5] Produces tears	ANSWER TO Q-21 **[3]** It is a word that takes parts of two words to create a new one. 54%

4. Which of these literary characters was called "The Great Man Mountain" by his captors?	[1] Paul Bunyan [2] Tarzan [3] Ali Baba [4] Gulliver [5] Frankenstein	ANSWER TO Q-3 [3] Crime was not sheriff Andy's biggest problem in the tiny town of Mayberry; Barney Fife was. 89%
4. The expression "Slow but steady wins the race" comes from a fable by:	[1] Aesop [2] The Brothers Grimm [3] Mother Goose [4] Uncle Remus [5] Mother Hubbard	ANSWER TO Q-3 [1] The novella is a story of a boy at sea. 23%
4. Which classic work is by an author whose name is unknown?	[1] Cyrano de Bergerac [2] Hunchback of Notre Dame [3] Doctor Faustus [4] Oedipus Rex [5] Beowulf	ANSWER TO Q-3 [5] It served as a model for its successor, the United Nations. 68%
4. This French novelist's work is considered to have a strong autobiographical basis:	[1] Victor Hugo [2] Emile Zola [3] Jean Cocteau [4] Marcel Proust [5] Gustave Flaubert	ANSWER TO Q-3 [3] The first wife tries to have Beauty burned at the stake but the prince rescues her. 67%
4. Which of these playing cards has the nickname "Suicide King"?	[1] King of Spades [2] King of Hearts [3] King of Clubs [4] King of Diamonds [5] One-eyed Jack	ANSWER TO Q-3 [4] Mitty dreamed of heroics in contrast to his mundane life in a short story by James Thurber. 89%

23 Which European ruler made a pope his prisoner?	[1] Ivan the Terrible [2] Attila the Hun [3] Napoleon Bonaparte [4] Adolf Hitler [5] Alexander the Great	ANSWER TO Q-22 [4] Witwatersrand is one of South Africa's major gold-producing regions. 43%
23 What makes the lantern fish so unique?	[1] Lamp on its head [2] Oily residue on skin [3] Wick-like tongue [4] Glowing body [5] Fluorescent scales	ANSWER TO Q-22 [3] Sigourney Weaver made her third and final appearance as Ripley in "Alien 3." 89%
23 In which novel would you read about the ship "Hispaniola"?	[1] Robinson Crusoe [2] Gulliver's Travels [3] Treasure Island [4] The Blue Lagoon [5] Swiss Family Robinson	ANSWER TO Q-22 [3] The Titanic sunk in 1912 with the loss of over 1500 lives. 79%
23 Which famous literary work is not written in verse?	[1] Beowulf [2] The Divine Comedy [3] Don Quixote [4] Oedipus Rex [5] The Odyssey	ANSWER TO Q-22 [5] A type of migrating soul, it enters the body of the living. 57%
23 Which of these common minerals is formed in very thin sheets?	[1] Marble [2] Quartz [3] Shale [4] Mica [5] Granite	ANSWER TO Q-22 [4] Along with elastic cartilage and fluid-filled sacs, it reduces friction in joints. 46%

3 What was Andy's relation to Barney Fife on the "Andy Griffith show"?	[1] Uncle [2] Father [3] Cousin [4] Brother-in-law [5] No relation	ANSWER TO Q-2 **[3]** "1984" and "Brave New World" are probably the most famous examples. 59%
3 "The Narrative of Arthur Gordon Pym" is the longest work of this author:	[1] Edgar Allan Poe [2] Nathaniel Hawthorne [3] Mark Twain [4] Joseph Conrad [5] Washington Irving	ANSWER TO Q-2 **[5]** Uriah Heep's false humility and Tartuffe's fake piety have become proverbial. 67%
3 The League of Nations was formed at the end of which war?	[1] Franco-Prussian [2] World War II [3] Russo-Turkish [4] Sino-Japanese [5] World War I	ANSWER TO Q-2 **[5]** "The Razor's Edge" takes place in America, Europe and India. 76%
3 Which is true of the prince in the earliest known version of "Sleeping Beauty"?	[1] He is an ugly beast [2] He loses his kingdom [3] He already has a wife [4] He is a hunchback [5] He abandons her	ANSWER TO Q-2 **[2]** HBO started in 1972, some sixteen years before Ted Turner began his first network. 67%
3 The character Walter Mitty was known for his:	[1] Gossip column [2] Friendship with Al Capone [3] Hot temper [4] Daydreaming [5] Economic advice	ANSWER TO Q-2 **[2]** Unlike "etc.," "et al." can refer to people as well as to things. 54%

WHAT IS NTN?

NTN Communications, Inc., located in beautiful Carlsbad, CA, is the creator of the NTN Entertainment Network, the world's first totally interactive television network. You not only watch what's happening—you participate in the action. Once you experience NTN, you'll never watch TV the same way again.

The network centers around thousands of subscribing bars, hotels, and restaurants across the USA, Canada, Australia, and South Africa. Players use a small wireless keyboard called a Playmaker™ to interact with what's happening on television monitors in each location.

WHAT'S ON?

NTN offers a wide variety of game shows. **Showdown,** the world's most all-encompassing game show, is a test of general knowledge. Music fans sing about **Playback.** Travel the world during **Passport,** which visits a different destination each week. **Spotlight** covers the hottest happenings in the entertainment industry. **Nightside** is for adults only. And, if you check box scores every day, come take our **Sports IQ** test. If you've ever seen the NTN Network, you've probably seen **Countdown,** a quick half-hour game played all day long.

Sports fan? If you like football, play **QB1** and call what the quarterback will do during live NFL games. **DiamondBall** players predict hits and runs during live baseball games. Boxing fans score a fight, round by round, during **UpperCut.** Hockey fanatic? Call shots on goal during **PowerPlay. Triples** players forecast which horses will finish first, second, and third during live horse races. Basketball aficionados can draft their own dream teams by participating in **Hoops.**

No matter what kind of program you're watching, you'll see scoreboards after each activity that show you how you're doing along with everyone else in your location. After the game, you'll see how well you did individually against the thousands of other players across the NTN Network and how your location ranked as well. Top scores are eligible for prizes, and we've given away everything from caps to cruises. The competition gets pretty fierce with all that bragging and booing going on, and it all adds up to a ton of fun.

HOW DOES IT WORK?

Briefly, we broadcast our programming via satellite to a computer at each subscribing location. The Playmakers™ function as receiving and transmitting devices between the player and the computer, which keeps track of everyone's activities during each game. After the game, each location contacts NTN via modem and transmits scoring information. Our computers then correlate and rank all the individuals and groups. Those rankings are then sent back out to each location within a few minutes.

CAN I PLAY NTN TRIVIA AT HOME?

You bet. If you have a computer and a modem, you can join us on a variety of online service providers. Currently, we can be found on America Online, GEnie, and the ImagiNation Network. See below for info on how to contact these services and establish your own account. Look for NTN's products on other online services in the near future. We can also be found on GTE Mainstreet, an interactive cable station offered in selected areas of the USA. Check with your cable company to see if they carry GTE Mainstreet.

WHAT'S DIFFERENT ABOUT PLAYING ONLINE?

Well, the drinks are free. Seriously, though, there are a few differences. Online, we offer a twenty-four-hour schedule and games are played in fifteen-minute rather than thirty-minute intervals. We offer a live chat feature that enables you to actually talk in real time to other players in the game. It's like being at your local hangout, except the person sitting next to you may be several miles or a continent away! Players who frequent our online games have made lasting friendships and have planned many fun get-togethers over the years. All our online players are competing right along with subscribing locations across the network, giving another dimension to the word interactive!

If you have internet mail access, feel free to drop us a note
with your questions, comments, or suggestions
at NTNMAIL@NTN.mhs.compuserve.com.

24 Which of these comedians played the film role of "Fletch"?	[1] Bill Murray [2] Steve Martin [3] Jim Belushi [4] Chevy Chase [5] John Candy	ANSWER TO Q-23 **[3]** Pius VII excommunicated Napoleon. The emperor retaliated by taking him to France as a prisoner. 23%
24 Barbara Stanwyck plays the matriarch of the Barkley family on this TV show:	[1] Bonanza [2] The Big Valley [3] Falcon Crest [4] Hotel [5] Eight is Enough	ANSWER TO Q-23 **[1]** Living in the dark of the deep oceans, it uses its built-in light to attract prey. 35%
24 Writer Anais Nin is best known for her ten-volume:	[1] History of the world [2] Diary [3] Women's encyclopedia [4] Lives of the presidents [5] Study of English	ANSWER TO Q-23 **[3]** Robert Louis Stevenson tells the tale of Jim Hawkins' search for buried treasure. 45%
24 Which Latin legal term means being caught red-handed?	[1] In curia [2] Habeas corpus [3] In flagrante delicto [4] Quid pro quo [5] In camera	ANSWER TO Q-23 **[3]** The Cervantes work is one of the earliest examples of a novel. 46%
24 The first programming language developed for business applications was:	[1] COBOL [2] FORTRAN [3] ALGOL [4] BASIC [5] PASCAL	ANSWER TO Q-23 **[4]** Sheet mica is used as an insulating material and in certain acoustic devices. 68%

2 What term describes a book that describes an imperfect imaginary society?	[1] Naturalistic [2] Satirical [3] Dystopian [4] Experimental [5] Postmodern	ANSWER TO Q-1 **[3]** Lt. Gerard is the police detective hot on the trail of the wrongly accused Dr. Richard Kimball. 68%
2 The biblical Pharisee, Moliere's Tartuffe and Dickens' Uriah Heep are examples of the:	[1] Rigid schoolmaster [2] Incompetent physician [3] Philandering husband [4] Absent-minded professor [5] Pious hypocrite	ANSWER TO Q-1 **[4]** Fearing General MacArthur would attack China, Pres. Truman relieved him of his Korean conflict duties. 57%
2 Which famous story is not set in Africa?	[1] Heart of Darkness [2] Tarzan of the Apes [3] King Solomon's Mines [4] The Snows of Kilimanjaro [5] The Razor's Edge	ANSWER TO Q-1 **[4]** This lip-synching duo's final #1 hit was "Blame It on the Rain" in 1989. 56%
2 Which is the oldest U.S. cable service?	[1] Showtime [2] HBO [3] MTV [4] TNT [5] Disney	ANSWER TO Q-1 **[5]** The mineral-rich area is home to a quarter of Poland's population. 45%
2 "Et al." is an appropriate abbreviation for use on an incomplete list of:	[1] Automobiles [2] People [3] Grocery items [4] City names [5] Universities	ANSWER TO Q-1 **[3]** Trygve Lie of Norway served as United Nations secretary-general from 1946 to 1953. 45%

25 This bird migrates from its Texas wintering grounds to Canada's N.W. Territories:	[1] Peregrine falcon [2] Pink flamingo [3] Whooping crane [4] Yellow-bellied sapsucker [5] Barn swallow	ANSWER TO Q-24 **[4]** Chevy Chase plays the investigative reporter and master of disguises. 89%
25 In legend, Lady Godiva rode naked through this English town:	[1] Plymouth [2] Leeds [3] Birmingham [4] Manchester [5] Coventry	ANSWER TO Q-24 **[2]** The family was continually fighting the lawless elements of the old West. 81%
25 Which literary classic was first published in the 19th century?	[1] Tom Jones [2] Gulliver's Travels [3] Dangerous Liaisons [4] Alice in Wonderland [5] Robinson Crusoe	ANSWER TO Q-24 **[2]** Nin's diary was published over a number of years, from 1966 to 1983. 79%
25 Which famous novel was published before 1950?	[1] Doctor Zhivago [2] The Catcher in the Rye [3] Lord of the Flies [4] 1984 [5] The Old Man and the Sea	ANSWER TO Q-24 **[3]** The others mean "in court," "court order," "fair exchange" and "in chambers." 81%
25 Which book features a love triangle among Ellen Olenska, Newland Archer & May Welland?	[1] Portrait of a Lady [2] The Edwardians [3] The Age of Innocence [4] A Room with a View [5] The Gilded Age	ANSWER TO Q-24 **[1]** COBOL was developed in 1959 under the leadership of Grace Hopper. 59%

1 Which TV series featured the nemesis, Lt. Gerard?	[1] Dragnet [2] Police Woman [3] The Fugitive [4] The Incredible Hulk [5] Adam-12	Turn to the top frame on the next left hand page for the correct answer and the next question.
1 General Ridgway succeeded this famous commander-in-chief:	[1] Patton [2] Montgomery [3] Sherman [4] MacArthur [5] Lee	Turn to the second frame on the next left hand page for the correct answer and the next question.
1 "Baby Don't Forget My Number" and "Girl I'm Gonna Miss You" were #1 hits by:	[1] Bad English [2] Simply Red [3] Fine Young Cannibals [4] Milli Vanilli [5] C & C Music Factory	Turn to the middle frame on the next left hand page for the correct answer and the next question.
1 Once the object of several wars, most of the region of Silesia lies in present-day:	[1] Italy [2] France [3] Greece [4] Spain [5] Poland	Turn to the fourth frame on the next left hand page for the correct answer and the next question.
1 Who was the first secretary-general of the United Nations?	[1] Sidney Holland [2] Reinhard Heydrich [3] Trygve Lie [4] U Thant [5] Dag Hammerskjold	Turn to the bottom frame on the next left hand page for the correct answer and the next question.

26 Which man never won the U.S. Tennis Open?	[1] Bjorn Borg [2] Ilie Nastase [3] Guillermo Vilas [4] Arthur Ashe [5] Mats Wilander	ANSWER TO Q-25 **[3]** They leave for Canada in late March and return to Texas around the middle of October. 43%
26 Which type of hard liquor is mismatched with the ingredient it's distilled from?	[1] Whiskey - grain [2] Rum - sugar cane [3] Vodka - potatoes [4] Brandy - fruit [5] Tequila - cactus	ANSWER TO Q-25 **[5]** The only person who looked at her as she rode became known as Peeping Tom. 69%
26 All of these are kinds of boats or ships except:	[1] Brigantine [2] Funicular [3] Ketch [4] Trimaran [5] Skipjack	ANSWER TO Q-25 **[4]** The other classics date from the 17th and 18th centuries. 51%
26 Those menu items described as "en croute" are served:	[1] Encased in pastry [2] In a casserole [3] With cheese on the side [4] Covered with crumbs [5] With gravy	ANSWER TO Q-25 **[4]** George Orwell wrote this prophetic novel in 1948. 58%
26 Which two countries are located on the same island?	[1] Haiti - Dominican Republic [2] Jamaica - Cuba [3] Trinidad - Tobago [4] Suriname - Guyana [5] Antigua - Bermuda	ANSWER TO Q-25 **[3]** This book is a satirical look at upper class life in New York City in the middle 19th century. 41%

GAME NUMBER 16

ANSWER TO Q-15

[3] It was the doctor, not the creature, who actually bore the name Frankenstein.

56%

GAME NUMBER 34

ANSWER TO Q-15

[1] The 4500-mile-long mountain range also passes through Chile and Venezuela.

45%

GAME NUMBER 52

ANSWER TO Q-15

[1] Readers hope Wolf got bored with Rip's snores and went home for supper.

34%

GAME NUMBER 70

ANSWER TO Q-15

[3] The third type of rock, sedimentary, is made by consolidation of wind and water-borne material.

54%

GAME NUMBER 88

ANSWER TO Q-15

[4] A red rose was the emblem of the House of Lancaster while a white rose represented York.

46%

27		
27 This extinct bird was a close relative of the puffin:	[1] Dodo bird [2] Pterodactyl [3] Passenger pigeon [4] Trumpeter swan [5] Great auk	ANSWER TO Q-26 **[1]** All of Borg's Grand Slam titles came at the French Open or Wimbledon. 52%
27 Which type of person could most accurately be called an epicure?	[1] Miser [2] Hypocrite [3] Religious fanatic [4] Gourmet [5] Political martyr	ANSWER TO Q-26 **[5]** Tequila is distilled from the sap of the agave, a native plant of Mexico. 61%
27 The first woman athlete to win over $100,000 in prize money during a single year was:	[1] Chris Evert [2] Pat Bradley [3] Peggy Fleming [4] Babe Didrikson [5] Billie Jean King	ANSWER TO Q-26 **[2]** A funicular is a mountain railway often suspended from cables. 69%
27 In Greek mythology, what is the fate of Actaeon after he sees Artemis bathing?	[1] Turned to stone [2] Killed by dogs [3] Has to marry her [4] His firstborn is cursed [5] Becomes immortal	ANSWER TO Q-26 **[1]** "Croute" is the French word for crust. 46%
27 Virgil's "Aeneid" is the epic poem of the _____.	[1] Roman Empire [2] Athenian democracy [3] Venetian Republic [4] Third Reich [5] Boer War	ANSWER TO Q-26 **[1]** Haiti is French-speaking while natives of the Dominican Republic speak Spanish. 81%

15 What classic horror novel is subtitled "The Modern Prometheus"?	[1] Shadow over Innsmouth [2] Diary of a Madman [3] Frankenstein [4] Lair of the White Worm [5] Dracula	ANSWER TO Q-14 [3] James Arness went on to gain stardom in the long-running television series "Gunsmoke." 67%
15 South America's Andes Mountains pass through all but one of these countries?	[1] Brazil [2] Argentina [3] Bolivia [4] Peru [5] Colombia	ANSWER TO Q-14 [2] It is the highest and most sacred in Japan. 68%
15 What was the name of Rip Van Winkle's faithful dog in Washington Irving's tale?	[1] Wolf [2] Dawg [3] Blackie [4] Nipper [5] Spot	ANSWER TO Q-14 [5] Neil Tennant was the lead singer for these London-based disco fanatics. 57%
15 Metamorphic rocks are made from intense heat and pressure. Igneous rocks are made from:	[1] Water-borne debris [2] Compressed crystals [3] Magma inside the earth [4] Plant and animal remains [5] Volcanic ash	ANSWER TO Q-14 [5] This rock on the Rhine River in Germany rises 430 feet above a point where the river narrows. 62%
15 Which English house finally won the War of the Roses?	[1] Tudor [2] York [3] Plantagenet [4] Lancaster [5] Stuart	ANSWER TO Q-14 [5] The Robert Benton film "Kramer vs. Kramer" bested Coppola for the Oscar in 1979. 45%

28 This film opens with "On Broadway," and closes with "Bye Bye Love":	[1] Bye Bye Birdie [2] All That Jazz [3] Grease [4] White Knights [5] A Chorus Line	ANSWER TO Q-27 **[5]** Hunted for its flesh, feathers and oil, it became extinct in 1844. 35%
28 In May of 1993, the nation of Eritrea declared itself independent of:	[1] Great Britain [2] Portugal [3] Ethiopia [4] Spain [5] France	ANSWER TO Q-27 **[4]** The term has come to stand for the ability to appreciate the finer material things in life. 69%
28 Who is credited with saying, "The unexamined life is not worth living"?	[1] Ben Franklin [2] Thomas Hobbes [3] Franklin D. Roosevelt [4] Moses [5] Socrates	ANSWER TO Q-27 **[5]** She's long been a crusader for equality in prize money given to women athletes. 58%
28 Which Disney film featured the mice Bernard and Bianca?	[1] Peter Pan [2] The Rescuers Down Under [3] Lady and the Tramp [4] The Sword in the Stone [5] Pinocchio	ANSWER TO Q-27 **[2]** She turns him into a stag and he is torn to pieces by his own hounds. 35%
28 Soybeans are used to make all of these products except:	[1] Soy milk [2] Tempeh [3] Tofu [4] Miso [5] Tapioca	ANSWER TO Q-27 **[1]** Legend had it that a prince of Troy, Aeneas, landed in Italy and laid its foundations. 46%

14 In the 1951 version of "The Thing," the carrotlike 'thing' was played by:

[1] Peter Graves
[2] Steve McQueen
[3] James Arness
[4] Michael Landon
[5] Leslie Nielsen

ANSWER TO Q-13
[4] The Polish-born director also made a horror comedy, "The Fearless Vampire Killers."
79%

---

14 This is the world's most painted, photographed and climbed mountain:

[1] Blanc
[2] Fuji
[3] McKinley
[4] Everest
[5] Kilimanjaro

ANSWER TO Q-13
[5] The Pyrenees ride along the border of France and Spain.
58%

---

14 Which recording was a 1986 hit for the Pet Shop Boys?

[1] Higher Love
[2] Give it Away
[3] Hotel California
[4] Another Day in Paradise
[5] West End Girls

ANSWER TO Q-13
[1] The baby leopard managed to cause one hilarious situation after the other.
79%

---

14 Which famous rock is not matched with its location?

[1] Plymouth - Massachusetts
[2] Blarney Stone - Ireland
[3] Stone of Scone - London
[4] Inscription - New Mexico
[5] Lorelei - Hawaii

ANSWER TO Q-13
[4] Rockford lived in a rusty trailer on Malibu Beach.
79%

---

14 Which of these war films never won the Academy Award for Best Picture?

[1] The Deer Hunter
[2] Patton
[3] From Here to Eternity
[4] Platoon
[5] Apocalypse Now

ANSWER TO Q-13
[2] The Orson Welles' Mercury Theatre radio broadcast caused mass panic, since many people believed it was true.
89%

29 Which real person was never portrayed in a film by Henry Fonda?	[1] Wyatt Earp [2] Abraham Lincoln [3] Glenn Miller [4] Frank James [5] Clarence Gideon	ANSWER TO Q-28 [2] Directed by Bob Fosse, it is said to be autobiographical. 69%
29 Which French city is the center for production of fine mustards?	[1] Bordeaux [2] Lyon [3] Dijon [4] Paris [5] Cannes	ANSWER TO Q-28 [3] Once part of the ancient kingdom of Aksum, it struggled for 31 years to gain independence. 5%
29 What religious group publishes the "Watchtower"?	[1] Scientology [2] Latter Day Saints [3] Seven Day Adventists [4] Hare Krishnas [5] Jehovah's Witnesses	ANSWER TO Q-28 [5] Along with Plato and Aristotle, he was one of the great teachers of ancient Greece. 54%
29 Which famous writer was not alive in 1940?	[1] Ernest Hemingway [2] Thomas Hardy [3] Dylan Thomas [4] Noel Coward [5] Robert Frost	ANSWER TO Q-28 [2] This animated film contained more computer animation than any other Disney film at the time. 61%
29 Which would be sung or spoken at a funeral?	[1] Dogma [2] Diatribe [3] Diphthong [4] Dirge [5] Doggerel	ANSWER TO Q-28 [5] Tapioca is made from the edible root of a tropical plant called the cassava. 46%

13 Who directed such horrific films "Rosemary's Baby," "The Tenant" and "Repulsion"?

[1] Orson Welles
[2] Alfred Hitchcock
[3] David Cronenberg
[4] Roman Polanski
[5] John Carpenter

ANSWER TO Q-12
[4] In this heart-warming tale, slimy sewer derelicts are mutated into cannibals by waste.
54%

---

13 This mountain range stretches 600 miles from the Mediterran-ean Sea to the Bay of Biscay:

[1] Alps
[2] Cascade
[3] Atlas
[4] Andes
[5] Pyrenees

ANSWER TO Q-12
[4] The world's 35 highest peaks are located either in the Himalayas or in Kashmir's Karakorams.
58%

---

13 In the Cary Grant and Katharine Hepburn film, "Bringing up Baby," what was baby?

[1] Leopard
[2] Chimpanzee
[3] Irish wolfhound
[4] Lion cub
[5] Gorilla

ANSWER TO Q-12
[3] If the cat's tail is tilted like a question mark the cat is still checking you out.
58%

---

13 Which is not true of private investigator Jim Rockford?

[1] Ex-convict
[2] Drove gold Camaro
[3] Lived in a trailer
[4] Worked in San Francisco
[5] Bachelor

ANSWER TO Q-12
[2] Rocks with more than 10% free quartz are called acid rocks, those with none are basic rocks.
45%

---

13 "War of the Worlds" spread the fear that forces from ____ had invaded U.S. soil in 1938.

[1] Russia
[2] Mars
[3] The Moon
[4] Germany
[5] Planet X

ANSWER TO Q-12
[2] War recorded two albums with Eric Burdon. "Spill the Wine" was their biggest hit.
45%

156

30 Chantilly, France is known the world over for producing:	[1] Red wines [2] Mustard [3] Champagne [4] Cheeses [5] Lace	ANSWER TO Q-29 [3] Jimmy Stewart played the famous bandleader in the film "The Glenn Miller Story." 46%
30 Which adjective describes something that is pipe-shaped?	[1] Fistular [2] Stellar [3] Fililos [4] Spatulate [5] Cuneiform	ANSWER TO Q-29 [3] The seeds of European and Asian mustard herbs are ground into a paste with vinegar or oil. 69%
30 Which film made famous the remark "What we have here is a failure to communicate"?	[1] M*A*S*H [2] Cool Hand Luke [3] Easy Rider [4] Sleeper [5] Myra Breckinridge	ANSWER TO Q-29 [5] All "Witnesses" are considered ministers, preaching door-to-door. 71%
30 What is curacao?	[1] Hot curry spice [2] Liqueur made of oranges [3] Brazilian parrot stew [4] Aged cheese [5] Unsweetened chocolate	ANSWER TO Q-29 [2] The author of "Tess of the D'Urbervilles" died in 1928. 48%
30 Bruno Hauptmann was executed for the murder of:	[1] William McKinley [2] Jimmy Hoffa [3] George Moscone [4] Jennifer Levin [5] Charles Lindbergh, Jr.	ANSWER TO Q-29 [4] A dirge is a lamentation composed for a funeral. 79%

12 The plot of the horror flick "C.H.U.D." features cannibalistic bad guys from:

[1] Lost city of Atlantis
[2] Planet Zypton
[3] Acting school
[4] The sewers
[5] A cult of giant insects

ANSWER TO Q-11

[2] Only at the very end of Clouzot's film does the viewer realize what is going on.
67%

---

12 The second tallest mountain in the world, K-2, is found in this range:

[1] Pyrenees
[2] Andes
[3] Canadian Rockies
[4] Karakoram
[5] Swiss Alps

ANSWER TO Q-11

[4] Fujiyama is actually the highest mountain in Japan, rising 12,388 ft.
56%

---

12 When a cat's tail is held straight up in the air, he is saying that he:

[1] Wants to play
[2] Is ready to fight
[3] Likes you
[4] Feels afraid
[5] Is mildly miffed

ANSWER TO Q-11

[5] The bassett hound rides along with another eccentric TV cop, Columbo.
89%

---

12 Rocks are graded as acidic or basic depending on the amount of ____ they contain.

[1] Iron
[2] Quartz
[3] Aluminum
[4] Carbon
[5] Gold

ANSWER TO Q-11

[4] This is a concert film of the Talking Heads; U2's rock film is titled "Rattle and Hum."
87%

---

12 Which British invasion singer fronted the funk band "War" in 1970?

[1] Peter Noone
[2] Eric Burdon
[3] Brian Jones
[4] Ray Davies
[5] Dave Clark

ANSWER TO Q-11

[5] In six days in June of 1967, the Israeli army soundly defeated their Arab enemies.
73%

BRAIN BUSTER

GAME NUMBER 4

ANSWER TO Q-30

[5] The first hand-made Chantilly lace produced in the town was black in color.

81%

BRAIN BUSTER

GAME NUMBER 22

ANSWER TO Q-30

[1] Fililos is thread-like; stellar is star-shaped; cuneiform is triangular; and spatulate is spoon-shaped.

69%

BRAIN BUSTER

GAME NUMBER 40

ANSWER TO Q-30

[2] Paul Newman starred as the never-say-"uncle" hero in this southern prison movie.

81%

BRAIN BUSTER

GAME NUMBER 58

ANSWER TO Q-30

[2] It takes its name from Curacao, the island off of Venezuela where it was first made.

79%

BRAIN BUSTER

GAME NUMBER 76

ANSWER TO Q-30

[5] The 20-month-old baby was killed even though a $50,000 ransom was paid.

81%

11 In which film does the Machiavellian plot focus on a man, his wife and his mistress?	[1] Vertigo [2] Diabolique [3] Rosemary's Baby [4] Spellbound [5] Dementia 13	ANSWER TO Q-10 [3] Robert Englund stars as the burn victim who attacks innocent teens in their dreams. 89%
11 This mountain is actually a dormant volcano that last erupted in 1707:	[1] The Matterhorn [2] Mt. McKinley [3] Sugarloaf Mountain [4] Mt. Fuji [5] Pikes Peak	ANSWER TO Q-10 [3] Mt. McKinley's height measures 20,320 feet, just above Mt. Logan's 19,850 feet. 78%
11 On the TV drama, big city cop Baretta lived in a rundown hotel with his pet:	[1] Bassett hound [2] Ferret [3] Cat [4] Hamster [5] Cockatoo	ANSWER TO Q-10 [1] Cats were so highly valued anyone who killed one would be punished by death. 21%
11 Which rock film and the band it centers on is mismatched?	[1] Quadrophenia - The Who [2] The Last Waltz - The Band [3] Gimme Shelter - Rolling Stones [4] Stop Making Sense - U2 [5] Help!-The Beatles	ANSWER TO Q-10 [4] Coach Knute Rockne led Notre Dame to three national titles and is known for his famous "Gipper" speech. 34%
11 The Israelis fought against ___ in the Six-Day War of 1967.	[1] Greece and Turkey [2] China and North Vietnam [3] Libya and Tunisia [4] USSR and Afghanistan [5] Egypt and Syria	ANSWER TO Q-10 [3] C.A. Pennebaker and Chris Hegedus give us a behind-the-scenes look at American politics. 34%

1 He became president of Mexico in 1867 after leading the uprising against Maximilian:	[1] General Santa Anna [2] Padre Hidalgo [3] Venustiano Carranza [4] Alvaro Obregon [5] Benito Juarez	Turn to the top frame on the next right hand page for the correct answer and the next question.
1 This quipster once said, "I can resist everything except temptation":	[1] Will Rogers [2] Groucho Marx [3] Oscar Wilde [4] Ernest Hemingway [5] W.C. Fields	Turn to the second frame on the next right hand page for the correct answer and the next question.
1 He played Philip Marlowe in Robert Altman's adaption of "The Long Goodbye":	[1] James Woods [2] William Hurt [3] Elliott Gould [4] Dustin Hoffman [5] Jerry Lewis	Turn to the middle frame on the next right hand page for the correct answer and the next question.
1 In the New Testament, the people referred to as "publicans" were:	[1] Tax collectors [2] Religious leaders [3] Slaves [4] Governors [5] Gentiles	Turn to the fourth frame on the next right hand page for the correct answer and the next question.
1 The Leakeys found many fossils at Olduvai Gorge, a small canyon in:	[1] China [2] Turkey [3] Tanzania [4] South Africa [5] Libya	Turn to the bottom frame on the next right hand page for the correct answer and the next question.

10 Which of these horror characters wears a fedora?	[1] Jason Vorhees [2] Michael Myers [3] Freddy Krueger [4] Norman Bates [5] Pinhead	ANSWER TO Q-9 **[3]** Flesh-hungry zombies are the problem in "Night of the Living Dead," not ghosts. 89%
10 The tallest mountain in North America is:	[1] Mt. Logan [2] Mt. Hood [3] Mt. McKinley [4] Mt. Rainer [5] Mt. Rushmore	ANSWER TO Q-9 **[4]** At 14,494 feet, Mount Whitney is 84 feet higher than Mt. Rainer in Washington. 57%
10 What did ancient Egyptians do as a sign of respect when the family cat died?	[1] Shaved their eyebrows [2] Fasted 7 days [3] Put ashes on their bed [4] Burned their clothes [5] Cut off a finger	ANSWER TO Q-9 **[5]** Steelheads are large rainbow trout found on the Pacific Coast. 45%
10 How did the legendary coach Knute Rockne die?	[1] Fire [2] Car wreck [3] War wound [4] Plane crash [5] Drowning	ANSWER TO Q-9 **[2]** Rocky takes his daily jog through the city's many famous historical landmarks. 92%
10 What is the subject of the documentary film, "The War Room"?	[1] Vietnam [2] Russian Revolution [3] The Clinton campaign [4] Punk rock and capitalism [5] Virtual reality	ANSWER TO Q-9 **[3]** In the Second Punic War, he set out to invade Italy through the Alps, using elephants. 51%

2 The U.S. president's retreat is Camp David. What is the British PM's country house called?	[1] Windsor [2] Wolf's Lair [3] Camp Larry [4] Coral Gables [5] Chequers	ANSWER TO Q-1 [5] As one Mexican president said, "Poor Mexico, so far from God and so close to the U.S." 35%
2 Which river begins in the Himalayas, and empties into the Arabian Sea?	[1] Orinoco [2] Indus [3] Tigris [4] Ganges [5] Danube	ANSWER TO Q-1 [3] This saying with a paradoxical twist is an example of an epigram. 47%
2 A villanelle is a type of:	[1] Pastry [2] Coat [3] Drama [4] Poem [5] Currency	ANSWER TO Q-1 [3] This version of the Raymond Chandler P.I. is very different from the Bogart interpretation. 43%
2 An "open space in Scotland" is the opening setting in this Shakespeare play:	[1] Hamlet [2] King Lear [3] Macbeth [4] Othello [5] Midsummer Night's Dream	ANSWER TO Q-1 [1] Those who became tax collectors for Rome were despised by their fellow countrymen. 57%
2 During WWII, American General Claire Chennault organized and led the:	[1] Hiroshima atom bomb raid [2] Flying Tigers [3] D-Day invasion [4] Screaming Eagles [5] Anti-U-boat campaign	ANSWER TO Q-1 [3] The fossils proved that human ancestors lived in the area 1.8 million years ago. 46%

9 The action in this classic horror film does not take place in a haunted building:	[1] The Shining [2] The Amityville Horror [3] Night of the Living Dead [4] Legend of Hell House [5] Poltergeist	ANSWER TO Q-8 **[3]** In each of these tales, the students get permanent summer vacations. 56%
9 The highest mountain peak in the continental United States is located in this state:	[1] Colorado [2] Nevada [3] Washington [4] California [5] Montana	ANSWER TO Q-8 **[5]** In 1883, this explosion blew the island off the face of the earth. 45%
9 All of these are common tropical fish for a home aquarium except:	[1] Neon tetra [2] Angelfish [3] Black molly [4] Pencilfish [5] Steelhead	ANSWER TO Q-8 **[3]** Albert was the delightful alligator in the "Pogo" comic strip. 89%
9 Famous film character Rocky Balboa's hometown was:	[1] Chicago [2] Philadelphia [3] New York [4] Boston [5] Newark	ANSWER TO Q-8 **[5]** He illustrated many "Saturday Evening Post" covers. 45%
9 Hannibal is associated with this series of wars:	[1] Micronesian [2] Seminole [3] Punic [4] Spanish Civil [5] Trojan	ANSWER TO Q-8 **[4]** The term originally applied to the tactics of the Napoleonic wars. 46%

3 Integration and differentiation are two processes in which branch of mathematics?	[1] Trigonometry [2] Calculus [3] Algebra [4] Geometry [5] Statistics	ANSWER TO Q-2 [5] The prime minister gets away to a Tudor mansion in Buckinghamshire, 35 miles north of London. 68%
3 What was Ingrid Bergman's last feature film?	[1] Cactus Flower [2] Indiscreet [3] Voyage to Italy [4] A Woman Called Golda [5] Autumn Sonata	ANSWER TO Q-2 [2] This 1800-mile river is not navigable, but is used for irrigation and hydroelectric power. 46%
3 If you limn something, you are ____ it.	[1] Singing [2] Drawing [3] Limping [4] Walking [5] Reading	ANSWER TO Q-2 [4] Dylan Thomas' "Do not go gentle into that good night" is an example of the form. 23%
3 What black athlete faced a court martial for refusing to sit at the back of a bus?	[1] Arthur Ashe [2] Sugar Ray Robinson [3] Jackie Robinson [4] Kareem Abdul-Jabbar [5] Joe Louis	ANSWER TO Q-2 [3] In this setting, the future King of Scotland encounters the famous 3 witches. 57%
3 Which nation's basic unit of currency is the inti?	[1] Peru [2] South Africa [3] Norway [4] China [5] Bulgaria	ANSWER TO Q-2 [2] His all-volunteer group of pilots battled the Japanese during early war action in China. 35%

8 Which bloody tale of chopped-up students have we made up?	[1] Massacre at Central High [2] Student Bodies [3] Professor Maniac [4] Splatter University [5] Dorm that Dripped Blood	ANSWER TO Q-7 [5] L. Frank Baum is known for his children's books. He is the author of the Oz books. 68%
8 The greatest single volcanic explosion in the last 3000 years was the eruption of:	[1] Mt. St. Helens [2] Vesuvius [3] Mauna Kea [4] Cotopaxi [5] Krakatoa	ANSWER TO Q-7 [4] The peak tops off at a mere 7,316 feet. 56%
8 All of these comic strip characters are dogs except:	[1] Daisy [2] Pluto [3] Albert [4] Ruff [5] Marmaduke	ANSWER TO Q-7 [3] Parrots live from 18 to 80 years, so owners should be prepared to grow old with them. 45%
8 Norman Rockwell created a well-known series of paintings called "The Four ____."	[1] Seasons [2] Stages of Childhood [3] Holidays [4] Embarrassing Moments [5] Freedoms	ANSWER TO Q-7 [3] Nick Cave took a recent turn at writing with his novel, "And the Ass Saw the Angel." 67%
8 This commonly used term literally means "little war":	[1] Kamikaze [2] Blitzkrieg [3] Quid pro quo [4] Guerrilla [5] Covert	ANSWER TO Q-7 [5] This John Wayne flick set in Vietnam was the only film made about the war while it was going on. 67%

4 Each size of champagne bottle has a specific name. The largest bottle is called a:

[1] Magnum
[2] Nebuchadnezzar
[3] Jeroboam
[4] Largesse
[5] Pontiff's

ANSWER TO Q-3
[2] Calculus is used to analyze quantities that continually vary over time.
58%

---

4 They were the only British rulers of the House of Orange:

[1] Victoria & Albert
[2] Heloise & Abelard
[3] William & Mary
[4] Elizabeth & Philip
[5] Edward & Wallis

ANSWER TO Q-3
[5] The 1978 drama was written and directed by fellow Swede Ingmar Bergman.
58%

---

4 Which feature of a novel would lead the French to classify it as a "Roman fleuve"?

[1] Based on actual events
[2] Composed of letters
[3] Set in prehistoric times
[4] Deals with crime
[5] Great length

ANSWER TO Q-3
[2] The word limn comes from the French "enluminer," which means to make light.
24%

---

4 Which modern American poet is associated with the Beat Generation of the 1950's?

[1] Grant Wood
[2] Conrad Aiken
[3] Langston Hughes
[4] Gary Snyder
[5] Ezra Pound

ANSWER TO Q-3
[3] A 1990 movie, "The Court Martial of Jackie Robinson," told the little-known story.
47%

---

4 A treatment which provides relief from, but does not cure, a disease is called:

[1] Placebo
[2] Velveteen
[3] Keratome
[4] Hypo-allergenic
[5] Palliative

ANSWER TO Q-3
[1] Its value is hard to calculate, as inflation has recently run as high as 45% a day(!).
35%

7 All these writers are known for their horror stories except:	[1] H.P. Lovecraft [2] Bram Stoker [3] Edgar Allan Poe [4] Ambrose Bierce [5] Frank L. Baum	ANSWER TO Q-6 **[3]** In "The Howling," a TV anchorwoman investigates a cult with members who turn into werewolves. 79%
7 Mount Kosciusko is the highest peak in this country:	[1] Korea [2] Japan [3] Philippines [4] Australia [5] Russia	ANSWER TO Q-6 **[4]** Mount Etna erupted as recently as 1981. 67%
7 All of these birds are members of the parrot family except:	[1] Budgerigar [2] African gray [3] Myna bird [4] Cockatiel [5] Yellow-headed amazon	ANSWER TO Q-6 **[3]** Lassie saved lives and brought joy to all for 17 seasons from 1954 to 1971. 69%
7 All these people are noted writers as well as musicians except for:	[1] Nick Cave [2] Jim Carroll [3] Axl Rose [4] Patti Smith [5] John Lennon	ANSWER TO Q-6 **[2]** Tycoon John D. Rockefeller founded the Standard Oil Company in 1870, which dominated the oil industry. 45%
7 Which war movie is incorrectly matched with the conflict it depicts?	[1] Platoon - Vietnam [2] The Dirty Dozen - WW II [3] Glory - Civil War [4] Gallipoli - WW I [5] The Green Berets - Korea	ANSWER TO Q-6 **[3]** Although the United States won many naval battles, attempts to take Canadian sites failed. 34%

5 Advocated by Emerson, Thoreau and Goethe, it was a philosophic and literary movement:	[1] Surrealism [2] Existentialism [3] Transcendent-alism [4] Expressionism [5] Fabianism	ANSWER TO Q-4 **[2]** Made for the extremely thirsty celebrator, it holds a gargantuan four U.S. gallons. 35%
5 "Dead Souls" is the best-known work of this Russian master of the grotesque:	[1] Anton Chekhov [2] Nikolai Gogol [3] Fyodor Dostoyevsky [4] Leo Tolstoy [5] Boris Pasternak	ANSWER TO Q-4 **[3]** William III and Mary II ruled jointly until she died in 1694. 68%
5 Which conflict ended under the command of general Creighton W. Abrams?	[1] World War I [2] World War II [3] Korea [4] Vietnam [5] Persian Gulf	ANSWER TO Q-4 **[5]** A designation for a long novel dealing with several generations, it means "river-novel." 23%
5 The Malthusian theories concern this issue:	[1] World overpopulation [2] The Big Bang [3] Evolution vs. creation [4] White supremacy [5] Euthanasia	ANSWER TO Q-4 **[4]** Snyder's poetry has been greatly influenced by Zen Buddhism. 63%
5 In its native tongue, this sovereign state's name is "Republik Osterreich":	[1] Lichtenstein [2] Austria [3] Switzerland [4] Finland [5] Germany	ANSWER TO Q-4 **[5]** The word is derived from the latin "palliatus," meaning "cloaked." 57%

6 Four of these are vampire films. Which one concerned a werewolf?

[1] Fright Night
[2] The Hunger
[3] The Howling
[4] Martin
[5] The Lost Boys

ANSWER TO Q-5
[4] "American Werewolf in London" is another film with a famous transformation scene.
89%

---

6 Where is the volcanic Mount Etna located?

[1] Cyprus
[2] Sardinia
[3] Greece
[4] Sicily
[5] Crete

ANSWER TO Q-5
[2] At 9,570 feet, the mythical home of the ancient gods is the highest peak in Greece.
87%

---

6 Which animal series ran for the greatest number of seasons?

[1] Flipper
[2] Gentle Ben
[3] Lassie
[4] Mr. Ed
[5] Grizzly Adams

ANSWER TO Q-5
[5] Tonkinese is a breed of domestic cat.
76%

---

6 John D. Rockefeller made his initial fortune in which business?

[1] Crops
[2] Oil
[3] Publishing
[4] Textiles
[5] Steel

ANSWER TO Q-5
[3] An aquifer is an underground rock through which groundwater can easily percolate.
54%

---

6 In which war did the United States attempt to gain territory in Canada?

[1] Spanish-American War
[2] Civil War
[3] War of 1812
[4] French-Indian War
[5] World War I

ANSWER TO Q-5
[4] With Prince Faisal, he carried out a guerrilla campaign against Turkish rail supply lines.
52%

6 This literary work features Homunculus, a miniature man in a vial:	[1] Arabian Nights [2] 1984 [3] Faust [4] The Divine Comedy [5] Brave New World	ANSWER TO Q-5 [3] They relied on direct experience, disregarding external authority and tradition. 51%
6 Which poet used the character Sweeney to symbolize brutal 20th-century mankind?	[1] Robert Frost [2] T.S. Eliot [3] Robert Lowell [4] Robinson Jeffers [5] E.E. Cummings	ANSWER TO Q-5 [2] Gogol was a major influence on later Russian writers such as Dostoyevsky and Nabokov. 23%
6 Felix Houphouet-Boigny ruled this country for 33 years, until 1993:	[1] Iceland [2] Lesotho [3] Ivory Coast [4] San Marino [5] Corsica	ANSWER TO Q-5 [4] Abrams had replaced Gen. Westmoreland, who had been promoted to chief of staff, in 1968. 35%
6 This novel's central character is the unscrupulous, greedy Becky Sharp:	[1] War of the Worlds [2] Vanity Fair [3] Brave New World [4] Gravity's Rainbow [5] A Christmas Carol	ANSWER TO Q-5 [1] 17th-century economist Thomas Malthus believed population would exceed earth's resources. 58%
6 French actress "The Divine Sarah" Bernhardt was known for this bizarre habit:	[1] Ate spiders [2] Impromptu strip dances [3] Slept in a coffin [4] Wore live animals [5] Bathed once a year	ANSWER TO Q-5 [2] Its large empire was destroyed in WWI, giving it the national boundaries it has today. 46%

5 Which movie does not feature a person who transforms into another creature?	[1] Dr. Jekyll and Mr. Hyde [2] The Thing [3] The Howling [4] Eraserhead [5] The Fly	ANSWER TO Q-4 **[4]** Fredric March played the double role in 1932. 56%
5 Where is Mt. Olympus?	[1] Italy [2] Greece [3] Cyprus [4] Albania [5] Bulgaria	ANSWER TO Q-4 **[3]** Kibo reaches a height of 19,340 feet; Mawenzi stands 17,564 feet. 45%
5 All of these are breeds of dogs except:	[1] Welsh Corgi [2] Basenji [3] Whippet [4] Hungarian Puli [5] Tonkinese	ANSWER TO Q-4 **[1]** This entertaining story also has a message: humane treatment for animals. 57%
5 Which type of rock would not make a good aquifer?	[1] Silica [2] Sandstone [3] Marble [4] Gravel [5] Limestone	ANSWER TO Q-4 **[5]** The characteristic feature of sedimentary rocks is their stratification. 45%
5 Lawrence of Arabia led the Arabs in war against which invading nation?	[1] Greece [2] Egypt [3] Afghanistan [4] Turkey [5] Russia	ANSWER TO Q-4 **[5]** The irony is that the territory was given back to North Korea at the armistice. 61%

7 ASCII is the common code of letters, numbers and symbols used in:	[1] Celestial navigation [2] Cryptography [3] Medical charts [4] Computers [5] The Periodic Table	ANSWER TO Q-6 [3] Homunculus leads Faust and Mephistopheles in this classic tale. 35%
7 Consort of Gaea and father of the Titans, he is the earliest supreme god of the Greeks:	[1] Pluto [2] Jupiter [3] Uranus [4] Mars [5] Mercury	ANSWER TO Q-6 [2] Among other things, godless Sweeney is a rapist and murderer. 35%
7 The character of Mrs. Grundy has come to symbolize someone who is a:	[1] Bumbling teacher [2] Big gossip [3] Domineering mother [4] Disapproving moralist [5] Evil adultress	ANSWER TO Q-6 [3] Houphouet-Boigny led the nation to independence in 1960 and spurred an economic renaissance. 23%
7 The art of illumination concerns:	[1] Meditation [2] Designing stained glass [3] Balancing objects [4] Ornamenting sacred texts [5] Walking on hot coals	ANSWER TO Q-6 [2] She gains wealth and power through cleverness in Thackeray's 19th century work. 46%
7 This Grace Metalious book climbed on the 1956 bestseller list and stayed there two years:	[1] Catch-22 [2] North by Northwest [3] Valley of the Dolls [4] The Manchurian Candidate [5] Peyton Place	ANSWER TO Q-6 [3] In 1912, she became the first great stage actress to appear in the new medium of film. 35%

4 This is the only horror character to win an Oscar for its portrayer:	[1] Count Dracula [2] Dr. Frankenstein [3] The Werewolf [4] Jekyll and Hyde [5] Phantom of the Opera	ANSWER TO Q-3 **[1]** "Audrey Rose" is about a young girl who dreams about fires and finds she's been reincarnated. 78%
4 Which mountain is divided into two peaks, Kibo and Mawenzi?	[1] Matterhorn [2] Mount Everest [3] Kilimanjaro [4] Mount Etna [5] Mount McKinley	ANSWER TO Q-3 **[4]** In 1953, he and Tenzing Norkay became the first men to reach the mount's summit. 56%
4 Which children's classic is the life story of an animal written from its point of view?	[1] Black Beauty [2] Lassie Come Home [3] Song of the South [4] Sounder [5] Old Yeller	ANSWER TO Q-3 **[2]** Paddy was PM Harold Wilson's dog; the others belonged to Clinton, FDR, Bush and Johnson, respectively. 65%
4 Which is not a sedimentary rock?	[1] Sandstone [2] Shale [3] Coal [4] Limestone [5] Marble	ANSWER TO Q-3 **[2]** "Crawdaddy" began publication in 1964. 45%
4 The battle of "Pork Chop Hill" was fought by the the U.S. Marines during the:	[1] Second World War [2] Vietnam War [3] American Civil War [4] American Revolution [5] Korean War	ANSWER TO Q-3 **[3]** Until then, crowded conditions provided an ideal environment for fast spreading of germs. 65%

8 This primary platform catapulted James Polk to victory in the 1845 U.S. presidential election:	[1] Abolitionist [2] Free silver movement [3] Populism [4] Manifest destiny [5] Reconstruction	ANSWER TO Q-7 **[4]** ASCII is a code for representing characters using numeric values. 81%
8 Parthia was an ancient empire located in what is now:	[1] Greece [2] Algeria [3] Iran [4] Spain [5] Italy	ANSWER TO Q-7 **[3]** Uranus is the sky god, while his consort Gaea embodies the Earth. 67%
8 What always appears on the anniversary cover of "The New Yorker" magazine?	[1] Broadway theater marquee [2] City skyline [3] Dollar bill sign [4] Monocled dandy [5] Pen and pad of paper	ANSWER TO Q-7 **[4]** Mrs. Grundys have a way of appearing on censorship committees. 35%
8 Who was the first actor to portray Hamlet, Lear and Macbeth?	[1] Edwin Booth [2] Henry Irving [3] John Drew [4] David Garrick [5] Richard Burbage	ANSWER TO Q-7 **[4]** Monks used silver and gold leaf, painting and calligraphy to decorate manuscripts. 46%
8 Dominican Friars of Santa Maria, Milan could dine in the shadow of this masterpiece:	[1] Mona Lisa [2] The Creation [3] Sistine Chapel [4] Christina's World [5] The Last Supper	ANSWER TO Q-7 **[5]** Her story of a country town's infidelities was made into a film and a television soap opera. 57%

3 What do "Audrey Rose," "The Bad Seed" and "It's Alive" have in common?	[1] Scary kids [2] Demonic animals [3] Anthony Hopkins [4] Blood-dripping walls [5] Mutant zombies	ANSWER TO Q-2 [2] "Ben" was a sequel to "Willard," which centered on killer rats. 91%
3 Who was the first to climb Mount Everest?	[1] Sir Francis Drake [2] Louis Mountbatten [3] Admiral Richard Byrd [4] Sir Edmund Hillary [5] Marco Polo	ANSWER TO Q-2 [5] Discovered perfectly intact in 1911, it was abandoned centuries ago for no known reason. 59%
3 All of these "First Pets" have had the chance to sniff around the White House except:	[1] Socks [2] Paddy [3] Fala [4] Millie [5] Him and Her	ANSWER TO Q-2 [5] Andy Capp is the beer-swilling couch potato constantly nagged by his cranky wife. 98%
3 Which was the first magazine devoted exclusively to rock music?	[1] Rolling Stone [2] Crawdaddy [3] Creem [4] Spin [5] Billboard	ANSWER TO Q-2 [4] The clear, hard sugar crystals were called rock sugar in England. 69%
3 Not until the ____ did combat exceed sickness as the number one killer of American soldiers.	[1] Korean War [2] Civil War [3] First World War [4] Vietnam War [5] Second World War	ANSWER TO Q-2 [3] Gen. Ulysses S. Grant accepted the South's surrender from Robert E. Lee at the courthouse. 61%

9 Without sextant, chart or compass, Polynesians navigated vast oceans. How did they do it?	[1] Read patterns of waves [2] Followed fish [3] Emerald talismans [4] Whalebone divining rods [5] With magnets	ANSWER TO Q-8 [4] Polk extended the Oregon Territory northward and acquired most of the Southwest from Mexico. 43%
9 This 17th-century artist did a series of allegorical paintings of Queen Marie de Medici:	[1] Jan Vermeer [2] Hieronymous Bosch [3] Rembrandt [4] Michelangelo [5] Peter Rubens	ANSWER TO Q-8 [3] The Parthians were successful in stopping the westward expansion of the Roman Empire. 42%
9 Jakob Ammann founded which conservative religious group in the 17th century?	[1] Anabaptists [2] Jehovah's Witnesses [3] Amish [4] Mormons [5] Puritans	ANSWER TO Q-8 [4] Eustace Tilly is the name of this widely recognized figure. 58%
9 The astronomer Percival Lowell is best remembered for championing this theory:	[1] Intelligent life on Mars [2] Ours is only galaxy [3] Sun will last forever [4] Black holes [5] Sun circles Earth	ANSWER TO Q-8 [5] Considered the first great English thespian, he premiered the plays of 7 different artists. 21%
9 What well-known liquor is made from the agave plant?	[1] Kahlua [2] Scotch Whiskey [3] Tequila [4] Vodka [5] Gin	ANSWER TO Q-8 [5] After 13 years of work, just one quarter of Da Vinci's work has been successfully restored. 35%

2 Of these horror films, which is not matched with its animal of terror?	[1] Jaws - shark [2] Ben - bear [3] Willard - rat [4] Orca - killer whale [5] King Kong - giant ape	ANSWER TO Q-1 [1] Steve McQueen starred in the 1958 classic. 76%
2 The Incas built a mountain citadel known as:	[1] Quetzalcoatl [2] Toltec [3] Yucatan [4] Tenochtitlan [5] Machu Picchu	ANSWER TO Q-1 [4] This Chilean mountain reaches a peak of 22,834 feet. 54%
2 Which cartoon character does not have a pet?	[1] Charlie Brown [2] Fred Flintstone [3] Little Orphan Annie [4] George Jetson [5] Andy Capp	ANSWER TO Q-1 [4] Guinea pigs are rodents and make good pets even though they are not much in the IQ department. 52%
2 Old-fashioned rock candy is made from:	[1] Marshmallows [2] Caramel [3] Peanuts and molasses [4] Sugar crystals [5] Taffy	ANSWER TO Q-1 [2] The DJ's name was Alan Freed, and his career ended with trumped-up charges of payola and scandal. 57%
2 Which war was ended at the Appomattox Courthouse?	[1] World War I [2] Spanish-American War [3] American Civil War [4] Korean War [5] World War II	ANSWER TO Q-1 [5] Historians consider the war a milestone in the development of national consciousness in Europe. 65%

10 It is the oldest country in all Europe, and the oldest republic in the world:

[1] Yugoslavia
[2] San Marino
[3] France
[4] Ireland
[5] Lichtenstein

ANSWER TO Q-9

[1] The islanders estimated their position by seeing how waves bounced off large ocean islands.

21%

---

10 Which insects use the substance propolis to glue together their homes?

[1] Termites
[2] Cockroaches
[3] Ants
[4] Flies
[5] Bees

ANSWER TO Q-9

[5] The series of large paintings can be seen at the Louvre in Paris.

24%

---

10 Which term refers to a theory that living matter can develop from nonliving material?

[1] Entropy
[2] Abiogenesis
[3] Anthropor-morphic
[4] Induration
[5] Adiabetic

ANSWER TO Q-9

[3] This Mennonite sect believes in literal interpretation of the bible.

57%

---

10 What did Cyrus the Great found?

[1] Russian Empire
[2] Persian Empire
[3] Ottoman Empire
[4] Greek Empire
[5] Roman Empire

ANSWER TO Q-9

[1] He thought the Martian "Canals" were an irrigation system built by a race of aliens.

46%

---

10 In chemistry, the corrosion-resistant metals of the platinum group are called:

[1] Noble metals
[2] Valence elements
[3] Inert metals
[4] Mendeleevium elements
[5] Salt-free metals

ANSWER TO Q-9

[3] It is actually the best brand of mescal, made only in and around the city of Tequila, Mexico.

69%

179

1 How did they finally get rid of "The Blob"?	[1] Froze it [2] Burned it [3] Blasted it [4] Sealed it in a cave [5] Buried it	Turn to the top frame on the next left hand page for the correct answer and the next question.
1 Which is the highest peak in the southern hemisphere?	[1] Kilamanjaro [2] McKinley [3] Vinson Massif [4] Aconcagua [5] Aneto	Turn to the second frame on the next left hand page for the correct answer and the next question.
1 Guinea pigs are called "pigs" because they:	[1] Enjoy mud [2] Are of the pig family [3] Get very fat [4] Oink [5] Have curly tails	Turn to the middle frame on the next left hand page for the correct answer and the next question.
1 In the 50's, a new style of music was coined "Rock-and-Roll" by:	[1] An R & B musician [2] A disc jockey [3] A reporter [4] A music critic [5] Elvis Presley	Turn to the fourth frame on the next left hand page for the correct answer and the next question.
1 The intermittent struggle called the "Hundred Years War" involved what nations?	[1] France - Germany [2] Poland - Austria [3] Austria - Italy [4] Italy - Spain [5] England - France	Turn to the bottom frame on the next left hand page for the correct answer and the next question.

SHOWDOWN **GAME NUMBER 5**	ANSWER TO Q-10 **[2]** Entirely inside Italy, the 24-square-mile republic was established in 1631. 68%
SHOWDOWN **GAME NUMBER 23**	ANSWER TO Q-10 **[5]** The waxy substance, also called bee glue, is collected from the buds of certain trees. 35%
SHOWDOWN **GAME NUMBER 41**	ANSWER TO Q-10 **[2]** The other terms are from the fields of geology, physics or chemistry. 23%
SHOWDOWN **GAME NUMBER 59**	ANSWER TO Q-10 **[2]** In the 5th century B.C., Cyrus the Great overthrew 3 empires and united the Middle East. 47%
SHOWDOWN **GAME NUMBER 77**	ANSWER TO Q-10 **[1]** This group includes the precious metals like gold, silver and sometimes rhenium. 51%

Horror

GAME NUMBER 15

ANSWER TO Q-30

[3] Mark Chapman identified with Holden Caulfield and thought John Lennon symbolized "phoniness."

89%

Mountains

GAME NUMBER 33

ANSWER TO Q-30

[5] Chard is a vegetable.

54%

Pet Shop

GAME NUMBER 51

ANSWER TO Q-30

[4] The classic by Henry David Thoreau was published in 1854.

65%

Rock

GAME NUMBER 69

ANSWER TO Q-30

[1] Adverbs describe verbs, adjectives and other adverbs.

65%

War

GAME NUMBER 87

ANSWER TO Q-30

[4] All the others played her later, either on stage or screen.

78%

1 Which movement was founded by the Reverend William Booth?	[1] Salvation Army [2] Jehovah's Witnesses [3] Black Panthers [4] Quakers [5] Suffragettes	Turn to the top frame on the next right hand page for the correct answer and the next question.
1 Which film is not about a blind woman?	[1] Jennifer 8 [2] Wait Until Dark [3] Awakenings [4] A Patch of Blue [5] See No Evil	Turn to the second frame on the next right hand page for the correct answer and the next question.
1 The literary work told thru Quentin Compson's conversations with his roommate is:	[1] East of Eden [2] The Red Badge of Courage [3] The Grapes of Wrath [4] Absalom, Absalom! [5] Ulysses	Turn to the middle frame on the next right hand page for the correct answer and the next question.
1 In which Tennessee Williams play is the hero an ex-jock?	[1] A Streetcar Named Desire [2] Cat on a Hot Tin Roof [3] Orpheus Descending [4] The Glass Menagerie [5] The Rose Tattoo	Turn to the fourth frame on the next right hand page for the correct answer and the next question.
1 Who authored such tales as "White Fang," "Call of the Wild" and "The Sea Wolf"?	[1] Stephen Crane [2] Jack London [3] Rudyard Kipling [4] Stephen King [5] Ernest Hemingway	Turn to the bottom frame on the next right hand page for the correct answer and the next question.

30 Which book was Mark Chapman carrying when he assassinated John Lennon?	[1] Atlas Shrugged [2] Lord of the Rings [3] Catcher in the Rye [4] Alice B. Toklas Cookbook [5] The Bible	ANSWER TO Q-29 **[5]** The smallest intervals in a chromatic scale are half-steps. 45%
30 Which of these is not an edible fish?	[1] Brill [2] Sole [3] Anchovy [4] Sturgeon [5] Chard	ANSWER TO Q-29 **[1]** "From Here to Eternity" is the first book of a trilogy written by James Jones. 65%
30 Which book was published in the 19th century?	[1] Ulysses [2] Animal Farm [3] The Jungle [4] Walden [5] Dr. Zhivago	ANSWER TO Q-29 **[3]** Released from prison in 1955, he went to Mexico to organize the revolt against Batista. 59%
30 What type of word is 'virtuously"?	[1] Adverb [2] Preposition [3] Article [4] Adjective [5] Gerund	ANSWER TO Q-29 **[3]** In French, saute means "to jump." 79%
30 Who portrayed Dolly Levi in the original Broadway production of "Hello Dolly"?	[1] Pearl Bailey [2] Ethel Merman [3] Mary Martin [4] Carol Channing [5] Barbra Streisand	ANSWER TO Q-29 **[5]** Ponce de Leon named the islands Tortuga (Spanish for turtle) when he discovered them. 43%

2 The House of Savoy was the ruling house of ____ until 1946.	[1] Italy [2] England [3] Austria [4] Russia [5] Belgium	ANSWER TO Q-1 **[1]** He wanted to help the unspeakably poor souls of London's grimy East End circa 1878. 53%
2 "A little learning is a dangerous thing" is a line from a poem by:	[1] Shakespeare [2] Walt Whitman [3] Alexander Pope [4] H.W. Longfellow [5] John Donne	ANSWER TO Q-1 **[3]** "Awakenings" stars Robert DeNiro as a man who awakens from a coma. 81%
2 Which character in "Alice in Wonderland" is seen always weeping?	[1] Mock Turtle [2] Queen of Hearts [3] Mad Hatter [4] March Hare [5] White Rabbit	ANSWER TO Q-1 **[4]** After telling the tale to his Harvard roommate, Compson later committed suicide. 45%
2 What game are you playing if you have the option to fold, call or raise?	[1] Gin rummy [2] Bridge [3] Pinochle [4] Cribbage [5] Poker	ANSWER TO Q-1 **[2]** Brick, played by Paul Newman on screen, can't forget his days of glory on the field. 46%
2 Which instrument is played by means of a vibrating reed?	[1] Piccolo [2] Flute [3] Oboe [4] French horn [5] Trombone	ANSWER TO Q-1 **[2]** He was a sailor, miner and war correspondent; like him, his work was adventurous and brutal. 79%

29 What is the space or distance between any two musical pitches called?

[1] Octave
[2] Measure
[3] Meter
[4] Note
[5] Interval

ANSWER TO Q-28
[1] The son of a goldsmith, author Camara Laye recorded his childhood with affection.
42%

---

29 Which novel was not written by Herman Wouk?

[1] From Here to Eternity
[2] War and Remembrance
[3] Marjorie Morningstar
[4] The Winds of War
[5] Caine Mutiny

ANSWER TO Q-28
[4] On October 2, 1980, the end of an era came at the hands of Holmes' 11th round TKO of Ali.
54%

---

29 Jailed for leading an abortive coup in 1953, he returned for a successful one in 1956:

[1] Che Guevara
[2] Idi Amin
[3] Fidel Castro
[4] Nelson Mandela
[5] Anastasio Somoza

ANSWER TO Q-28
[3] The author of "Robinson Crusoe" traveled widely, but not beyond Europe.
43%

---

29 The cooking term "saute" means to:

[1] Soak in cooking sherry
[2] Broil in broth
[3] Fry rapidly using butter
[4] Garnish with fruit
[5] Serve lightly

ANSWER TO Q-28
[2] The Jupiter satellite is approximately one and a half times the size of the Earth's moon.
67%

---

29 The Tortuga Islands are off the coast of:

[1] California
[2] British Columbia
[3] West Africa
[4] Argentina
[5] Florida

ANSWER TO Q-28
[2] Not only is the fruit delicious, but the pear tree's wood is valued for cabinetmaking.
78%

3 What part of the eye is affected by cataracts?	[1] Lens [2] Iris [3] Pupil [4] Cornea [5] Optic nerve	ANSWER TO Q-2 [1] The crown was the ancient family's reward for its contributions to Italian unification. 47%
3 Which film critic had a cameo role in "Superman"?	[1] Roger Ebert [2] Rex Reed [3] Mary Hart [4] Gene Shalit [5] Gene Siskel	ANSWER TO Q-2 [3] "Fools rush in where angels fear to tread" is another famous line from "An Essay in Criticism." 46%
3 This man directed films of "Hamlet," "Romeo and Juliet" and "The Taming of the Shrew":	[1] Franco Zeffirelli [2] Laurence Olivier [3] Orson Welles [4] Kenneth Branagh [5] Peter Brooks	ANSWER TO Q-2 [1] The Mock Turtle's conversation consists largely of puns and a play on words. 79%
3 France entered this conflict on the side of the U.S.:	[1] Spanish-American War [2] War of 1812 [3] American Revolution [4] Mexican War [5] Crimean War	ANSWER TO Q-2 [5] You can either hold the best hand, or bluff your way through. 94%
3 These women writers are all known for their science fiction novels except:	[1] Ursula Leguin [2] Octavia Butler [3] Joan Didion [4] Mary Shelley [5] Doris Lessing	ANSWER TO Q-2 [3] The clarinet is also played by means of a vibrating reed. 88%

28 A classic of African literature, it is an autobiography set in a traditional village:

[1] The Dark Child
[2] Madmen and Specialists
[3] Ambiguous Adventure
[4] Bound to Violence
[5] Wretched of the Earth

ANSWER TO Q-27
[4] Vegetable purees are used in soups, baby foods and many sauces.
79%

28 Who's the only man to knock out Muhammad Ali in a heavyweight title fight?

[1] Sonny Liston
[2] Ken Norton
[3] Joe Frazier
[4] Larry Holmes
[5] Leon Spinks

ANSWER TO Q-27
[4] Insectivores are mammals which subsist on insects.
51%

28 Which famous writer did not visit and write about life in the Pacific islands?

[1] Mark Twain
[2] Robert L. Stevenson
[3] Daniel Defoe
[4] Herman Melville
[5] Joseph Conrad

ANSWER TO Q-27
[5] The Murray is Australia's longest river.
51%

28 Ganymede is the largest ____ in the solar system.

[1] Star
[2] Moon
[3] Black hole
[4] Galaxy
[5] Crater

ANSWER TO Q-27
[4] Amy Tan and Maxine Hong Kingston are the authors of these acclaimed books.
87%

28 The Anjou is a variety of:

[1] Apple
[2] Pear
[3] Grape
[4] Orange
[5] Plum

ANSWER TO Q-27
[2] Watts is known for his books about drug and occult experiences.
56%

4 All these countries are ruled by monarchs except:	[1] Saudi Arabia [2] Austria [3] Bhutan [4] Spain [5] Jordan	ANSWER TO Q-3 **[1]** They are corrected when the lens is surgically removed and replaced with an artificial one. 78%
4 Which legendary woman was married to Earl Leofric of Mercia?	[1] Helen of Troy [2] Mary Magdalene [3] Queen Guinevere [4] Lady Godiva [5] Queen Jezebel	ANSWER TO Q-3 **[2]** He also underwent a sex change in that film masterpiece, "Myra Breckenridge." 79%
4 Gastrin is a hormone that is produced by glands found in the:	[1] Kidney [2] Stomach [3] Liver [4] Pancreas [5] Small intestine	ANSWER TO Q-3 **[1]** Actor Mel Gibson's "Hamlet" is the most recent of his Shakespearean ventures. 58%
4 Which prefix translates as "in some sense or degree"?	[1] Proto [2] Trans [3] Quasi [4] Ambi [5] Omni	ANSWER TO Q-3 **[3]** The Americans were joined by the French in defeating the British at Yorktown in 1781. 61%
4 Andorra, Liechtenstein and Monaco are all considered:	[1] Commonwealths [2] Republics [3] Confederations [4] Principalities [5] Democracies	ANSWER TO Q-3 **[3]** Didion is known for her essays and novels about life on the West Coast. 58%

27 Which of these food terms means to mash or pulp into a thick paste?

[1] Shirr
[2] Braise
[3] Parboil
[4] Puree
[5] Dice

ANSWER TO Q-26
[2] Alsatian is spoken in Alsace, a part of France near the German border.
64%

---

27 Moles, shrews, and hedgehogs are all considered:

[1] Reptiles
[2] Arachnids
[3] Ruminants
[4] Insectivores
[5] Marsupials

ANSWER TO Q-26
[5] The thick mixture of herbs and water is applied to sore or infected body areas.
69%

---

27 Which river is not in the United Kingdom?

[1] Humber
[2] Thames
[3] Avon
[4] Mersey
[5] Murray

ANSWER TO Q-26
[4] The bird takes revenge on Sinbad by dropping rocks on his ship until it sinks.
65%

---

27 "The Joy Luck Club" and "The Woman Warrior" are books about:

[1] Vietnamese boat people
[2] Louisiana's Cajuns
[3] Mexican-Americans
[4] Chinese-Americans
[5] Haitian refugees

ANSWER TO Q-26
[1] Along with Donald Klopfer, he founded Random House.
69%

---

27 Which writer is not known for his work in journalism?

[1] Murray Kempton
[2] Alan Watts
[3] Jimmy Breslin
[4] William Safire
[5] George F. Will

ANSWER TO Q-26
[3] An Iowa farmer builds a fantasy baseball field and old baseball heroes live out their dreams.
89%

5 Which animal is not a rodent?	[1] Capybara [2] Prairie dog [3] Titmouse [4] Squirrel [5] Porcupine	ANSWER TO Q-4 **[2]** This small European nation is governed by a president and parliament. 71%
5 What kind of saw is operated by two persons to cut timber?	[1] Saber saw [2] Whipsaw [3] Hacksaw [4] Band saw [5] Coping saw	ANSWER TO Q-4 **[4]** She took her famous nude ride in order to get her husband to lower the people's taxes. 46%
5 Which branch of mathematics does topology fall under?	[1] Computer science [2] Calculus [3] Physics [4] Geometry [5] Statistics	ANSWER TO Q-4 **[2]** Gastrin stimulates the secretion of gastric juice. 35%
5 Avogadro's law and Avogadro's number both have to do with:	[1] Molecules [2] Genetic traits [3] Electricity [4] Plant reproduction [5] The solar system	ANSWER TO Q-4 **[3]** A document, for example, can be "quasi-official," while a person may be a "quasi-intellectual." 59%
5 Which major city is slowly sinking into the ground?	[1] Paris [2] Rome [3] London [4] New York [5] Mexico City	ANSWER TO Q-4 **[4]** A principality is just like a kingdom, except that is ruled by a prince. 58%

26 Which is a dialect of German?

[1] Breton
[2] Alsatian
[3] Provencal
[4] Basque
[5] Catalan

ANSWER TO Q-25

[2] His concept of an inflationary universe solved problems arising from the older theory.

65%

---

26 Poultices, commonly used in folk medicine, are:

[1] Soups
[2] Salt solutions
[3] Herb teas
[4] Camphor rubs
[5] Hot paste mixtures

ANSWER TO Q-25

[4] Wilder's works run the gamut from exotic historical fantasies to homey realistic plays.

54%

---

26 In which place did Sinbad the Sailor encounter a legendary giant bird?

[1] Mihragian Kingdom
[2] Great Cliffs of Tartar
[3] Diamond Mountain
[4] Island of the Roc
[5] Ape Valley

ANSWER TO Q-25

[1] It is a solution of "lac," a substance exuded by scale insects.

57%

---

26 Bennett Cerf is an important name in American:

[1] Publishing
[2] Politics
[3] Sports
[4] Science
[5] Architecture

ANSWER TO Q-25

[1] Hadrian ruled Rome from 117 to 138 A.D.

59%

---

26 Who was the central baseball figure used in the 1988 film "Field of Dreams"?

[1] Sultan of Swat Babe Ruth
[2] Georgia Peach Ty Cobb
[3] Shoeless Joe Jackson
[4] Iron Horse Lou Gehrig
[5] Smoky Joe Wood

ANSWER TO Q-25

[1] It is also a unit of liquid measure for ale or liquor equal to 1/4 pint.

45%

6 Which telescope was the largest in the world when it was built in 1948?

[1] Mayall
[2] Hubble
[3] Sagan
[4] Shapley
[5] Hale

ANSWER TO Q-5
[3] The titmouse is actually a type of bird.
59%

---

6 In philosophy, a monist is the opposite of a:

[1] Sophist
[2] Theist
[3] Existentialist
[4] Dualist
[5] Realist

ANSWER TO Q-5
[2] The two-man crosscut saw is used frequently in the lumber industry.
71%

---

6 A supercilious person is:

[1] Shallow
[2] Ignorant
[3] Silly
[4] Arrogant
[5] Demanding

ANSWER TO Q-5
[4] It is the study of those properties of geometric figures that remain unchanged.
69%

---

6 Which word can refer to a spy, a small mammal or a dark eruption on the skin?

[1] Gerbil
[2] Sleeper
[3] Mole
[4] Ganglion
[5] Zit

ANSWER TO Q-5
[1] The English chemist was especially interested in the quantity and weight of molecules.
46%

---

6 What drink is made from ginger ale, grenadine and a cherry?

[1] Candy cocktail
[2] Cherry bang
[3] Pink lady
[4] Smoky Mary
[5] Shirley Temple

ANSWER TO Q-5
[5] The exploding population has drawn heavily on the water table; it sank 35 feet in 100 years.
69%

25 In 1980, Alan Guth proposed a theory that significantly modified the ____ theory.	[1] Darwinian evolutionary [2] Big bang [3] Einstein relativity [4] Leakey African origins [5] Global warming	ANSWER TO Q-24 [2] In some loans, the balance can increase even when the borrower is making the payments. 76%
25 Who wrote such modern American classics as "The Bridge of San Luis Rey" & "Our Town"?	[1] Theodore Dreiser [2] Sinclair Lewis [3] Willa Cather [4] Thornton Wilder [5] Edith Wharton	ANSWER TO Q-24 [3] The commercial tomato is one of seven species of the genus that botanists know as lycopersicon. 43%
25 What is shellac made from?	[1] Insect secretions [2] Tree sap [3] Gum resin [4] Linseed oil [5] Camphor leaves	ANSWER TO Q-24 [3] The work, "The Decameron," is made up of prose tales told by aristo-crats trying to escape the plague. 32%
25 Which of these historical leaders came first?	[1] Hadrian [2] Eric the Red [3] Genghis Khan [4] Charlemagne [5] Attila the Hun	ANSWER TO Q-24 [5] Linnaeus devel-oped the animal and plant classification system in 1735. 54%
25 What is a noggin?	[1] Small cup or mug [2] Wooden block [3] V-shaped cut [4] Soup ladle [5] Punch bowl	ANSWER TO Q-24 [5] A surety guaran-tees payment to a lending institution in case the debtor defaults. 47%

7 Budgie is another name for what bird?	[1] Parakeet [2] Parrot [3] Canary [4] Mynah [5] Cockatoo	ANSWER TO Q-6 **[5]** The Hale telescope is at the Palomar observatory near San Diego, California. 58%
7 Which hormone is called the growth hormone?	[1] Glucagon [2] Somatotropin [3] Vasopressin [4] Secretin [5] Norepinephrine	ANSWER TO Q-6 **[4]** Monists believe that all things are unified. Dualists say some things are always opposed. 71%
7 The Witch of Endor is a sorceress in:	[1] The Bible [2] Roman mythology [3] Shakespeare's "Macbeth" [4] The Salem witch trials [5] Goethe's "Faust"	ANSWER TO Q-6 **[4]** The word comes from the Latin for "eyebrow," since arched eyebrows indicate haughtiness. 79%
7 England's Aethelred the Unready was unready for the:	[1] Industrial Revolution [2] Norman Conquest [3] Protestant Reformation [4] Invading Danes [5] Spanish Armada	ANSWER TO Q-6 **[3]** A mole is also a powerful boring machine used in constructing tunnels. 81%
7 Which baseball player topped Babe Ruth's single-season home run record?	[1] Roger Maris [2] Hank Aaron [3] Willie Mays [4] Joe DiMaggio [5] Mickey Mantle	ANSWER TO Q-6 **[5]** The other cocktails are all made with alcohol. 79%

24 The term "negative amortization" is used when discussing:	[1] Savings bonds [2] Home loans [3] Mutual funds [4] Stock purchases [5] Coin investments	ANSWER TO Q-23 [3] The others are by Mandelshtam, Nabokov, Gorky and Tolstoy. 34%
24 Which plant listed was originally native only to western parts of South America?	[1] Artichoke [2] Rhubarb [3] Tomato [4] Ginkgo [5] Fern	ANSWER TO Q-23 [3] The first and last lines have five syllables. The middle line has seven. 68%
24 Of all these medieval works, which is not primarily written in verse?	[1] The Canterbury Tales [2] The Divine Comedy [3] The Decameron [4] The Romance of the Rose [5] Parsifal	ANSWER TO Q-23 [5] It has since been proven that children's games very similar to baseball existed long before. 89%
24 In the 18th century, the Swedish scientist Carolus Linnaeus developed the:	[1] Periodic table [2] Centigrade scale [3] Metric system [4] Geiger counter [5] Plant classification	ANSWER TO Q-23 [3] Although named for Christopher Columbus, Spanish explorer Alonso de Ojeda arrived three years earlier. 63%
24 A corporation might need a surety if it is:	[1] Located overseas [2] Family-owned [3] Multinational [4] A mail order business [5] In financial trouble	ANSWER TO Q-23 [4] Sour cherries usually come frozen or in cans, and are used primarily for sauces and pies. 65%

8 Which Mexican general set siege to the Alamo, killing Crockett and Bowie?	[1] Santa Anna [2] Emiliano Zapata [3] Pancho Villa [4] Alvarez Obregon [5] Manuel de la Madrid	ANSWER TO Q-7 [1] Budgie comes from the Australian outback word for "pretty good." 81%
8 Gravenstein is a variety of:	[1] Apple [2] Pear [3] Grape [4] Plum [5] Cherry	ANSWER TO Q-7 [2] Often abbreviated to STP, it stimulates both bone and muscle growth. 34%
8 How can you sense a pheromone?	[1] Sight [2] Hearing [3] Smell [4] Touch [5] Taste	ANSWER TO Q-7 [1] King Saul asked her to call up the spirit of the prophet Samuel so he could consult him. 81%
8 Blue sky laws deal with:	[1] Alcoholic beverages [2] Wilderness areas [3] Marriage and divorce [4] Copyrights [5] Stocks and bonds	ANSWER TO Q-7 [4] During his reign in the 10th century, the Danes plundered England. 35%
8 All of these "Z" places are in Africa except:	[1] Zululand [2] Zimbawe [3] Zuni [4] Zaire [5] Zambia	ANSWER TO Q-7 [1] Maris made sports history by hitting 61 home runs in 1961. 52%

23 Which memoir is written by Aleksandr Solzhenitsyn?	[1] The Noise of Time [2] Speak, Memory [3] The Oak and the Calf [4] I Cannot be Silent [5] My Universities	ANSWER TO Q-22 **[1]** The combination of tongues enables foreigners and natives to communicate business. 56%
23 The Japanese poetic form known as haiku must have:	[1] Internal rhymes [2] Several cantos [3] Seventeen syllables [4] Heroic couplets [5] Fourteen lines	ANSWER TO Q-22 **[3]** Permanent magnets and jet engines require these special alloys made with cobalt. 43%
23 Civil War General Abner Doubleday allegedly invented ___ in Cooperstown, New York.	[1] Steamboats [2] Cotton gin [3] Electric light bulbs [4] Eyeglasses [5] Baseball	ANSWER TO Q-22 **[4]** Billy Joel is "The Piano Man"; the others are known for their guitar work. 78%
23 Which is the northern-most country in South America?	[1] Ecuador [2] Guyana [3] Colombia [4] Brazil [5] Bolivia	ANSWER TO Q-22 **[1]** It has been used since ancient times for beads and small ornaments. 67%
23 The Montmorency is a sour type of:	[1] Plum [2] Grape [3] Apple [4] Cherry [5] Rhubarb	ANSWER TO Q-22 **[1]** "Costal" comes from the Latin word for rib and means of or near a rib. 51%

9 This island nation's capital is Velletta:

[1] Madagascar
[2] Corsica
[3] Sicily
[4] Cyprus
[5] Malta

ANSWER TO Q-8

[1] Santa Ana, four times president of Mexico, fought to keep Texas as part of his country.

58%

---

9 Which term denoted a southern supporter of the reconstruction after the Civil War?

[1] Carpetbagger
[2] Jim Crow
[3] Mugwumper
[4] Teetotaler
[5] Scalawag

ANSWER TO Q-8

[1] Gravensteins are large, yellow apples with red streaks.

69%

---

9 Which country ceased being a monarchy in 1974?

[1] Spain
[2] Brazil
[3] Greece
[4] Luxembourg
[5] Philippines

ANSWER TO Q-8

[3] Pheromones are chemical scents released to produce a response in another organism.

82%

---

9 Which song is considered the African-American national anthem?

[1] Lift Every Voice & Sing
[2] St. Louis Blues
[3] Respect
[4] We Shall Overcome
[5] Go Down Moses

ANSWER TO Q-8

[5] It regulates the sale of stocks and bonds to protect the public from fraud.

77%

---

9 Homiletics is the art of:

[1] Cooking and sewing
[2] Preaching sermons
[3] Natural medicine
[4] Reading minds
[5] Perfect pitch

ANSWER TO Q-8

[3] This area in western New Mexico is home to the Zuni Indians.

68%

22 "Lingua franca" is Italian for a:

[1] Hybrid language
[2] Monetary coin
[3] Party dress
[4] Sausage
[5] Kindergarten

ANSWER TO Q-21

[5] The Grand Duchy of Luxembourg is an independent nation.

65%

---

22 Most of the world's production of ___ is used for heat-resistant and magnetic alloys:

[1] Selenium
[2] Fluorine
[3] Cobalt
[4] Mercury
[5] Carbon

ANSWER TO Q-21

[2] The language is also called Persian.

79%

---

22 Which of these musicians is "instrumentally" out of place on this list?

[1] Chuck Berry
[2] Jeff Beck
[3] Keith Richards
[4] Billy Joel
[5] Slash

ANSWER TO Q-21

[5] Mauritius is located in the southwest Indian Ocean, about 500 miles east of Madagascar.

56%

---

22 What gem is blue and usually flecked?

[1] Lapis lazuli
[2] Garnet
[3] Moonstone
[4] Aquamarine
[5] Amethyst

ANSWER TO Q-21

[3] Previous methods of smallpox inoculation were fatal 2% of the time.

67%

---

22 The intercostal muscle and nerve are located between the:

[1] Ribs
[2] Heart chambers
[3] Spinal column
[4] Lower arm bones
[5] Neck and shoulder

ANSWER TO Q-21

[1] Trapunto is a decorative design in high relief which is padded from the underside.

56%

10 Which was the only "M*A*S*H" character to go permanently AWOL?	[1] Benjamin Pierce [2] B.J. Hunnicut [3] Frank Burns [4] Radar O'Reilly [5] Max Klinger	ANSWER TO Q-9 [5] Malta's largest city is Sliema, with a population of over 20,000. 45%
10 What caused the death of James Dean?	[1] Airplane crash [2] Car wreck [3] Drug overdose [4] Suicide [5] Gunshot wound	ANSWER TO Q-9 [5] Carpetbaggers were northerners who went south to take part in Reconstruction. 79%
10 "Al dente" is a cooking term used in reference to this food:	[1] Pasta [2] Fish [3] Potato [4] Fruit pie [5] Egg	ANSWER TO Q-9 [3] The republic now has a president and a premier responsible to a 300-member parliament. 69%
10 Which tool would you not find in a chemistry lab?	[1] Crucible [2] Burette [3] Leyden jar [4] Bunsen burner [5] Mattock	ANSWER TO Q-9 [1] Poet and scholar James Weldon Johnson wrote the words to the stirring hymn. 47%
10 Which major airport is mismatched with its city?	[1] Heathrow - London [2] Stapleton - Denver [3] Kennedy - New York [4] Logan - St. Louis [5] O'Hare - Chicago	ANSWER TO Q-9 [2] A homily, however, far from being an artful sermon, is a tedious and moralizing lecture. 35%

21 Which is not a region in France?

[1] Brittany
[2] Anjou
[3] Burgundy
[4] Alsace
[5] Luxembourg

ANSWER TO Q-20
[1] Semolina cereal is the main ingredient of couscous.
78%

---

21 Farsi is the official language of:

[1] Saudi Arabia
[2] Iran
[3] Jordan
[4] Syria
[5] Turkey

ANSWER TO Q-20
[2] Armour was the first businessman to introduce the refrigerated railroad car.
69%

---

21 Which is an island country?

[1] Laos
[2] Suriname
[3] Gabon
[4] Senegal
[5] Mauritius

ANSWER TO Q-20
[1] Vast bodies of magma give off heat that is a potential source of energy.
79%

---

21 Edward Jenner is credited with perfecting the:

[1] Printing press
[2] Birth control pill
[3] Smallpox vaccine
[4] Steam engine
[5] Radio

ANSWER TO Q-20
[5] Bamboo can grow as much as 35 inches a day!
66%

---

21 "Trapunto" is a technique used in:

[1] Quilting
[2] Singing
[3] Horseriding
[4] Target shooting
[5] Cooking

ANSWER TO Q-20
[2] A tercel is the male of any species of falcon.
45%

11 The drug mecamylamine serves this purpose:	[1] Kills bacteria [2] Increases adrenalin flow [3] Fights glaucoma [4] Promotes hair growth [5] Lowers blood pressure	ANSWER TO Q-10 [3] After Burns' AWOL, he was transferred to another hospital and never returned to 4077. 81%
11 Which Bronte sister wrote the novel "Jane Eyre"?	[1] Charlotte [2] Emily [3] Anne [4] Ellis [5] Jane	ANSWER TO Q-10 [2] His real name was James Byron. He died in a Porsche Spyder in 1955. 87%
11 Which painter and his famous work are mismatched?	[1] Michelangelo - Last Supper [2] Rembrandt - Night Watch [3] Van Gogh - Starry Night [4] Da Vinci - Mona Lisa [5] Monet -Haystacks	ANSWER TO Q-10 [1] Pasta "al dente" is cooked but firm to the bite. 89%
11 Where is Cleopatra's Needle?	[1] Cairo [2] Athens [3] London [4] Rome [5] China	ANSWER TO Q-10 [5] A mattock is like a pickax with one broad end for loosening soil. 58%
11 Which film does not feature an orphaned character?	[1] Oliver Twist [2] Annie [3] Escape to Witch Mountain [4] Raggedy Man [5] Dick Tracy	ANSWER TO Q-10 [4] Logan International Airport is in Boston. 81%

20
Couscous is a dietary staple in which part of the world?

[1] North Africa
[2] Far East
[3] India and Pakistan
[4] Latin American
[5] Indonesia

ANSWER TO Q-19

[3] Chlorophyll, the green pigment in plants, is responsible for forming hydrogen and carbon.
64%

---

20 The 19th century tycoon Philip D. Armour made his fortune in this industry:

[1] Five-and-dime stores
[2] Meat packing
[3] Fur trading
[4] Steel
[5] Copper mining

ANSWER TO Q-19

[2] Darren often suffered from curses inflicted by his witch of a mother-in-law, Endora.
95%

---

20 What is magma?

[1] Molten rock
[2] An ethanol derivative
[3] Dried plasma
[4] Liquid methane gas
[5] Coal-derived oil

ANSWER TO Q-19

[1] Both horses stand stuffed in the couple's museum in California.
78%

---

20 What is the fastest growing plant on earth?

[1] Seaweed
[2] Onion
[3] Grass
[4] Ivy
[5] Bamboo

ANSWER TO Q-19

[5] The first champ under the new rules was Jim Corbett, who knocked out John L. Sullivan.
59%

---

20 What type of animal is a tercel?

[1] Gopher
[2] Falcon
[3] Antelope
[4] Hare
[5] Snake

ANSWER TO Q-19

[4] Richard Harris and Anthony Hopkins are among the most famous actors to have played Richard I.
57%

12 What is a boll weevil?	[1] Insect [2] Dog [3] Wild pig [4] Bird [5] Fish	ANSWER TO Q-11 [5] It uses a ganglionic blocking agent to effect a rapid lowering of high blood pressure. 35%
12 Which tennis star never won the Grand Slam?	[1] Rod Laver [2] Martina Navratilova [3] Margaret Court Smith [4] Maureen Connolly [5] Steffi Graf	ANSWER TO Q-11 [1] She based the novel on her own miserable experience at a boarding school for girls. 58%
12 Sidon, Byblos and Tyre were the major cities of this ancient civilization:	[1] Babylonia [2] Byzantium [3] Phoenicia [4] Mali [5] Assyria	ANSWER TO Q-11 [1] This famous painting of Christ's Last Supper was painted by Leonardo Da Vinci. 59%
12 This animal comes in two distinct types, the bush and the forest varieties:	[1] Boa constrictor [2] African elephant [3] Golden pheasant [4] Crocodile [5] Snapping turtle	ANSWER TO Q-11 [3] Although having no direct connection to Cleo, Egypt gifted the U.S. and England with these ancient granite obelisks in 1876. 59%
12 The largest seeds come from this kind of plant:	[1] Ginkgo [2] Palm [3] Rubber [4] Sequoia [5] Redwood	ANSWER TO Q-11 [4] Sissy Spacek stars in this film as a lonely small town mother raising two children. 81%

19 Which of these is not part of an animal cell?	[1] Ribosomes [2] Mitochondria [3] Chlorophyll [4] Chromatin [5] Golgi apparatus	ANSWER TO Q-18 **[3]** Released in 1975, "Captain Fantastic" was Elton John's semi-autobiographical album. 76%
19 Which television dad worked for the ad agency "McMahon and Tate"?	[1] Mike Brady [2] Darren Stevens [3] Ward Cleaver [4] Steve Douglas [5] Ozzie Nelson	ANSWER TO Q-18 **[1]** These unique fish can temporarily live on shore and have the ability to climb trees. 42%
19 Roy Rogers' horse was named Trigger. What was Dale Evans' horse named?	[1] Buttermilk [2] Honeysuckle [3] Buttercup [4] Daisy [5] Scout	ANSWER TO Q-18 **[2]** The faint white band crossing the stars of our galaxy looks like spilled milk. 63%
19 Other than three-minute rounds, what did the Queensberry Rules bring to boxing?	[1] Referees [2] Legalized gambling [3] 15-round limit [4] Interracial bouts [5] Gloves	ANSWER TO Q-18 **[4]** The short plate also comes from the stomach. 54%
19 Errol Flynn played all of these famous people in the movies except:	[1] Robin Hood [2] Gentleman Jim Corbett [3] General Custer [4] Richard the Lionheart [5] John Barrymore	ANSWER TO Q-18 **[2]** His "Leningrad Symphony" was composed during the seige of Leningrad and gave him great success. 34%

13 The world's second largest coral reef is off the coast of:	[1] Argentina [2] Belize [3] Japan [4] Madagascar [5] South Africa	ANSWER TO Q-12 [1] It is a small, grayish beetle whose larvae hatch in and damage cotton balls. 89%
13 All of these performers died of gunshot wounds, except:	[1] John Lennon [2] Kurt Cobain [3] Sam Cooke [4] John Belushi [5] Marvin Gaye	ANSWER TO Q-12 [2] Tennis star Martina Navratilova won all of the events consecutively, but not in one calendar year. 61%
13 In which state is the world-famous Mayo Clinic?	[1] Minnesota [2] New York [3] Pennsylvania [4] Massachusetts [5] Illinois	ANSWER TO Q-12 [3] From 1100 to 332 B.C., the Phoenicians held sway in what is now Palestine. 58%
13 Which is not a disease of the eye?	[1] Astigmatism [2] Cataract [3] Otitis [4] Glaucoma [5] Retinitis	ANSWER TO Q-12 [2] Their habitats make them so different some scientists consider them distinct species. 61%
13 Which of these is not a drum?	[1] Conga [2] Timbal [3] Marimba [4] Tabor [5] Tom-tom	ANSWER TO Q-12 [2] The coco-de-mer, which grows in the Seychelles, produces seeds that can weigh up to 50 pounds. 58%

18 Which character was created by Elton John?	[1] Ziggy Stardust [2] Napoleon Dynamite [3] Captain Fantastic [4] Alladin Sane [5] The Impostor	ANSWER TO Q-17 **[4]** Ken Howard played coach, teacher and friend to an inner-city basketball team. 89%
18 A mudskipper is a:	[1] Fish [2] Bird [3] Mammal [4] Insect [5] Reptile	ANSWER TO Q-17 **[3]** Alabaster is used in ornaments and for sculpture. 45%
18 The Greek word "galaxy" means:	[1] Home of the gods [2] Milk [3] Star path [4] Far away [5] Sky-islands	ANSWER TO Q-17 **[4]** "Here lies Butch/ we planted him raw/ quick on the trigger/ slow on the draw." 57%
18 The flank cut comes from this part of the steer:	[1] Rump [2] Breast [3] Back [4] Belly [5] Shoulder	ANSWER TO Q-17 **[5]** Nearly 2000 lines long, the work is considered Walt Whitman's most significant effort. 59%
18 "Lady Macbeth of Mtsensk" and "The Nose" are works by this Russian composer:	[1] Peter Tchaikovsky [2] Dmitri Shostakovich [3] Nikolai Glinka [4] Sergei Rachmaninoff [5] Igor Stravinsky	ANSWER TO Q-17 **[4]** The Imperial is made by Chrysler. 78%

14 Which is not a term for a young mammal?

[1] Cub
[2] Fledgling
[3] Kid
[4] Foal
[5] Whelp

ANSWER TO Q-13
[2] Australia's Great Barrier Reef is the world's largest.
45%

---

14 What water does the term "high seas" refer to?

[1] Atlantic Ocean
[2] Mediterranean Sea
[3] Areas with large waves
[4] Unowned waters
[5] Pacific Ocean

ANSWER TO Q-13
[4] John Belushi died from a drug overdose.
91%

---

14 These are rounded rocks or nodules with crystals inside:

[1] Sodalites
[2] Geodes
[3] Conchinas
[4] Hematites
[5] Tiger eyes

ANSWER TO Q-13
[1] The clinic was founded by surgeon brothers, Charles and William Mayo.
65%

---

14 Dorothea Brooke is the heroine of this classic novel:

[1] Portrait of a Lady
[2] The Scarlet Letter
[3] Bleak House
[4] Middlemarch
[5] Vanity Fair

ANSWER TO Q-13
[3] Otitis in an inflammation of the ear, especially the middle ear.
68%

---

14 Which word means a universal remedy or cure-all?

[1] Curare
[2] Placebo
[3] Alchemy
[4] Panacea
[5] Analgesic

ANSWER TO Q-13
[3] The marimba, a latin version of the xylophone, is played with soft mallets.
79%

209

17 Which of these television shows centered around a high school basketball coach?	[1] Fast Break [2] Head of the Class [3] Charles in Charge [4] White Shadow [5] Coach	ANSWER TO Q-16 **[4]** George Eliot, Mark Twain and George Orwell are examples of nom de plumes. 79%
17 Which mineral is incorrectly matched with its product or use?	[1] Dolomite - building [2] Graphite - pencil lead [3] Alabaster - insulation [4] Corundum - gemstone [5] Talc - powder	ANSWER TO Q-16 **[1]** After being wrongly imprisoned, Dantes avenged himself from the island of Monte Cristo. 67%
17 Where would you expect to find an epitaph?	[1] Restaurant [2] Insurance policy [3] Grocery store [4] Gravestone [5] Sports arena	ANSWER TO Q-16 **[2]** Williams plays the great running back whose best friend and teammate is dying of cancer. 89%
17 Poet Walt Whitman penned which of these works?	[1] Songs of Innocence [2] Song of Hiawatha [3] Song of Solomon [4] Song of Bernadette [5] Songs of Myself	ANSWER TO Q-16 **[5]** Exocrine glands release chemicals through tubes called ducts. 67%
17 Which of these is not a GM car?	[1] Chevrolet [2] Oldsmobile [3] Cadillac [4] Imperial [5] Saturn	ANSWER TO Q-16 **[5]** Glandular activity is regulated involuntarily by the nervous system. 45%

15 Where was Martin Luther King Jr. when he made his famed "I have a dream" speech?	[1] Lincoln Memorial [2] Ebenezer Baptist Church [3] Birmingham Jail [4] Pettus Bridge [5] White House lawn	ANSWER TO Q-14 **[2]** A fledgling is a general term used to describe the young of all birds. 69%
15 Which TV game show did not feature a panel of celebrities?	[1] What's My Line [2] I've Got a Secret [3] Beat the Clock [4] The Match Game [5] Hollywood Squares	ANSWER TO Q-14 **[4]** The high seas belong to no nation just as the "high road" is one everybody can use. 58%
15 Which is a high office in Islamic tradition?	[1] Oba [2] Rajah [3] Pharisee [4] Viceroy [5] Caliph	ANSWER TO Q-14 **[2]** Tiny geodes are commonly called ocos. 59%
15 Which entertainer of Latin descent does not use a stage name?	[1] Martin Sheen [2] Vicki Carr [3] Linda Ronstadt [4] Raquel Welch [5] Rita Moreno	ANSWER TO Q-14 **[4]** George Eliot's brainy and willful heroine creates continual problems for herself. 46%
15 Which writer created Holly Golightly?	[1] James Thurber [2] Anita Loos [3] F. Scott Fitzgerald [4] Truman Capote [5] Gore Vidal	ANSWER TO Q-14 **[4]** Example: in election years, candidates offer voters panaceas for society's ills. 79%

16 A pen name is also known as a:

[1] Acronym
[2] Neologism
[3] Eponym
[4] Nom de plume
[5] Sobriquet

ANSWER TO Q-15

[3] The Persian sage, Mani, founded this religion in the 3rd century A.D.

21%

16 Alexandre Dumas' character Edmond Dantes called himself the ____.

[1] Count of Monte Cristo
[2] Emperor of Ice Cream
[3] King of Paris
[4] Baron Frankenstein
[5] Prince of Thieves

ANSWER TO Q-15

[2] After signing with Geffen, the Eagles produced their first hit single, "Take it Easy."

57%

16 Who portrays NFL great Gale Sayers in the movie "Brian's Song"?

[1] Sidney Poitier
[2] Billy Dee Williams
[3] Danny Glover
[4] Richard Roundtree
[5] Louis Gossett, Jr.

ANSWER TO Q-15

[1] The mudpuppy is found in permanent ponds and lakes from Canada to the Gulf of Mexico.

45%

16 In the human body, the exocrine glands are considered part of this system:

[1] Nervous
[2] Respiratory
[3] Circulatory
[4] Reproductive
[5] Digestive

ANSWER TO Q-15

[4] Drones are dedicated to the queen and are the first to go during winter cutbacks in population.

57%

16 The submaxillary, sublingual, and parotid are your three pairs of major:

[1] Lacrimal glands
[2] Sebaceous glands
[3] Sweat glands
[4] Endocrine glands
[5] Salivary glands

ANSWER TO Q-15

[2] Originally "Skid Road," bull teams dragged heavy logs over cross ties called skids.

45%

16 In his last will and testament, what did Hitler say he liked most about Eva Braun?	[1] Legs [2] Wit [3] Lack of intellect [4] Cooking [5] Clothes	ANSWER TO Q-15 [1] The speech, based on biblical phraseology, emphasized the brotherhood of all men. 66%
16 The vole is a European relative of this North American animal:	[1] Muskrat [2] Woodchuck [3] Badger [4] Mountain goat [5] Coyote	ANSWER TO Q-15 [3] On "Beat the Clock," couples performed stunts in a certain time period. 81%
16 What is a Molotov cocktail?	[1] Automobile [2] Mixed drink [3] Songbird [4] Assault gun [5] Explosive	ANSWER TO Q-15 [5] Abu Bakr was elected the first caliph in 632 A.D. 58%
16 Operation "Sea Lion" was Hitler's plan for:	[1] Invading England [2] Mining the Mediterranean [3] Allying with Mexico [4] Eliminating ethnicity [5] Sinking ships	ANSWER TO Q-15 [3] The biggest star of Latin heritage was Rita Hayworth, who was born Margarita Casino. 78%
16 When King Arthur wed Queen Guinevere, he received this celebrated gift:	[1] Excalibur sword [2] Island of Avalon [3] The Round Table [4] Camelot [5] Merlin the magician	ANSWER TO Q-15 [4] The heroine of "Breakfast at Tiffany's" is an eccentric New York playgirl. 68%

15 Christianity was an influence on the founder of this religion:	[1] Buddhism [2] Taoism [3] Manichaeism [4] Shinto [5] Orphism	ANSWER TO Q-14 **[4]** Gene Hackman stars as Popeye Doyle, a cop out to locate a drug kingpin in this film. 89%
15 Which group started as a backup band for Linda Ronstadt?	[1] Lynyrd Skynyrd [2] The Eagles [3] Fleetwood Mac [4] The Allman Brothers [5] The Pretenders	ANSWER TO Q-14 **[3]** The atoll was subjected to 22 nuclear detonations between 1946 and 1958. 68%
15 What is the mudpuppy?	[1] Amphibian [2] Shore bird [3] Catfish [4] Beetle [5] Jellyfish	ANSWER TO Q-14 **[1]** Zurich has a population of 345,000. 56%
15 The drones in a beehive are:	[1] Queens [2] Asexual workers [3] Domestic worker bees [4] Fertile males [5] Unfertile females	ANSWER TO Q-14 **[2]** One of the basic ethnic groups of north Africa, their culture dates back before 2400 B.C. 34%
15 Where was the original "Skid Row"?	[1] New York City [2] Seattle [3] San Francisco [4] Chicago [5] New Orleans	ANSWER TO Q-14 **[2]** This is a game where players add their cards, trying to come as close as they can to 9 or 19. 68%

17 Which prefix means "beneath"?

[1] Ante-
[2] Infra-
[3] Ambi-
[4] Supra-
[5] Tropo-

ANSWER TO Q-16

[3] We must agree; she said she'd go to her death with him "at her own wish."
64%

---

17 Which mythological figure was not a king?

[1] Oedipus
[2] Midas
[3] Eros
[4] Pygmalion
[5] Agamemnon

ANSWER TO Q-16

[1] The muskrat is one of the few American animals introduced into Europe, where it is a pest.
57%

---

17 An "aficionado" is a:

[1] Pasta dish
[2] South american ranch
[3] Fan or devotee
[4] Flagship
[5] Seafood soup

ANSWER TO Q-16

[5] The crude bomb was named after a foreign minister of the USSR during the 1940's.
81%

---

17 Hard red, soft white and durum are classes of:

[1] Corn
[2] Wheat
[3] Rice
[4] Beans
[5] Oats

ANSWER TO Q-16

[1] Britain's staunch resistance to aerial attacks delayed the operation indefinitely.
57%

---

17 Although known primarily as poets, all these writers except ____ wrote plays as well.

[1] T.S. Eliot
[2] Emily Dickinson
[3] William Butler Yeats
[4] Archibald Macleish
[5] Robert Lowell

ANSWER TO Q-16

[3] In many versions, the donator of the famous table is Guinevere's father.
68%

14 Which film does not center around valuable jewels?	[1] The Maltese Falcon [2] A Fish Called Wanda [3] The Pink Panther [4] The French Connection [5] Family Plot	ANSWER TO Q-13 [1] Created by Agnes DeMille in 1942, who later choreographed "Oklahoma!" 78%
14 Bikini Atoll is located in this island group:	[1] Caroline Islands [2] Society Islands [3] Marshall Islands [4] Coral Sea Islands [5] Solomon Islands	ANSWER TO Q-13 [2] All these drugs are made from the sap of the unripe seed pods, not the seed itself. 56%
14 Which is the most populous city in Switzerland?	[1] Zurich [2] Bern [3] Basel [4] Geneva [5] Lausanne	ANSWER TO Q-13 [2] Just for a change of taste from his homemade brew. 78%
14 Ancient north African states like Numidia and Mauritania were formed by:	[1] Incas [2] Berbers [3] Visigoths [4] Philistines [5] Ethiopians	ANSWER TO Q-13 [4] Born without scales, most fish add these growth rings as they age. 56%
14 Which game does not involve moving pieces off the playing area?	[1] Chess [2] Baccarat [3] Marbles [4] Backgammon [5] Checkers	ANSWER TO Q-13 [4] Formed in 1969, the organization of activists protests environmental wrongs. 68%

18 The mainstay of a porcupine's diet is:

[1] Tree bark
[2] Small rodents
[3] Berries
[4] Leaves
[5] Moss and lichens

ANSWER TO Q-17
[2] This is exemplified in terms such as infrastructure, infrared, and infrasonic.
57%

---

18 A shtreimel and bekesheh are articles of clothing worn by a/an:

[1] Catholic Pope
[2] African Shaman
[3] Hasidic Jew
[4] Islamic leader
[5] Sherpa guide

ANSWER TO Q-17
[3] Also known as Amor and Cupid, Eros is the god of love.
69%

---

18 Which metallic element is also called wolfram?

[1] Tungsten
[2] Calcium
[3] Silver
[4] Sodium
[5] Platinum

ANSWER TO Q-17
[3] Originally used for bullfight enthusiasts, now the term has a more general meaning.
81%

---

18 The great Australian Bight is a:

[1] Coral reef
[2] Mountain range
[3] Gold mine
[4] Bay
[5] Desert

ANSWER TO Q-17
[2] Classes are determined by planting season and the color of the kernel.
77%

---

18 Which Sullivan was half of the "Gilbert and Sullivan" musical team?

[1] Harry Stack Sullivan
[2] John L. Sullivan
[3] Arthur Sullivan
[4] Louis Henry Sullivan
[5] Anne Sullivan

ANSWER TO Q-17
[2] Dickinson's writings were confined to short lyrics.
65%

217

13 "Rodeo" is considered the first major American:	[1] Ballet [2] Western [3] Musical comedy [4] Circus [5] Opera	ANSWER TO Q-12 [3] Sweet peppers register at 0 scoville units, jalapenos at 4,000 units and habaneros at up to 300,000 units. 45%
13 Which narcotic is not produced from the poppy?	[1] Heroin [2] Cocaine [3] Opium [4] Morphine [5] Codeine	ANSWER TO Q-12 [2] Tanzania, formerly Tanganyika, has the highest mountain in Africa, Mt. Kilimanjaro. 67%
13 M*A*S*H's Capt. Hawkeye Pierce usually orders what at the Officer's Club?	[1] Gin and tonic [2] Dry martini [3] Shot of whiskey [4] Scotch and water [5] Grape Nehi	ANSWER TO Q-12 [5] For example, pates are usually prepared and served in terrines. 68%
13 To determine the age of a fish, it is best to look at this part of its body:	[1] Teeth [2] Fins [3] Eyes [4] Scales [5] Gills	ANSWER TO Q-12 [2] Zenith is Sinclair Lewis' satirical composite picture of the typical small town. 56%
13 When Americans and Canadians joined forces to protest ___, Greenpeace was created:	[1] The Vietnam War [2] Air pollution [3] Ocean degradation [4] Nuclear bomb testing [5] Soviet whaling	ANSWER TO Q-12 [2] This relative of the ibis feeds on minute crustaceans. 56%

19 The word "rigmarole" refers to:	[1] Children's games [2] Meaningless talk [3] Rock strata [4] Accumulated frost [5] X-ray units	ANSWER TO Q-18 [1] Porcupines forage in trees at night for the inner bark they crave. 46%
19 A lampoon is a:	[1] Large eel [2] Buffoonish person [3] Satire [4] Kerosene lamp [5] Hurricane	ANSWER TO Q-18 [3] A shtreimel is a hat and the long coat is called a bekesheh. 68%
19 A relationship from which two organisms mutually benefit is called:	[1] Photosynthesis [2] Hybridization [3] Osmosis [4] Organic [5] Symbiosis	ANSWER TO Q-18 [1] The atomic symbol "W" comes from the German wolfram; tungsten is a Swedish term. 58%
19 What is a penchant?	[1] Strong liking [2] Suspended ornament [3] Small flag [4] Supreme chief [5] Wing	ANSWER TO Q-18 [4] This large bay indents the southern coast. The lesser Gulf of Carpathia carves the north. 59%
19 His use of brick and unvarnished wood came to be known as the Prairie Style:	[1] Christopher Wren [2] I.M. Pei [3] Buckminster Fuller [4] Frank Lloyd Wright [5] Walter Gropius	ANSWER TO Q-18 [3] Sullivan wrote the music while Gilbert wrote the witty words to their musicals. 52%

12 In cooking, what is measured in scoville units?

[1] Yeast activity
[2] Pie crust
[3] Heat of peppers
[4] Alcohol content
[5] Degree of evaporation

ANSWER TO Q-11

[3] Billy Wilder's "Sunset Boulevard" was released in 1951.
65%

---

12 The African nation of Tanzania includes this well-known island:

[1] Madagascar
[2] Zanzibar
[3] Santa Cruz
[4] Las Palmas
[5] St. Helena

ANSWER TO Q-11

[3] Capsicums include the red peppers, cayenne and ancho, and jalapeno and seriano green peppers.
43%

---

12 Which term refers to both a utensil and a mixed meat preparation?

[1] Canard
[2] Torte
[3] Tendron
[4] Capucin
[5] Terrine

ANSWER TO Q-11

[2] The archipelago of Fiji is in the southwest Pacific Ocean.
51%

---

12 The 1920's city of Zenith is the setting for which famous novel?

[1] The Grapes of Wrath
[2] Babbitt
[3] East of Eden
[4] Mainstreet
[5] The Great Gatsby

ANSWER TO Q-11

[1] Sponges are the most primitive of the multicellular organisms.
54%

---

12 Which bird is not a flesh-eater?

[1] Owl
[2] Spoonbill
[3] Raptor
[4] Kestrel
[5] Osprey

ANSWER TO Q-11

[3] As the origin of the word in Latin suggests, it means to "cook it up."
64%

20 Which body organ produces hydrochloric acid?	[1] Gall bladder [2] Small intestine [3] Stomach [4] Pancreas [5] Diaphragm	ANSWER TO Q-19 **[2]** The term evolved from "ragman roll," a 13th century name for any official document. 81%
20 Which of these is not an ailment of the intestinal tract?	[1] Amoebic dysentery [2] Crohn's disease [3] Colitis [4] Diverticulitis [5] Meniere's disease	ANSWER TO Q-19 **[3]** Broadly satirical, lampoons attack personalities or institutions. 89%
20 "The Waterworks" is a book by the author of:	[1] The Firm [2] Billy Bathgate [3] The Stand [4] Lonesome Dove [5] Lasher	ANSWER TO Q-19 **[5]** The organisms must be of different species; an example is fungus and lichen forming algae. 89%
20 During litigation, someone who appears "amicus curiae" is:	[1] Charged with a crime [2] A court employee [3] A defense attorney [4] A friend of the court [5] Part of the prosecution	ANSWER TO Q-19 **[1]** The others are pendant, pennant, pendragon and pennon, respectively. 78%
20 Beatrix became queen of the Netherlands upon the abdication of her mother:	[1] Juliana [2] Phillipa [3] Madeleine [4] Wilhelmina [5] Margrethe	ANSWER TO Q-19 **[4]** Among Wright's buildings are NYC's Guggenheim Museum and Chicago's Robie House. 68%

11 All these movies were released during the 1930's except:	[1] King Kong [2] The Thin Man [3] Sunset Boulevard [4] Top Hat [5] Duck Soup	ANSWER TO Q-10 **[1]** It means to provoke or encourage some expression of unrest. 87%
11 What kind of vegetables are capsicums?	[1] Oranges [2] Mushrooms [3] Peppers [4] Onions [5] Cabbage	ANSWER TO Q-10 **[2]** These tales are told by Scheherazade in order to stave off the king's punishment. 68%
11 The islands of Vanua Levu and Viti Levu are the two largest islands of:	[1] The Philippines [2] Fiji [3] Greenland [4] Sri Lanka [5] New Guinea	ANSWER TO Q-10 **[1]** The raw fish "cooks" in a vinegar-type marinade. 64%
11 Which invertebrates are the lone occupants of phylum Porifera?	[1] Sponges [2] Sea urchins [3] Corals [4] Jellyfish [5] Starfish	ANSWER TO Q-10 **[5]** This D.H. Lawrence classic was published in 1928. 52%
11 Which of these words suggests the most unorganized way of putting things together?	[1] Compose [2] Compile [3] Concoct [4] Arrange [5] Constitute	ANSWER TO Q-10 **[1]** Babe Ruth made baseball our national pastime with his heroics at the Yankees' new stadium. 85%

21 Which song was Simon and Garfunkel's first #1 hit?	[1] Mrs. Robinson [2] The Sounds of Silence [3] Homeward Bound [4] The Boxer [5] Scarborough Fair	ANSWER TO Q-20 **[3]** Excess secretion of it causes gastric ulcers. A deficient amount impairs digestion. 81%
21 This 1892 ballad became the first pop smash hit by selling a million copies of sheet music:	[1] After The Ball [2] Sonny Boy [3] My Melancholy Baby [4] Alexander's Ragtime Band [5] Together	ANSWER TO Q-20 **[5]** Meniere's disease is a disorder of the inner ear. 72%
21 Which famous Russian was not a composer?	[1] Sergei Rachmaninoff [2] Dmitri Shostakovich [3] Igor Stravinsky [4] Nikolai Gogol [5] Sergei Prokofiev	ANSWER TO Q-20 **[2]** The E.L. Doctorow novel is set in post-Civil War New York City. 51%
21 Which is not a part of the human eye?	[1] Vitreous humor [2] Retina [3] Choroid [4] Iris [5] Alveoli	ANSWER TO Q-20 **[4]** This type of appearance allows parties not named in a suit to give the court information. 57%
21 All of these nicknames belonged to baseball players except:	[1] Sultan of Swat [2] Georgia Peach [3] Say Hey Kid [4] Iron Horse [5] Ambling Alp	ANSWER TO Q-20 **[1]** Beatrix, Juliana's firstborn child, has three sons with her German husband. 79%

10 One might foment a:	[1] Riot [2] Marriage [3] Meal [4] Movie review [5] Hairstyle	ANSWER TO Q-9 **[5]** A traditional string quartet is composed of two violins, a viola, and a cello. 78%
10 In which story from the Arabian Nights does the expression "Open Sesame" occur?	[1] The Thief of Baghdad [2] Ali Baba & Forty Thieves [3] The Alhambra [4] The Red-Haired Demon [5] Sinbad the Sailor	ANSWER TO Q-9 **[1]** The novel inspired the movie "Charly," for which Cliff Robertson won an Academy Award. 79%
10 What is used to make ceviche?	[1] Seafood [2] Cheese [3] Mushrooms [4] Toast [5] Chicken livers	ANSWER TO Q-9 **[4]** "I," said the sparrow, "With my bow and arrow, I killed Cock Robin." 68%
10 Of these literary works, which was not written during the 19th century?	[1] Uncle Tom's Cabin [2] Vanity Fair [3] Walden [4] Jane Eyre [5] Lady Chatterley's Lover	ANSWER TO Q-9 **[5]** Most other citrus fruits have their origins in Southeast Asia. 54%
10 Yankee Stadium is commonly known as "The house that ___ built."	[1] Ruth [2] LaGuardia [3] New York [4] Mantle [5] We	ANSWER TO Q-9 **[2]** The large port on the Rhine river is an industrial city that produces iron and steel. 59%

22 Before it was banned, thalidomide was used as a/an:	[1] Analgesic [2] Emetic [3] Sedative [4] Appetite suppressant [5] Stimulant	ANSWER TO Q-21 **[2]** It topped the charts for two weeks back in 1965. 52%
22 In French cooking, if something is "en brouchette," how is it cooked?	[1] On a skewer [2] Encased in pastry [3] Garnished with mushrooms [4] Baked in paper [5] In olive oil	ANSWER TO Q-21 **[1]** The other songs are hits of the teens and twenties. 32%
22 Which term is used to refer to a place where oysters are cultivated?	[1] Herd [2] Band [3] Litter [4] Bed [5] Pack	ANSWER TO Q-21 **[4]** Gogol was a 19th-century author whose works include "Dead Souls" and "The Inspector General." 56%
22 The Victoria was the name of the first ship to:	[1] Round Cape of Good Hope [2] Enter the Panama Canal [3] Sail on Hudson Bay [4] Circumnavigate the globe [5] Reach Antarctica	ANSWER TO Q-21 **[5]** The alveoli are the tiny air sacs that do most of the work in the human lungs. 81%
22 Which legal defense is also referred to as "The Nuremberg Defense"?	[1] Accident [2] Insanity [3] Doing the Lord's work [4] Self-defense [5] Just following orders	ANSWER TO Q-21 **[5]** The Ambling Alp was Italian heavyweight boxer Primo Carnera. 61%

9 In the world of music, Budapest, Julliard and Cleveland are all prominent:

[1] Symphony orchestras
[2] Music schools
[3] Opera houses
[4] Jazz festivals
[5] String quartets

ANSWER TO Q-8

[5] Other famous people born out of wedlock include Da Vinci, Cezanne, Juan Peron and Willy Brandt.

68%

---

9 In which book will you find the story of a man who has his IQ raised from 68 to 200?

[1] Flowers for Algernon
[2] The Andromeda Strain
[3] On the Beach
[4] Fahrenheit 451
[5] The Lost World

ANSWER TO Q-8

[2] Malta is an island in the Mediterranean Sea.

67%

---

9 In the nursery rhyme, "Cock Robin" was killed by the:

[1] Hunter
[2] Buzzard
[3] Farmer
[4] Sparrow
[5] Maiden

ANSWER TO Q-8

[2] Frelimo is the Marxist guerrilla group which won independence for Mozambique.

35%

---

9 Which fruit originated in the West Indies?

[1] Orange
[2] Lime
[3] Lemon
[4] Tangerine
[5] Grapefruit

ANSWER TO Q-8

[1] Naturalist writer Zola attempted to present a chunk of life complete, without modification.

67%

---

9 The European city of Cologne is located in:

[1] France
[2] Germany
[3] Norway
[4] Spain
[5] Belgium

ANSWER TO Q-8

[2] Preferred by many Europeans, this drink is coffee at its strongest.

76%

23 Which word would not refer to a servile person?	[1] Subservient [2] Peremptory [3] Menial [4] Obsequious [5] Sycophantic	ANSWER TO Q-22 **[3]** The only remaining legitimate use is as a treatment for leprosy. 79%
23 Which war novel is by Norman Mailer?	[1] The Naked and the Dead [2] From Here to Eternity [3] The Young Lions [4] In a Narrow Grave [5] Crossing the Line	ANSWER TO Q-22 **[1]** This is a fancy way of saying, "kabobs." 76%
23 Which was founded by Pierre de Coubertin in the late 19th century?	[1] Interpol [2] Cannes film festival [3] Modern Olympic games [4] Red Cross [5] Boy Scouts	ANSWER TO Q-22 **[4]** The term refers to both artificial and natural locations. 81%
23 Israel is bordered by all but which of these Arab countries?	[1] Egypt [2] Jordan [3] Lebanon [4] Syria [5] Saudi Arabia	ANSWER TO Q-22 **[4]** Magellan's ship returned to Seville in 1522. 68%
23 Alexander Borodin is a major Russian:	[1] Statesman [2] Writer [3] General [4] Scientist [5] Composer	ANSWER TO Q-22 **[5]** It got its name from the unsuccessful defense many Nazis used when on trial for war crimes. 81%

8 Which of the following famous people was not an illegitimate child?	[1] Marilyn Monroe [2] Sophia Loren [3] Charles Manson [4] Eric Clapton [5] Paul McCartney	ANSWER TO Q-7 [4] A yellow jacket is a wasp. The others are birds. 65%
8 These are all peninsulas except:	[1] Baja California [2] Malta [3] Nova Scotia [4] Jutland [5] Iberia	ANSWER TO Q-7 [4] Young Alex and his "droogs" (friends) were violent gang members in "A Clockwork Orange." 54%
8 Which of these African political groups is incorrectly matched with its country?	[1] ANC - South Africa [2] Frelimo - Somalia [3] Unita - Angola [4] Zanu - Zimbabwe [5] Mau Mau - Kenya	ANSWER TO Q-7 [3] Claude Monet's painting was entitled, "Impression, Sunrise." 78%
8 The plotless type of fiction that strives to give an impression of daily life is called:	[1] Slice of life [2] Stream of consciousness [3] Postmodern [4] Expressionistic [5] Picaresque	ANSWER TO Q-7 [5] Williams batted .406 for the Boston Red Sox in 1941. 69%
8 Which of these coffee drinks never includes milk or cream in any form?	[1] Irish coffee [2] Espresso [3] Cafe au lait [4] Viennese coffee [5] Cappucino	ANSWER TO Q-7 [5] Cedar is a durable, red-colored wood used for construction and cabinetry. 53%

24 Whose first color film was titled "Cries and Whispers"?	[1] Bernardo Bertolucci [2] Alfred Hitchcock [3] Federico Fellini [4] Roberto Rossellini [5] Ingmar Bergman	ANSWER TO Q-23 [2] A peremptory person is dictatorial and dogmatic. 82%
24 Which is the first African country due east of Morocco?	[1] Mauritania [2] Algeria [3] Niger [4] Chad [5] Mali	ANSWER TO Q-23 [1] His first novel is based on his experiences in World War II. 75%
24 Which character is not the heroine of a historical romance?	[1] Rebecca [2] Lorna Doone [3] Scarlett O'Hara [4] Lucie Manette [5] Esmeraida	ANSWER TO Q-23 [3] The Olympics returned in 1896 after a 1700-year hiatus. 54%
24 Dr. Seuss is the nom de plume of:	[1] William Sidney [2] Theodore Geisel [3] Shel Silverstein [4] Charles Perrault [5] A.A. Milne	ANSWER TO Q-23 [5] Jordan lies between the two. 57%
24 Which medieval poet has the reputation of being an outlaw and thief as well as a great writer?	[1] Dante [2] Petrarch [3] Rabelais [4] Villon [5] Chaucer	ANSWER TO Q-23 [5] Borodin is known for an extensive use of local folk music in his works. 81%

7 Which "yellow" animal is a fish?	[1] Yellowhammer [2] Yellow jacket [3] Yellowthroat [4] Yellowtail [5] Yellow-rumped warbler	ANSWER TO Q-6 **[4]** Ceylon, now Sri Lanka, in 1960 elected Srimavo Bandaranaike prime minister. 32%
7 Which is not a term from George Orwell's novel "1984"?	[1] Big Brother [2] Oceania [3] Thought Police [4] Droogs [5] Inner Party	ANSWER TO Q-6 **[4]** It also marked his last performance in a feature film. 78%
7 The term "Impression-ism" was prompted by an 1872 painting by:	[1] Edgar Degas [2] Vincent Van Gogh [3] Claude Monet [4] Paul Cezanne [5] Paul Gauguin	ANSWER TO Q-6 **[5]** The gods made Medea fall in love with Jason so he could succeed in a quest for the golden fleece. 57%
7 The famed Ted Williams is the last major league baseball player to:	[1] Hit 60 home runs [2] Win Triple Crown [3] Have 56-game hitting streak [4] Pitch a perfect game [5] Bat .400	ANSWER TO Q-6 **[2]** Sakharov was forced out of his Moscow home and into an "internal exile" in the city of Gorky. 68%
7 Cyprus, atlas and deodar are all types of:	[1] Maple [2] Mahogany [3] Elm [4] Fig [5] Cedar	ANSWER TO Q-6 **[3]** Martha Reeves was backed up by the fabulous Vandellas. 78%

25 Which New Testament event took place on the Eve of the Passion?

[1] Wedding at Cana
[2] Last Supper
[3] Flight into Egypt
[4] Laying on of hands
[5] Slaughter of innocents

ANSWER TO Q-24

[5] Like many later Bergman films, it explores family relationships.

79%

---

25 The tip, vamp, throat, collar and shank are all parts of this familiar item:

[1] Woman's shoe
[2] Hair dryer
[3] Table lamp
[4] Garbage disposal
[5] Pencil sharpener

ANSWER TO Q-24

[2] This giant country is almost four times larger than the state of Texas.

52%

---

25 A wicked scheme could be called any of these terms except:

[1] Nefarious
[2] Vituperative
[3] Machievellian
[4] Malevolent
[5] Iniquitous

ANSWER TO Q-24

[1] Daphne du Maurier's tale has a modern setting and Rebecca is the dead wife, not the heroine.

57%

---

25 Which creature thrives on starch from clothing, wallpaper and book bindings?

[1] Silverfish
[2] Lady bugs
[3] Centipedes
[4] Dragonflies
[5] Fireflies

ANSWER TO Q-24

[2] Geisel was famous for his "Cat in the Hat" series as well as "The Grinch Who Stole Christmas" and "Green Eggs & Ham."

69%

---

25 Louis Malle directed all these films except:

[1] Pretty Paby
[2] My Dinner with Andre
[3] Rosemary's Baby
[4] Damage
[5] Atlantic City

ANSWER TO Q-24

[4] After receiving an excellent education, he lived the life of a rogue.

41%

---

6 Which was the first country to elect a woman as a prime minister?	[1] Pakistan [2] India [3] Israel [4] Sri Lanka [5] Indonesia	ANSWER TO Q-5 [3] Cantor was known for his rolling eyes and high-toned voice. 54%
6 Who returned to the movies in the 1981 film "Ragtime" after a twenty-year hiatus?	[1] Mae West [2] Karl Malden [3] Gloria Swanson [4] James Cagney [5] Lee Marvin	ANSWER TO Q-5 [3] Petruchio masters the shrew, Katarina, and ensures a happy married life for himself. 61%
6 In Greek mythology, Medea became the wife of:	[1] Perseus [2] Theseus [3] Ulysses [4] Achilles [5] Jason	ANSWER TO Q-5 [4] The successor of Moses, Joshua was the conqueror of Jericho. 54%
6 Which Russian Nobel Prize winner was not exiled to some part of the western world?	[1] Bunin [2] Sakharov [3] Solzhenitsyn [4] Brodsky [5] Sinyavsky	ANSWER TO Q-5 [3] James Joyce's "Ulysses" takes place during a single day in Dublin, Ireland. 45%
6 Which singer and backup group are not correctly paired?	[1] Junior Walker - All Stars [2] Freddy - Dreamers [3] Martha - Blue Caps [4] Gary Puckett - Union Gap [5] Dion - Belmonts	ANSWER TO Q-5 [1] Rue McClanahan, later appearing as Blanche Devereaux, was Maude's next door neighbor. 78%

232

26 In the Lewis Carroll classic, Alice increases or decreases her size by:	[1] Reading a magic spell [2] Turning a ring [3] Eating a mushroom [4] Winning a chess game [5] Tapping her foot	ANSWER TO Q-25 [2] At that time Christ instituted the sacrament of Communion. 81%
26 What was the first toy ever advertised on TV?	[1] Tinker Toys [2] Erector sets [3] Barbie dolls [4] Lincoln logs [5] Mr. Potato Head	ANSWER TO Q-25 [1] Notice that a pump grips both the toe and the heel, while a slingback grips the toe only. 46%
26 Which of these is not a lighter-than-air craft?	[1] Zeppelin [2] Dirigible [3] Heliotrope [4] Blimp [5] Hot air balloon	ANSWER TO Q-25 [2] "Vituperative" means in a scolding manner. 68%
26 Which person would you go to if you needed to have a barrel repaired?	[1] Gaffer [2] Wainwright [3] Taxidermist [4] Cooper [5] Podiatrist	ANSWER TO Q-25 [1] These pests prefer cool damp areas such as basements as their habitats. 69%
26 The Heisman trophy is awarded to:	[1] Amateur boxers [2] Pro basketball players [3] College football players [4] Gymnasts [5] Tennis pros	ANSWER TO Q-25 [3] This one is Roman Polanski's "baby." 71%

5 "Makin" Whoopee" & "If You Knew Susie" are songs associated with this vaudevillian:	[1] George M. Cohan [2] W.C. Fields [3] Eddie Cantor [4] George Burns [5] Al Jolson	ANSWER TO Q-4 **[2]** In order to send messages from nerve cell to nerve cell, this gap must be crossed. 65%
5 Petruchio is a character in:	[1] Romeo and Juliet [2] Othello [3] Taming of the Shrew [4] As You Like It [5] Richard III	ANSWER TO Q-4 **[4]** Denmark is separated from Belgium by Germany and the Netherlands. 68%
5 Which statement about Old Testament figure Aaron is inaccurate?	[1] First Hebrew high priest [2] Performed miracles [3] Created the golden calf [4] Destroyed Jericho [5] Brother of Moses	ANSWER TO Q-4 **[5]** Two philosophical books, "The Tao of Pooh" and "The Te of Piglet," were inspired by A.A. Milne. 45%
5 Blazes Boylan and Buck Mulligan are minor characters in this classic novel:	[1] Lolita [2] To the Lighthouse [3] Ulysses [4] Dr. Zhivago [5] Nausea	ANSWER TO Q-4 **[1]** John Cleland wrote "Fanny Hill" while in London's Newgate prison. 62%
5 "Golden Girl" Dorothy Zbornak, played by Bea Arthur, first starred in this sitcom:	[1] Maude [2] Gimme a Break [3] All in the Family [4] Mama's Family [5] Flying Nun	ANSWER TO Q-4 **[5]** Every lounge singer on earth sings that song. 89%

27 Most species of this fish have the ability to change colors in response to stimuli:	[1] Shark [2] Sturgeon [3] Grouper [4] Trout [5] Halibut	ANSWER TO Q-26 [3] The classic features her adventures with the Mad Hatter, the Mock Turtle and the Cheshire Cat. 89%
27 Which science is concerned with methods of punishment and prevention of crime?	[1] Penology [2] Forensics [3] Phrenology [4] Recidivism [5] Phytography	ANSWER TO Q-26 [5] When the stick-in pieces were deemed unsafe, real potatoes were replaced with the plastic spuds. 47%
27 Which of the great lakes is farthest east?	[1] Lake Superior [2] Lake Huron [3] Lake Erie [4] Lake Michigan [5] Lake Ontario	ANSWER TO Q-26 [3] A heliotrope is a kind of plant that follows the sun. 71%
27 Which body of water does not border Africa?	[1] Mediterranean Sea [2] Gulf of Guinea [3] Mozambique Channel [4] Bay of Biscay [5] Red Sea	ANSWER TO Q-26 [4] A cooper makes and repairs barrels; they're not much in demand these days. 71%
27 "Faust," "Iphigenia in Tauris" and "The Sorrows of Young Werther" are works by:	[1] Thomas Mann [2] Heinrich Heine [3] Alexander Pushkin [4] Franz Kafka [5] Goethe	ANSWER TO Q-26 [3] Sportswriters and sportscasters are polled each year and vote for the winner. 89%

4 The tiny space between two nerve cells is called a:

[1] Dendrite
[2] Synapse
[3] Motrin
[4] Abalin
[5] Myelin sheath

ANSWER TO Q-3

[1] A stage and movie actor in character roles, he played a bit part in son John's "Maltese Falcon."
65%

---

4 Belgium borders all of these countries except:

[1] France
[2] Netherlands
[3] Germany
[4] Denmark
[5] Luxembourg

ANSWER TO Q-3

[4] "Ivanhoe" is set in the middle ages, but the historical novel dates from the late 1800's.
53%

---

4 Who lives in the Hundred Acre Wood?

[1] Peter Rabbit
[2] Babar
[3] Beauty and the Beast
[4] Horton the Who
[5] Winnie the Pooh

ANSWER TO Q-3

[1] Debuting in 1971, it was the first TV comedy to deal with social issues that were taboo.
98%

---

4 Which sex classic was written while in prison to pay the author's debts?

[1] Fanny Hill
[2] Tropic of Cancer
[3] Casanova's Memoirs
[4] Fear of Flying
[5] Lady Chatterley's Lover

ANSWER TO Q-3

[1] The macula is the central part of the retina that gives us our sharp vision.
67%

---

4 The line, "Play it, Sam," refers to what song in the classic movie "Casablanca"?

[1] Time After Time
[2] Some Sunday Morning
[3] Endlessly
[4] More & More
[5] As Time Goes By

ANSWER TO Q-3

[3] Although Tracy and Hepburn were involved for years, he never divorced his wife.
78%

28 Frank Shorter became the first American to win this Olympic event in 64 years in 1972:	[1] Marathon [2] Weightlifting [3] Discus throw [4] Giant slalom [5] Biathlon	ANSWER TO Q-27 [3] Most groupers also undergo a sex change from male to female during their lifespan. 35%
28 Each of these is a type of tea, except:	[1] Darjeeling [2] Lapsang souchong [3] Oolong [4] Keemun [5] Ouagadougou	ANSWER TO Q-27 [1] The root word of this term means to pay, atone or compensate. 81%
28 Which word means next to the last?	[1] Foregoing [2] Proximate [3] Terminal [4] Penultimate [5] Preeminent	ANSWER TO Q-27 [5] The Saint Lawrence Seaway opened Lake Ontario to oceangoing vessels in 1959. 68%
28 Which is not associated with the legendary King Arthur?	[1] Atlantis [2] Camelot [3] Excalibur [4] Merlin [5] Avalon	ANSWER TO Q-27 [4] The Bay of Biscay lies off the northern shores of France and Spain. 57%
28 Rick Wright, David Gilmour, Nick Mason & Roger Waters were the original members of:	[1] Fleetwood Mac [2] Roxy Music [3] Pink Floyd [4] Yes [5] The Kinks	ANSWER TO Q-27 [5] Goethe is considered Germany's greatest poet. 46%

3 What relationship does Walter Huston have to Anjelica Huston?	[1] Grandfather [2] Brother [3] Husband [4] Father [5] Adopted son	ANSWER TO Q-2 **[4]** Speed has been racing professionally since 1983, and has earned close to $2 million. 79%
3 Which work was not written during medieval times?	[1] Reynard the Fox [2] Everyman [3] The Song of Roland [4] Ivanhoe [5] Tristan and Isolde	ANSWER TO Q-2 **[4]** Mr. Piszek used his partner, Mr. Paul, as the inspiration for his frozen fish line. 76%
3 Where would you hear the phrases "Stifle yourself," "Meathead," and "Dingbat"?	[1] All in the Family [2] Cheers [3] Beverly Hillbillies [4] Taxi [5] Green Acres	ANSWER TO Q-2 **[4]** Remembered for its identification of the four basic freedoms, it was signed in 1941. 56%
3 Which part of the body contains the macula?	[1] Eye [2] Ear [3] Nose [4] Mouth [5] Throat	ANSWER TO Q-2 **[5]** The stories usually involve legendary events and historical personalities. 79%
3 All these screen couples were married in real life except:	[1] Gable - Lombard [2] Olivier - Vivien Leigh [3] Tracy - Hepburn [4] Bogart - Bacall [5] Fairbanks - Pickford	ANSWER TO Q-2 **[2]** Presbyopia is a condition that causes nearby objects to appear blurred. 56%

29 In which Humphrey Bogart film does he play a salty captain of a small riverboat?	[1] The Harder They Fall [2] Key Largo [3] To Have and Have Not [4] The African Queen [5] Caine Mutiny	ANSWER TO Q-28 **[1]** No American runner has won the Olympic marathon since Shorter did it in 1972. 79%
29 During the Revolutionary War, what was a "Tory"?	[1] American saboteur [2] Navy admiral [3] Sailing vessel [4] British supporter [5] Type of rifle	ANSWER TO Q-28 **[5]** Ouagadougou is the capital of the west African nation of Burkina Faso. 69%
29 Which designation would apply to Peter Paul Rubens?	[1] Flemish master [2] Balkan liberator [3] Nordic seafarer [4] Prussian martinet [5] German wunderkind	ANSWER TO Q-28 **[4]** A "penult" is the second to the last syllable of a word. 69%
29 Which is not part of an airplane?	[1] Fuselage [2] Bilge [3] Rudder [4] Stabilizer [5] Landing gear	ANSWER TO Q-28 **[1]** Atlantis was a mythological island that was swallowed in an earthquake. 81%
29 Which wine is not chilled before serving?	[1] Blush [2] White [3] Red [4] Rose [5] Champagne	ANSWER TO Q-28 **[3]** Their 1973 album "The Dark Side of the Moon" has been on the charts longer than any other. 68%

2 Each of the following are real names of people. Which one is the pro race car driver?	[1] Mike Quick [2] Howard Fast [3] Mac Speedie [4] Lake Speed [5] Jonathan Swift	ANSWER TO Q-1 **[3]** It can be any drink served with lots of finely crushed ice. 56%
2 Which of these company figureheads was not a real person?	[1] Mama Celeste [2] Jim Beam [3] Philip Morris [4] Mrs. Paul [5] Sara Lee	ANSWER TO Q-1 **[3]** It is about the murder of St. Thomas à Becket. 57%
2 He was a signer of the human rights document, "The Atlantic Charter":	[1] Woodrow Wilson [2] Karl Marx [3] Henry the Navigator [4] Winston Churchill [5] Pope John Paul II	ANSWER TO Q-1 **[1]** Moore took over the role from Sean Connery with this 1973 release. 67%
2 Which type of poem always tells a story?	[1] Ode [2] Sonnet [3] Limerick [4] Couplet [5] Ballad	ANSWER TO Q-1 **[1]** In his world, the animals run the zoo. 78%
2 Which part of the body is affected by the condition presbyopia?	[1] Brain [2] Eye [3] Ear [4] Heart [5] Lung	ANSWER TO Q-1 **[2]** Harriet Stowe claimed that her book was written by God. 79%

30 When the body can't supply sufficient blood to its tissues, the result is:

[1] Arteriosclerosis
[2] Heart attack
[3] Shock
[4] Hypertension
[5] Sciatica

ANSWER TO Q-29

[4] Humphrey Bogart spars with prim and proper Katharine Hepburn in this adventure classic.

92%

---

30 The scientific study of insects is known as:

[1] Ophthalmology
[2] Etymology
[3] Ichthyology
[4] Paleontology
[5] Entomology

ANSWER TO Q-29

[4] The term is now used to describe members of the Conservative party in Britain.

88%

---

30 The tonsure is a kind of haircut associated with:

[1] Gangsta rappers
[2] 18th century courtiers
[3] Hippies
[4] Military personnel
[5] Monks

ANSWER TO Q-29

[1] This grouping refers to the great 16th and 17th century painters of Flanders.

89%

---

30 "Danny Boy" was the theme song for this television show:

[1] You Bet Your Life
[2] My Favorite Husband
[3] Make Room for Daddy
[4] Father Knows Best
[5] Leave It to Beaver

ANSWER TO Q-29

[2] The bilge is the rounded portion of a ship's bottom.

81%

---

30 Harry Blackstone, Jr., Doug Henning, and Siegfried Fischbecker are names of famous:

[1] Psychics
[2] Disc jockeys
[3] Magicians
[4] Industrialists
[5] World War I pilots

ANSWER TO Q-29

[3] Red wine should be served cool or at room temperature (65 to 68 degrees).

81%

1 A frappe is a beverage that always contains:	[1] Fruit [2] Vanilla [3] Crushed ice [4] Rum [5] Mint leaves	Turn to the top frame on the next left hand page for the correct answer and the next question.
1 Which T.S. Eliot work is a play?	[1] The Wasteland [2] The Four Quartets [3] Murder in the Cathedral [4] Ash Wednesday [5] The Hollow Men	Turn to the second frame on the next left hand page for the correct answer and the next question.
1 What was the first James Bond film in which Roger Moore played the title character?	[1] Live and Let Die [2] Diamonds are Forever [3] Never Say Never Again [4] The Spy Who Loved Me [5] Thunderball	Turn to the middle frame on the next left hand page for the correct answer and the next question.
1 Which cartoonist created "The Far Side"?	[1] Gary Larson [2] Bill Watterson [3] Johnny Hart [4] Berke Breathed [5] Matt Groening	Turn to the fourth frame on the next left hand page for the correct answer and the next question.
1 The death of Little Eva and Eliza being pursued over the ice floes are scenes from this book:	[1] David Copperfield [2] Uncle Tom's Cabin [3] The Scarlet Letter [4] Crime and Punishment [5] Les Miserables	Turn to the bottom frame on the next left hand page for the correct answer and the next question.

American Lit

GAME NUMBER 6

ANSWER TO Q-30

[3] Shock can be fatal and immediate emergency treatment is essential.

69%

Family Fare

GAME NUMBER 24

ANSWER TO Q-30

[5] Over one million species of insects have been identified with more discovered each year.

81%

Foreign Food

GAME NUMBER 42

ANSWER TO Q-30

[5] The crown of the head is shaved with a rim of lower hair remaining.

71%

Gambling

GAME NUMBER 60

ANSWER TO Q-30

[3] It starred Danny Thomas as the nightclub singer and comedian, Danny Williams.

75%

Sports

GAME NUMBER 78

ANSWER TO Q-30

[3] Siegfried Fischbecker, with his assistant Roy Horn, was known for making large animals disappear.

81%

GAME NUMBER 14

ANSWER TO Q-10

[5] He's been credited with hits such as "Student Bodies" and "Death of a Gunfighter."

32%

GAME NUMBER 32

ANSWER TO Q-10

[4] All his tragedies had unity of time and place, violence, bombast, revenge and ghosts.

21%

GAME NUMBER 50

ANSWER TO Q-10

[2] Kirk defeats the Gorn captain in a duel, but spares the helpless enemy's life at the end.

67%

GAME NUMBER 68

ANSWER TO Q-10

[4] This martial art is a form of basic jujitsu that stresses blows with the side of the hand.

43%

GAME NUMBER 86

ANSWER TO Q-10

[1] The body's fat is deposited as tiny droplets that later fuse to form one large drop.

56%

1 Which famous American author has been a recluse since the 1960's?	[1] E.L. Doctorow [2] J.D. Salinger [3] Tom Wolfe [4] Hunter S. Thompson [5] Saul Bellow	Turn to the top frame on the next right hand page for the correct answer and the next question.
1 Which television family made the hit recording "I Think I Love You"?	[1] Huxtable [2] Brady [3] Partridge [4] Cleaver [5] Nielson	Turn to the second frame on the next right hand page for the correct answer and the next question.
1 What is the primary ingredient of the famous German dish sauerbraten?	[1] Sausage [2] Pork loin [3] Sauerkraut [4] Potatoes [5] Beef roast	Turn to the middle frame on the next right hand page for the correct answer and the next question.
1 "Shoot the Moon" is a term used in this card game:	[1] Hearts [2] Poker [3] Bridge [4] Pinochle [5] Gin rummy	Turn to the fourth frame on the next right hand page for the correct answer and the next question.
1 Which National League stadium has the deepest center field?	[1] Joe Robbie Stadium [2] Mile High Stadium [3] Wrigley Field [4] Three Rivers Stadium [5] Busch Stadium	Turn to the bottom frame on the next right hand page for the correct answer and the next question.

10 This pseudonym is used by producers when a film is a disaster & they wish anonymity:	[1] Rex Reed [2] Brooks De Soto [3] Seasil B. De Mille [4] Wilma Flintstone [5] Allen Smithee	ANSWER TO Q-9 [2] He was the prime mover in the discovery of plutonium, a key element in atomic bombs. 32%
10 Tragedies of Marlowe & Shakespeare followed conventions established by this Roman:	[1] Cicero [2] Euripides [3] Octavius [4] Seneca [5] Hortensius	ANSWER TO Q-9 [1] Betty Friedan's work is also referred to as the "Uncle Tom's Cabin of the women's movement." 66%
10 On which T.V. show did a race of lizard-like aliens called "Gorn" appear?	[1] Alf [2] Star Trek [3] Mork & Mindy [4] Land of the Lost [5] Space: 1999	ANSWER TO Q-9 [2] This is why such importance is given to the Monegasque kings' production of heirs. 23%
10 Translated to English, this Japanese word means "an empty hand":	[1] Hara-kiri [2] Sumo [3] Samurai [4] Karate [5] Mitsubishi	ANSWER TO Q-9 [1] Kane is the sheriff who saves a small town from villainous thugs in the classic film. 45%
10 The fatty connective tissue in your body is called:	[1] Adipose tissue [2] Arachnoid membrane [3] Alimentary tissue [4] Nephron membrane [5] Bile tissue	ANSWER TO Q-9 [4] Light from distant stars shifts to lower wavelengths like a siren does when moving away. 52%

2 Which novel was not written by Saul Bellow?	[1] Henderson the Rain King [2] Herzog [3] Humboldt's Gift [4] Seize the Day [5] Portnoy's Complaint	ANSWER TO Q-1 **[2]** 1951's "The Catcher in the Rye" is his only novel. Some people believe that J.D. Salinger is in fact author Thomas Pynchon. 71%
2 Which animated film is not a Walt Disney production?	[1] Beauty and the Beast [2] Fantasia [3] Lady and the Tramp [4] Thumbelina [5] Cinderella	ANSWER TO Q-1 **[3]** Except for David Cassidy and Shirley Jones, studio musicians sang on the Partridge Family records. 81%
2 Which words on a French menu tell you that the food is topped with cheese?	[1] Dijonnaise [2] Au poivre [3] Au gratin [4] Amandine [5] Au oignons	ANSWER TO Q-1 **[5]** The meat is marinated for 2-3 days in a blend of red wine and spices before it is cooked. 65%
2 Which of these poker hands ranks highest?	[1] Four of a kind [2] Straight [3] Full house [4] Two pair [5] Straight flush	ANSWER TO Q-1 **[1]** It means to win all the counting cards. 81%
2 These two teams played in the first World Series:	[1] Pittsburgh-Boston [2] Boston-New York [3] Cincinnati-New York [4] Detroit-Philadelphia [5] Detroit-Chicago	ANSWER TO Q-1 **[2]** It is 423 feet to straightaway center at Mile High Stadium. 46%

9 Glenn T. Seaborg was a key player in this field of science:

[1] Astronomy
[2] Physics
[3] Engineering
[4] Mathematics
[5] Biology

ANSWER TO Q-8
[4] A flageolet is similar in range and tone to a piccolo.
23%

---

9 This 1963 Betty Friedan book is credited with reviving the U.S. women's movement:

[1] Feminine Mystique
[2] The Woman's Room
[3] Living Contradictions
[4] Significant Sisters
[5] Being a Woman

ANSWER TO Q-8
[2] Cleveland actually won the popular vote in 1888 but lost the election in the Electoral College.
41%

---

9 By a 1919 agreement, a vacancy in its crown forces Monaco to become a protectorate of:

[1] India
[2] France
[3] Belgium
[4] England
[5] Italy

ANSWER TO Q-8
[5] Dirhams are hard to come by in Morocco; the gross national product runs at about $510 per capita.
32%

---

9 Will Kane is the name of the western sheriff in:

[1] High Noon
[2] My Darling Clementine
[3] Stagecoach
[4] The Virginian
[5] Unforgiven

ANSWER TO Q-8
[4] A 1903 "revolt" forcibly secured U.S. rights to build the canal, which was finished in 1914.
34%

---

9 In the field of astronomy, "Hubble's Law" mathematically expresses:

[1] A star's rotation
[2] The orbit of planets
[3] Gravity between 2 bodies
[4] The expanding universe
[5] The speed of light

ANSWER TO Q-8
[5] Like bones, teeth are made of calcium.
65%

3 This literary character was murdered because he protected Daisy Buchanan:	[1] Tom Joad [2] Doc Burton [3] Nick Adams [4] Jay Gatsby [5] Jean Valjean	ANSWER TO Q-2 [5] "Portnoy's Complaint" is by Philip Roth. 69%
3 Which of these popular children's book characters is a big red dog?	[1] Clifford [2] Babar [3] Curious George [4] Charlotte [5] Magellan	ANSWER TO Q-2 [4] "Thumbelina" is a Warner Bros. production. 81%
3 What are cepe, porcini, boletus and shitaki?	[1] Mushrooms [2] Cold cuts [3] Sweet breads [4] Rice [5] Pastas	ANSWER TO Q-2 [3] The others mean with mustard, pepper, almonds and onions. 68%
3 Which of these expressions did not originate in the world of gambling?	[1] Follow suit [2] Go for broke [3] Overboard [4] No dice [5] Above board	ANSWER TO Q-2 [5] A straight flush (five cards of the same suit in sequence) defeats four of a kind. 79%
3 Which pitcher allowed the most grand slams in baseball history?	[1] Jerry Reuss [2] Nolan Ryan [3] Wilbur Wood [4] Jerry Koosman [5] Milt Pappas	ANSWER TO Q-2 [1] In 1903, the Boston Pilgrims beat the Pirates 5 games to 3 in a best of nine series. 57%

8 What kind of musical instrument is a flageolet?

[1] Irish harp
[2] Steel drum
[3] Mouth organ
[4] Small flute
[5] Recorder

ANSWER TO Q-7

[5] Born in 1917, J.F.K. would be the oldest, with Marilyn Monroe next with a 1926 birthdate.

88%

---

8 Who won the presidency over Grover Cleveland in 1888, then lost it to him in 1892?

[1] Woodrow Wilson
[2] Benjamin Harrison
[3] John Adams
[4] Andrew Johnson
[5] William Taft

ANSWER TO Q-7

[4] A patron of the arts, Athens reached its zenith during his 14-year reign.

45%

---

8 Which country's basic unit of currency is the dirham?

[1] Bolivia
[2] Thailand
[3] Belize
[4] Liechtenstein
[5] Morocco

ANSWER TO Q-7

[4] The city is the setting of "Tom Sawyer" and three other books including "Huckleberry Finn."

56%

---

8 Which event took place the same year that World War I began?

[1] Perry reaches North Pole
[2] Wright brothers' flight
[3] San Francisco earthquake
[4] Panama Canal opened
[5] McKinley shot

ANSWER TO Q-7

[5] The vitreous humor is the gelatinous fluid that passes light from lens to retina.

68%

---

8 All of these are evolutionary adaptations of epidermis (skin) except:

[1] Horns
[2] Hooves
[3] Hair
[4] Feathers
[5] Teeth

ANSWER TO Q-7

[3] Highly photoelectric, it may be put in plasma propulsion engines for deep space exploration.

34%

4 "King Rat" is based on this author's experience as a Japanese P.O.W. in World War II:	[1] James Clavell [2] Gore Vidal [3] Herman Wouk [4] Norman Mailer [5] Joseph Heller	ANSWER TO Q-3 [4] Daisy runs over a woman while driving his car, and the woman's husband shoots Gatsby in error. 58%
4 All of these were children of TV's large Walton family except:	[1] John-Boy [2] Ben [3] Mary Ellen [4] Robin [5] Elizabeth	ANSWER TO Q-3 [1] The others are an elephant, monkey, spider and dragon, respectively. 57%
4 What gives Russian borscht its red color?	[1] Strawberries [2] Tomato sauce [3] Food coloring [4] Duck's blood [5] Beets	ANSWER TO Q-3 [1] Boletus, porcini and cepe are from Europe but shitaki is an oriental favorite. 68%
4 Which boxer testified to the U.S. Senate that he purposely lost a fight?	[1] Gene Tunney [2] Jake Lamotta [3] Sonny Liston [4] Rocky Graziano [5] Max Schmeling	ANSWER TO Q-3 [3] The board here refers to the sides of ships. In storms, ship parts were thrown overboard. 79%
4 Addressing his chronic hemorrhoids, he quipped, "My problems are all behind me":	[1] George Halas [2] Bob Uecker [3] Marv Albert [4] George Brett [5] John McEnroe	ANSWER TO Q-3 [2] Ryan gave up 10 grand slams during his career. 57%

7 Which celebrity would be oldest if he or she were alive today?	[1] Marilyn Monroe [2] Elvis Presley [3] Martin Luther King [4] James Dean [5] John F. Kennedy	ANSWER TO Q-6 **[1]** The expression comes from a Greek story about a warrior who traded gold armor for brass. 43%
7 The Athenian statesman Pericles was responsible for:	[1] Condemning Socrates [2] First Olympic Games [3] Starting Persian wars [4] Building the Parthenon [5] Destroying Sparta	ANSWER TO Q-6 **[1]** Policies like FDR's New Deal were in place from 1933 until the Reagan era of the 1980's. 45%
7 The town St. Petersburg, Mississippi is a popular setting in the books of this writer:	[1] William Faulkner [2] Truman Capote [3] Tennessee Williams [4] Mark Twain [5] Flannery O'Connor	ANSWER TO Q-6 **[2]** Spinal manipulation was widely used by ancient Egyptians, Hindus and Chinese. 45%
7 Where in the human body is the vitreous humor located?	[1] Elbow [2] Throat [3] Lower back [4] Stomach [5] Eye	ANSWER TO Q-6 **[2]** They're thought to be the people who etched huge, linear patterns into the Peruvian mesa. 34%
7 It reacts explosively with water, and is used in T.V. cameras & atomic clocks:	[1] Cobalt [2] Cetyl alcohol [3] Cesium [4] Ether [5] Arsenic	ANSWER TO Q-6 **[2]** Chamberlain was the British prime minister who preceded Winston Churchill. 54%

5 Which author is not primarily a writer of science fiction?

[1] Arthur C. Clarke
[2] Isaac Asimov
[3] Aldous Huxley
[4] Robert Heinlein
[5] Frank Herbert

ANSWER TO Q-4

[1] Subsequent works such as "Shogun" and "Noble House" are historical novels set in Asia.
57%

---

5 In which city can a family visit the Experimental Prototype Community of Tomorrow?

[1] Dallas
[2] Paris
[3] Orlando
[4] Seattle
[5] Amsterdam

ANSWER TO Q-4

[4] The remaining three Walton children were Jim-Bob, Erin and Jason.
81%

---

5 Miso, a basic ingredient in Japanese cooking, is made from:

[1] Seaweed
[2] Horseradish
[3] Fermented rice
[4] Soybean paste
[5] Mung bean

ANSWER TO Q-4

[5] The flavorful beet soup is always served with a hefty dollop of sour cream.
79%

---

5 Most gambling visitors to Atlantic City and Las Vegas pour their money into:

[1] Blackjack
[2] Roulette
[3] Slot machines
[4] Keno
[5] Craps

ANSWER TO Q-4

[2] There is specu- lation that Lamotta was paid off by gamblers to lose the fight to Billy Fox.
57%

---

5 This major league pitcher never gave up a grand slam in his career:

[1] Nolan Ryan
[2] Jim Palmer
[3] Bob Gibson
[4] Tom Seaver
[5] Catfish Hunter

ANSWER TO Q-4

[4] He actually had to miss some World Series games due to the severe pain they caused him.
46%

6 A diomedian swap is an exchange in which ___ benefits.	[1] Only one side [2] Both parties [3] No one [4] An outside party [5] The underdog	ANSWER TO Q-5 **[2]** They repopulated the world by throwing stones that turned into men and women. 34%
6 According to Keynes, the way to end an economic depression is to increase:	[1] Government spending [2] The money supply [3] Tax rates [4] Interest rates [5] Import tariffs	ANSWER TO Q-5 **[4]** This stage is one undergone by certain other insects during an "incomplete" cycle. 54%
6 Canadian D.D. Palmer redeveloped which ancient medical treatment?	[1] Acupuncture [2] Chiropractics [3] Homeopathy [4] Herbalism [5] Reflexology	ANSWER TO Q-5 **[4]** Deposing his father Uranus, he ruled the world until overthrown himself by son Zeus. 56%
6 The ancient culture of the Nazcas was located in present day:	[1] Mexico [2] Peru [3] Egypt [4] India [5] Greenland	ANSWER TO Q-5 **[5]** The famed Welsh poet and "tortured artist" died at 39 after drinking 18 straight whiskey shots. 43%
6 Which man could not possibly have affected the outcome of World War I?	[1] Georges Clemenceau [2] Neville Chamberlain [3] David Lloyd George [4] Woodrow Wilson [5] Kaiser Wilhelm II	ANSWER TO Q-5 **[3]** Making up 8% of the country's population, they are self-sufficient and culturally unique. 67%

6 This classic novel by Thomas Wolfe describes the childhood and youth of Eugene Gant:	[1] The Long Voyage Home [2] Look Homeward, Angel [3] Homeward Bound [4] You Can't Go Home Again [5] Harvest Home	ANSWER TO Q-5 [3] Although Huxley's best known book is "Brave New World," most of his work is not sci-fi. 57%
6 Kermit the Frog was the master of ceremonies on:	[1] Sesame Street [2] The Muppet Show [3] Captain Kangaroo [4] Winky Dink and You [5] Howdy Doody	ANSWER TO Q-5 [3] The EPCOT Center and Walt Disney World attract families from all over the world. 81%
6 What do Israelis call light dumplings served with a savory filling?	[1] Polenta [2] Knishes [3] Matzo balls [4] Bagels [5] Challah	ANSWER TO Q-5 [4] The others are used in dashi stock, wasabi, saki and cellophane noodles. 68%
6 A pool in which the bettor must pick the horses to come in 1st & 2nd in a race is called:	[1] Daily Double [2] Parimutuel [3] Trifecta [4] Exacta [5] Over-under	ANSWER TO Q-5 [3] Players are drawn to the slot machines by the exciting sounds of coins falling into the aluminum payoff trays. 68%
6 Who was the only American to win a gold medal at the 1968 Winter Olympics?	[1] Peter Mueller [2] Peggy Fleming [3] Bill Toomey [4] Dick Button [5] Al Oerter	ANSWER TO Q-5 [2] Palmer was a 20-game winner 8 times, earned 3 Cy Youngs and compiled a 268-152 record. 54%

5 According to Greek myth, ____ and his wife were the only mortals who survived the deluge.	[1] Pygmalion [2] Deucalion [3] Uranus [4] Midas [5] Odysseus	ANSWER TO Q-4 **[3]** Twain became cynical after the tragic deaths of his wife and two daughters. 43%
5 A butterfly undergoes four stages during its metamorphosis; which is not one of them?	[1] Egg [2] Larva [3] Pupa [4] Nymph [5] Imago	ANSWER TO Q-4 **[4]** He split the 1912 Republican vote by opposing incumbent William H. Taft. 34%
5 The youngest Titan, he is the Greek equivalent of the Roman god Saturn:	[1] Hades [2] Icarus [3] Achilles [4] Cronus [5] Poseidon	ANSWER TO Q-4 **[2]** Influenced by French Romanticism, his work included patriotic "Le Vieux Soldat Canadien." 21%
5 Who wrote the quasi-autobiographical work "Portrait of the Artist as a Young Dog"?	[1] James Joyce [2] Woody Allen [3] James Thurber [4] Norman Mailer [5] Dylan Thomas	ANSWER TO Q-4 **[5]** His "White on White" series of works is the best example of this semi-geometrical style. 21%
5 The Maori are descendants of ancient Polynesians who canoed to this land:	[1] Hungary [2] Japan [3] New Zealand [4] Aleutian Islands [5] Mexico	ANSWER TO Q-4 **[2]** Yuri Gagarin made the world's first manned spaceflight during the Soviet Vostok program. 67%

7 The characters in this Pulitzer Prize-winning novel include Celie, Mister, Harpo and Shug:	[1] Song of Solomon [2] To Kill a Mockingbird [3] Native Son [4] The Color Purple [5] The Reivers	ANSWER TO Q-6 **[2]** A novelist with intense individualism, he wrote it as a cruel portrait of town and family. 57%
7 Which "Sesame Street" character makes his home in a garbage can?	[1] Oscar [2] Cookie Monster [3] Ernie [4] Grover [5] Bert	ANSWER TO Q-6 **[2]** Jim Henson and company created the lovable puppets that made TV history. 92%
7 What is the mainstay of Cuban cooking?	[1] Black beans [2] Bulghur wheat [3] Corn [4] Beef [5] Sour cream	ANSWER TO Q-6 **[2]** The most common fillings are cheese or a potato-onion mixture. 46%
7 The most popular casino table game is:	[1] Craps [2] Baccarat [3] Roulette [4] Blackjack [5] Poker	ANSWER TO Q-6 **[4]** The trifecta is picking 3 horses to finish 1-2-3, and the daily double is picking 2 horses to win. 68%
7 Who was the first NHL defenseman to win a scoring championship?	[1] Paul Coffey [2] Larry Robinson [3] Bobby Orr [4] Rod Langway [5] Ray Bourque	ANSWER TO Q-6 **[2]** Peggy Fleming won the women's individual figure skating gold medal. 79%

4 What witty writer's later books, such as "What is Man?" show his growing pessimism?	[1] Jonathan Swift [2] Lewis Carroll [3] Mark Twain [4] Charles Dickens [5] Voltaire	ANSWER TO Q-3 **[3]** The ides are on the 13th day of the other months. 21%
4 Which U.S. president headed the "Bull Moose," or Progressive, party?	[1] William McKinley [2] Abraham Lincoln [3] Woodrow Wilson [4] Theodore Roosevelt [5] Ulysses S. Grant	ANSWER TO Q-3 **[2]** He was in the Detroit eatery on July 30, 1975; now check the end zone in the Meadowlands. 43%
4 Octave Cremazie is known as the father of ____.	[1] The harpsichord [2] French-Canadian poetry [3] Modern Hungary [4] Cell biology [5] The theory of evolution	ANSWER TO Q-3 **[1]** Some Cree adopted the plains buffalo culture; the Woodland Cree kept alive the deer culture. 32%
4 The term "Suprematist" is associated with this founding father of abstract art:	[1] Salvador Dali [2] Vincent Van Gogh [3] Pablo Picasso [4] Andy Warhol [5] Kasimir Malevich	ANSWER TO Q-3 **[5]** Sandburg's portrait of his hero of democracy won the Pulitzer Prize. 45%
4 Soyuz, Vostok, Salyut and Venera are all names of:	[1] Types of sewing stitches [2] Soviet space programs [3] Polish beer festivals [4] Egyptian goddesses [5] Black Sea islets	ANSWER TO Q-3 **[4]** An adept swimmer, the Asian elephant needs to eat 300 pounds of feed a day. 50%

8 This writer was with the Los Angeles police department for 14 years:	[1] Joseph Wambaugh [2] Lawrence Sanders [3] Robert Ludlum [4] John D. Macdonald [5] Elmore Leonard	ANSWER TO Q-7 **[4]** This moving novel takes the form of a series of letters between Celie and her sister Nettie. 76%
8 Which "G" rated film contains a strong message about the environment?	[1] The Little Mermaid [2] Field of Dreams [3] Ferngully [4] Willow [5] Moonstruck	ANSWER TO Q-7 **[1]** Oscar the Grouch is a favorite on the multiple Emmy-winning program. 99%
8 What Spanish rice dish includes meat, seafood, veggies and almost anything else?	[1] Risotto [2] Kedgeree [3] Gazpacho [4] Caldo gallego [5] Paella	ANSWER TO Q-7 **[1]** A blend of spicy black beans and rice is found on every Cuban table. 46%
8 Who was the only White Sox baseball player banned in the 1919 "Black Sox" scandal?	[1] Eddie Collins [2] Ray Schalk [3] Nemo Leibold [4] Joe Jackson [5] Red Faber	ANSWER TO Q-7 **[4]** The object is to get as close to or equal to 21, without going over. 67%
8 The first gymnast to record a perfect "10" in the Olympics came from this country:	[1] Russia [2] China [3] Bulgaria [4] Romania [5] Japan	ANSWER TO Q-7 **[3]** The leading defenseman from 1968 through 1975 was leading scorer in 1970 and 1975. 52%

3 In the Julian Calendar, "ides" fall on the 15th of any of these months except:	[1] March [2] May [3] December [4] October [5] July	ANSWER TO Q-2 [2] The rape victim central to "Sanctuary" appears many years afterward in "Requiem for a Nun." 33%
3 What missing person was last seen at the Machus Red Fox Restaurant?	[1] Charles Lindbergh, Jr. [2] Jimmy Hoffa [3] Fatty Arbuckle [4] Bruce Lee [5] Jim Morrison	ANSWER TO Q-2 [4] Related to sharks, some manta rays grow as large as 22 feet long, and weigh 3,000 pounds. 21%
3 Which of these Indian tribes originally inhabited the Canadian province of Manitoba?	[1] Cree [2] Seminole [3] Shawnee [4] Iroquois [5] Apache	ANSWER TO Q-2 [5] Considering his various arrests, including one on a rape charge, the book is aptly titled. 67%
3 Poet Carl Sandburg wrote a six-volume biography of this great American:	[1] Andrew Jackson [2] John D. Rockefeller [3] Mark Twain [4] Henry Ford [5] Abraham Lincoln	ANSWER TO Q-2 [4] When Daniel survived, King Darius ordered the tricksters into the den themselves. 54%
3 Which animal cries when in distress?	[1] Black rhinoceros [2] Gorilla [3] Red kangaroo [4] Asian elephant [5] Humpback whale	ANSWER TO Q-2 [1] In Judeo-Christian tradition, the Sabbath is a day of the week set aside for rest and worship. 43%

9 Stephen King's novel, "The Tommy-knockers," concerns which of these phenomena?	[1] Poltergeists [2] Extraterrestrials [3] Demonic possession [4] Vampires [5] Werewolves	ANSWER TO Q-8 [1] He tells of life behind the badge in "The Blue Knight," "The Choirboys," & "The New Centurions." 68%
9 Which of these books by Dr. Seuss was written for adults?	[1] You're Only Old Once [2] The Cat in the Hat [3] Horton Hatches the Egg [4] Happy Birthday To You [5] Yertle the Turtle	ANSWER TO Q-8 [3] The animated film about a rain forest beset by pollution teaches while it entertains. 72%
9 Which Middle Eastern food is a light paste made from toasted sesame seeds?	[1] Tahini [2] Basmati [3] Phyllo [4] Ghee [5] Tabouleh	ANSWER TO Q-8 [5] The name "paella" refers to the big round pan in which the dish is cooked. 79%
9 Immortal-ized in song, he was the English gambler who "broke the bank at Monte Carlo":	[1] James Bond [2] Casanova [3] Damon Runyan [4] Blackie Sherrod [5] Charles Wells	ANSWER TO Q-8 [4] Many feel that Joe Jackson's play in the Series was proof that he was trying not to lose. 58%
9 Which NBA player won both the Most Valuable Player award and Sixth Man award?	[1] Bob McAdoo [2] Dave Cowens [3] Kevin McHale [4] Bill Walton [5] Wes Unseld	ANSWER TO Q-8 [4] Nadia Comaneci of Romania was awarded seven perfect tens at the 1976 Montreal games. 91%

261

2 "Requiem for a Nun" and "Sanctuary" are among this author's lesser-known novels:	[1] Ernest Hemingway [2] William Faulkner [3] John Steinbeck [4] F. Scott Fitzgerald [5] Henry James	ANSWER TO Q-1 [5] De Soto became the first European to visit the huge delta mouth in 1541 A.D. 52%
2 Which animal is included in the order Batoidea?	[1] Aphid [2] Ostrich [3] Kangaroo [4] Manta ray [5] Salamander	ANSWER TO Q-1 [3] The 3 goddesses of vengeance, they punished wrongs committed by blood relatives. 21%
2 His 1959 autobiography was titled "My Wicked, Wicked Ways":	[1] Sen. Joseph McCarthy [2] Ernest Hemingway [3] Winston Churchill [4] Walt Disney [5] Errol Flynn	ANSWER TO Q-1 [2] She was born in San Antonio in 1908, and originally named Lucille Le Sueur. 82%
2 In an Old Testament story, King Darius was tricked into testing the faith of:	[1] Solomon [2] Jacob [3] David [4] Daniel [5] Samson	ANSWER TO Q-1 [1] He crossed the Delaware on Christmas night to catch the hated German troops. 21%
2 What is the Hebrew meaning of the word "Sabbath"?	[1] Repose [2] Sanctification [3] Medieval [4] Conflict [5] The last day	ANSWER TO Q-1 [2] Shelley's second wife Mary wrote the strange and terrible saga of the monster Frankenstein. 31%

10 The children's classics "Trumpet of the Swan" and "Charlotte's Web" are by:	[1] P.L. Travers [2] J.R.R. Tolkien [3] L. Frank Baum [4] E.B. White [5] A.A. Milne	ANSWER TO Q-9 **[2]** "Tommyknockers" is less a horror novel and more a science fictional critique of technology. 64%
10 Which family film was based on a story by "James Bond" creator Ian Fleming?	[1] The Little Princess [2] Frosty the Snowman [3] The Gnome-mobile [4] Chitty Chitty Bang Bang [5] 101 Dalmatians	ANSWER TO Q-9 **[1]** "You're Only Old Once" is a humorous message about aging gracefully. 69%
10 In which city are you most likely to be served couscous?	[1] Paris [2] Casablanca [3] Hong Kong [4] Rio de Janeiro [5] Munich	ANSWER TO Q-9 **[1]** The others are rice, flaky dough, melted butter and bulgur wheat. 69%
10 Who was holding aces and eights when he was killed?	[1] Billy the Kid [2] Doc Holiday [3] Wyatt Earp [4] "Wild Bill" Hickok [5] Jesse James	ANSWER TO Q-9 **[5]** In 1891, he broke the 100,000 franc banks at 3 roulette tables and left with over $1 million. 35%
10 Which horse denied Alysheba the Triple Crown by winning the 1987 Belmont Stakes?	[1] Spend A Buck [2] Risen Star [3] Ferdinand [4] Bet Twice [5] Strike the Gold	ANSWER TO Q-9 **[4]** He won the MVP with Portland in 1978 and was best off the bench for Boston in 1986. 35%

1 Spanish explorer Hernan de Soto was the first European to visit the mouth of this river:	[1] Amazon [2] Nile [3] Yellow [4] Congo [5] Mississippi	Turn to the top frame on the next left hand page for the correct answer and the next question.
1 The Furies were born of the blood of ___ when he was castrated by his son, Cronus.	[1] Jupiter [2] Apollo [3] Uranus [4] Bacchus [5] Mercury	Turn to the second frame on the next left hand page for the correct answer and the next question.
1 She took her husband's job as director of Pepsi-Cola after his death in 1959:	[1] Nancy Truman [2] Joan Crawford [3] Helen Wills Moody [4] June Iaccocca [5] Phoenix McCarthy	Turn to the middle frame on the next left hand page for the correct answer and the next question.
1 George Washington's successful 1776 attack on Trenton boosted morale because its target was:	[1] Hessian mercenaries [2] A fleet of tea ships [3] British regulars [4] Tory sympathizers [5] Indians	Turn to the fourth frame on the next left hand page for the correct answer and the next question.
1 This English poet fell from the boat "Ariel" and drowned during a storm on July 8, 1822:	[1] Lord Byron [2] Percy Bysshe Shelley [3] Samuel Taylor Coleridge [4] William Wordsworth [5] John Keats	Turn to the bottom frame on the next left hand page for the correct answer and the next question.

11 Which fictional sleuth was not invented by a U.S. writer?	[1] Sherlock Holmes [2] Philip Marlowe [3] Nero Wolfe [4] Mike Hammer [5] Charlie Chan	ANSWER TO Q-10 **[4]** White incorporated his satirical observations of culture into his novels for children. 69%
11 Based on computer analysis, the space most often landed on in the game Monopoly is:	[1] Illinois Avenue [2] Go [3] Jail [4] Reading Railroad [5] Connecticut Avenue	ANSWER TO Q-10 **[4]** Dick Van Dyke and Sally Ann Howes starred in the film about an inventor and his car. 78%
11 Which of these foods would you not find on a Swedish smorgasbord?	[1] Pickled herring [2] Loin of pork [3] Swedish meatball [4] Welsh rarebit [5] Lingonberry pancakes	ANSWER TO Q-10 **[2]** The steamed, processed wheat dish is usually eaten with the fingers, not with cutlery. 57%
11 Pete Rose was banned for betting on baseball games by which baseball commissioner?	[1] Peter Uebberoth [2] A. Bartlett Giamatti [3] David Stern [4] Fay Vincent [5] Paul Tagliabue	ANSWER TO Q-10 **[4]** Aces and eights are now known as the "Dead Man's Hand." 57%
11 Which NHL team did Bobby Clarke lead to consecutive Stanley Cup titles?	[1] Montreal Canadiens [2] Detroit Red Wings [3] Philadelphia Flyers [4] New York Islanders [5] Boston Bruins	ANSWER TO Q-10 **[4]** Ridden by Craig Perret, Bet Twice outran Alysheba, who finished in fourth place. 46%

BRAIN BUSTER

GAME NUMBER 13

ANSWER TO Q-30

[2] "Cheers" centers on the bar owner Sam and regulars Norm, Cliff, Carla and Frazier.

98%

BRAIN BUSTER

GAME NUMBER 31

ANSWER TO Q-30

[3] Timothy Hutton plays a vengeful graffiti artist fighting to secure his brother's pension.

79%

BRAIN BUSTER

GAME NUMBER 49

ANSWER TO Q-30

[2] The dall is native to Canada, the mouflon to Corsica and the shapu to western Asia.

67%

BRAIN BUSTER

GAME NUMBER 67

ANSWER TO Q-30

[4] Founded immediately after World War I, the influential group lasted until 1929.

56%

BRAIN BUSTER

GAME NUMBER 85

ANSWER TO Q-30

[4] A "laconic" speaker is one who uses few words.

65%

12 Who does not belong on this list of American writers?

[1] E.E. Cummings
[2] D.H. Lawrence
[3] J.D. Salinger
[4] H.L. Mencken
[5] B.F. Skinner

ANSWER TO Q-11

[1] British writer Sir Arthur Conan Doyle created Holmes.

81%

---

12 The award given to the illustrator of the most distinguished picture book for children is:

[1] Christopher Award
[2] Lincoln Prize
[3] Bollingen Prize
[4] Caldecott Medal
[5] Academy Award

ANSWER TO Q-11

[1] "Chance" card directions increase the odds for a player to land on the popular red property, Illinois Avenue.

54%

---

12 Which of these sausages is a favorite in what used to be called Yugoslavia?

[1] Cevapeci
[2] Kielbasa
[3] Knockwurst
[4] Chorizo
[5] Pepperoni

ANSWER TO Q-11

[4] An elaborate buffet, the word smorgasbord means "bread and butter" in Swedish.

79%

---

12 Which college basketball team was photographed in a hot tub with a convicted game-fixer?

[1] Duke
[2] Kentucky
[3] Nevada-Las Vegas
[4] Michigan State
[5] Tulane

ANSWER TO Q-11

[4] Perhaps overtaxed from the arduous ordeal, Giamatti died days after banning Rose.

61%

---

12 The year this player won the league MVP, his team finished in sixth place:

[1] Andre Dawson
[2] Willie McGee
[3] Kirk Gibson
[4] Barry Bonds
[5] Terry Pendleton

ANSWER TO Q-11

[3] The team honored Clarke, who led the Flyers to titles in 1974 and 1975, by retiring his #16 jersey.

61%

30 Which TV show's theme song is titled "Where Everybody Knows Your Name"?	[1] A Different World [2] Cheers [3] Dear John [4] Head of the Class [5] Moonlighting	ANSWER TO Q-29 **[5]** The film is responsible for launching Jack Nicholson into stardom. 68%
30 Which movie does not tell the story of political intrigue, assassination or espionage?	[1] The Eagle has Landed [2] The Eiger Sanction [3] Turk 182 [4] The Day of the Jackal [5] Little Nikita	ANSWER TO Q-29 **[2]** Richard Wright wrote "Black Boy" as well as "Native Son." 59%
30 The dall, mouflon and argali are all types of this animal:	[1] Parrot [2] Sheep [3] Dog [4] Deer [5] Monkey	ANSWER TO Q-29 **[3]** Rinzai stresses the study of enigmatic sayings while Soto concentrates on meditation. 21%
30 The Provincetown Players theater group discovered this major playwright:	[1] Arthur Miller [2] Tennessee Williams [3] Noel Coward [4] Eugene O'Neill [5] Samuel Beckett	ANSWER TO Q-29 **[5]** Also called a plexor, this small hammer with a rubber head is used to test reflexes. 43%
30 Which word does not mean "talkative"?	[1] Garrulous [2] Loquacious [3] Voluble [4] Laconic [5] Effusive	ANSWER TO Q-29 **[1]** The palm has four while the finger has three. 43%

13 Members of the Snopes family appear in several novels and stories by this author:	[1] Edgar Allan Poe [2] William Faulkner [3] John Steinbeck [4] Pearl Buck [5] Stephen King	ANSWER TO Q-12 **[2]** This Englishman's works include "Women in Love," "Lady Chatterly's Lover" and "Sons and Lovers." 62%
13 Which family lived in the "Little House on the Prairie"?	[1] Ingalls [2] Andersons [3] Bundys [4] Hansens [5] Cartwrights	ANSWER TO Q-12 **[4]** The annual award was named in honor of English illustrator Randolph Caldecott. 53%
13 Yorkshire pudding, the British go-along with roast beef, is similar to an American:	[1] Corn fritter [2] Popover [3] Mint jelly [4] Tapioca [5] Dumpling	ANSWER TO Q-12 **[1]** The others are Polish, German, Mexican and Italian sausages. 42%
13 What is the first throw in a craps shooter's turn called?	[1] Point throw [2] Control [3] Natural toss [4] Basic [5] Come-out throw	ANSWER TO Q-12 **[3]** Weeks after the photo, Jerry Tarkanian announced his resignation. 43%
13 What animal is the University of Arkansas football team named for?	[1] Raccoon [2] Tomcat [3] Garter snake [4] Beaver [5] Razorback hog	ANSWER TO Q-12 **[1]** Dawson hit 49 home runs and had 137 RBIs in his 1987 MVP year. 45%

29 The last line of this Nicholson movie was: "We blew it!"	[1] Psych-Out [2] Cuckoo's Nest [3] Studs Lonigan [4] The Missouri Breaks [5] Easy Rider	ANSWER TO Q-28 **[3]** This John Sayles film chronicles the events of the 1919 Black Sox scandal. 79%
29 Which author and work are mismatched?	[1] Baraka - The Dutchman [2] Baldwin - Black Boy [3] Ellison - Invisible Man [4] Wright - Native Son [5] Morrison - Sula	ANSWER TO Q-28 **[2]** The Panama Canal officially opened on August 15, 1914. 56%
29 Rinzai and Soto are the two principal groupings of:	[1] Chinese ideograms [2] Acupuncturists [3] Zen Buddhists [4] Himalayan peaks [5] Martial arts	ANSWER TO Q-28 **[3]** Commonwealths are autonomous states equal in status and united in allegiance to a power. 57%
29 What kind of medical tool is a plessor?	[1] Stethoscope [2] Blood pressure gauge [3] Thermometer [4] Tongue depressor [5] Reflex hammer	ANSWER TO Q-28 **[2]** The poplar's small, flat-stemmed leaves tremble in the slightest breeze. 43%
29 Which body part has eight bones?	[1] Wrist [2] Palm [3] Finger [4] Elbow [5] Ankle	ANSWER TO Q-28 **[2]** The head of the African National Congress has been honored with the Nobel Peace Prize. 82%

14 Leon Uris wrote with depth and clarity about the Jews in "Exodus" and the Arabs in:	[1] Mila 18 [2] The Angry Hills [3] Qb VII [4] Trinity [5] The Haj	ANSWER TO Q-13 **[2]** The Snopeses typify the vicious and inhuman aspects of modern commercial civilization. 65%
14 Which daughter or son of a famous pop vocalist had the #1 hit single in 1977?	[1] Liza Minelli [2] Gary Crosby [3] Natalie Cole [4] Nancy Sinatra [5] Debbie Boone	ANSWER TO Q-13 **[1]** The TV series was based on the "Little House" books by Laura Ingalls Wilder. 91%
14 What is the most essential spice in Hungarian cooking?	[1] Rosemary [2] Oregano [3] Paprika [4] Saffron [5] Curry	ANSWER TO Q-13 **[2]** The British version is baked in the drippings from the roasted meat. 65%
14 Which of these is neither a standard poker game nor a variation of poker?	[1] Five-card draw [2] Acey-deucey [3] Lowball [4] Miami [5] Seven-card stud	ANSWER TO Q-13 **[5]** The shooter can keep "coming out" until he rolls a seven, called a "sevens out." 65%
14 Which first baseman is the only player to wear a helmet while playing at his position?	[1] Will Clark [2] Kent Hrbek [3] Mark Grace [4] Wally Joyner [5] John Olerud	ANSWER TO Q-13 **[5]** The wild hog with the bristly ridge on its back is a product of Ozark legend. 61%

28 Which baseball film is based on a true story?

[1] The Natural
[2] Major League
[3] Eight Men Out
[4] Bull Durham
[5] Bad News Bears

ANSWER TO Q-27
[1] The others were Bashful, Sleepy and Dopey.
94%

---

28 Which event did not occur during the 1930's?

[1] Al Capone convicted
[2] Panama Canal opened
[3] Lindbergh baby kidnapped
[4] Joe Louis becomes champ
[5] Will Rogers killed

ANSWER TO Q-27
[1] The home of the Gordian knot, the city was on the trade route from Troy to Antioch.
31%

---

28 Which classification applies to such countries as Australia and Canada?

[1] Mandate
[2] Protectorate
[3] Commonwealth
[4] Colony
[5] Dependency

ANSWER TO Q-27
[5] Monkeys are divided into two distantly related families: Old World and New World.
78%

---

28 What tree is commonly called "the quaking aspen"?

[1] Oak
[2] American poplar
[3] Blue spruce
[4] Hemlock
[5] Cottonwood

ANSWER TO Q-27
[2] Internal parts and some extremities of an animal are classified as offal.
52%

---

28 This Black leader was imprisoned for 27 years, 19 of them on Robben Island:

[1] Idi Amin Dada
[2] Nelson Mandela
[3] Malcolm X
[4] Steven Biko
[5] Martin Luther King, Jr.

ANSWER TO Q-27
[4] Sequester means to set apart, isolate or segregate.
68%

15 Who is considered the father of American literature?	[1] Washington Irving [2] Booker T. Washington [3] Ralph Waldo Emerson [4] James Fenimore Cooper [5] Benjamin Franklin	ANSWER TO Q-14 [5] He depicts the lives of Palestinian Arabs from World War I to the Suez War of 1956. 55%
15 Where does the Byrd family live on the TV drama, "The Byrds of Paradise"?	[1] Hawaii [2] Jamaica [3] Tahiti [4] Puerto Rico [5] French Riviera	ANSWER TO Q-14 [5] Her "Light Up My Life" followed in the footsteps of father Pat's wholesome songs. 57%
15 Which kind of pancake bread is a favorite in Norway?	[1] Crepes [2] Pita [3] Blini [4] Lefse [5] Tortilla	ANSWER TO Q-14 [3] The best paprika is made in Hungary where the red pepper is tamed to make the sweet spice. 62%
15 In craps, if your first roll is a two, three or ____ you lose.	[1] Five [2] Seven [3] Nine [4] Eleven [5] Twelve	ANSWER TO Q-14 [4] There are two poker variations named after cities, Cincinnati and Chicago. 53%
15 Who became the first golfer to win two different major events in the 1990's?	[1] Fred Couples [2] Nick Faldo [3] Tom Kite [4] Payne Stewart [5] Nick Price	ANSWER TO Q-14 [5] Olerud won his first batting title with a .363 average for the Toronto Blue Jays. 42%

27 Each of these was one of the seven dwarfs except:	[1] Gabby [2] Doc [3] Happy [4] Sneezy [5] Grumpy	ANSWER TO Q-26 **[5]** Their religious centers with temple mounds were located near the present city of Vera Cruz. 63%
27 The ancient city of Gordium was known as the:	[1] Gateway to Asia [2] Second Rome [3] Hub of the Aegean [4] Megalopolis [5] City of Angels	ANSWER TO Q-26 **[2]** The Isle of Man is a self-governing dependency of the United Kingdom. 65%
27 Howler, spider, ringtail and rhesus are all types of:	[1] Parrots [2] Vipers [3] Owls [4] Sturgeon [5] Monkeys	ANSWER TO Q-26 **[1]** The solemn Woody Allen shows the influence of Ingmar Bergman. 89%
27 Which edible would be considered offal?	[1] Candy [2] Liver [3] Cracker [4] Fish fillet [5] Whipped cream	ANSWER TO Q-26 **[2]** The process sometimes consists of frying food, while vigorously shaking the pan. 65%
27 Which term does not mean to stimulate or to excite?	[1] Induce [2] Provoke [3] Whet [4] Sequester [5] Pique	ANSWER TO Q-26 **[3]** The Stanley Works is the world's leading maker of hand tools. 57%

GAME NUMBER 7

ANSWER TO Q-15

[1] "The Sketch Book" was the greatest success of this "First American Man of Letters."

51%

GAME NUMBER 25

ANSWER TO Q-15

[1] "Byrds of Paradise" was a mild tearjerker about a widower and his three kids.

81%

GAME NUMBER 43

ANSWER TO Q-15

[4] The others are from France, the Middle East, Russia and Mexico.

52%

![SHOWDOWN]

GAME NUMBER 61

ANSWER TO Q-15

[5] Box cars, snake eyes, or acey-ducey on your first roll will end your turn and crap out.

53%

![SHOWDOWN]

GAME NUMBER 79

ANSWER TO Q-15

[2] Faldo won the Masters in 1990 and won the British Open in 1990 and 1992.

45%

26 The remnants of the Olmec civilization of Mesoamerica are found here:	[1] Panama [2] Peru [3] Guatemala [4] Colombia [5] Mexico	ANSWER TO Q-25 **[3]** Lebanon is bordered by Israel, Syria and the Mediterranean Sea. 62%
26 The Isle of Man is located between these two countries:	[1] Finland - Sweden [2] Ireland - Great Britain [3] Italy - Sicily [4] Denmark - Norway [5] Belgium - The Netherlands	ANSWER TO Q-25 **[3]** Meiosis is the process of division in a cell by which the chromosomes are reduced by half. 68%
26 "Another Woman," "September" and "Interiors" are solemn films made by this comedic talent:	[1] Woody Allen [2] Charlie Chaplin [3] Jerry Lewis [4] Marcel Marceau [5] Peter Sellers	ANSWER TO Q-25 **[2]** Revolt leader Vaclav Havel became the first President of the Czech Republic in 1993. 51%
26 In cooking, what does saute mean?	[1] With cheese [2] Fry lightly [3] Soak in wine [4] Flavored with garlic [5] Boil rapidly	ANSWER TO Q-25 **[3]** Common salt, pottery glazes, glass and chlorine are derived from halite. 21%
26 Which of these companies is not an engineering & construction firm?	[1] Bechtel [2] Flour [3] The Stanley Works [4] Ashland [5] Baker Hughes	ANSWER TO Q-25 **[4]** Other marginal seas of the Arctic include Greenland Sea, Laptev Sea and Kara Sea. 52%

1 John Dunbar is the central character of this award-winning western:	[1] **Red River** [2] **Dances with Wolves** [3] **Unforgiven** [4] **Pale Rider** [5] **Silverado**	Turn to the top frame on the next right hand page for the correct answer and the next question.
1 In Kurt Vonnegut's "Slaughter-house-Five," the protagonist survives this WWII event:	[1] **The Battle of Midway** [2] **Firebombing of Dresden** [3] **Pearl Harbor** [4] **The Yalta Conference** [5] **Hiroshima**	Turn to the second frame on the next right hand page for the correct answer and the next question.
1 Somalia, Djibouti and _____ are the countries that make up the Horn of Africa.	[1] **Ethiopia** [2] **Sudan** [3] **Kenya** [4] **Mozambique** [5] **Egypt**	Turn to the middle frame on the next right hand page for the correct answer and the next question.
1 A cherry is an example of this kind of fruit:	[1] **Berry** [2] **Nut** [3] **Drupe** [4] **Tuber** [5] **Legume**	Turn to the fourth frame on the next right hand page for the correct answer and the next question.
1 Which James Bond film does not star Roger Moore?	[1] **View to a Kill** [2] **Live and Let Die** [3] **Moonraker** [4] **Never Say Never Again** [5] **The Spy Who Loved Me**	Turn to the bottom frame on the next right hand page for the correct answer and the next question.

25 Which country does not share a land border with Saudi Arabia?	[1] Jordan [2] Iraq [3] Lebanon [4] Oman [5] Kuwait	ANSWER TO Q-24 **[2]** It is the small piece of flesh which hangs from the palate above the back of the tongue. 65%
25 What is the term for sex cell division?	[1] Biosis [2] Entropy [3] Meiosis [4] Osmosis [5] Symbiosis	ANSWER TO Q-24 **[1]** European naval powers found it easier to pay tribute to the brigands than to destroy them. 54%
25 The revolt which overthrew Soviet-style Communism in Czechoslovakia was the:	[1] Six-Day War [2] Velvet Revolution [3] Catiline Conspiracy [4] Defenestration of Prague [5] Tet Offensive	ANSWER TO Q-24 **[3]** People for the ethical treatment of animals routinely protest the wearing of furs. 53%
25 Which mineral is not correctly matched with one of its uses or products?	[1] Alabaster - sculpture [2] Graphite - pencil lead [3] Halite - sulfur [4] Corundum - gemstones [5] Dolomite - cement	ANSWER TO Q-24 **[4]** New techniques allow it to be treated without resorting to open heart surgery. 73%
25 The Beaufort Sea, Baffin Bay and Barents Sea are all marginal seas of this body of water:	[1] Pacific [2] Atlantic [3] Indian [4] Arctic [5] Mediterranean	ANSWER TO Q-24 **[3]** "Platypus" means flatfooted. 56%

2 What kind of poisoning is plumbism?	[1] Lead [2] Food [3] Radiation [4] Blood [5] Alcohol	ANSWER TO Q-1 **[2]** "Two Socks" is his elusive wolf companion while "Cisco" is his horse. 81%
2 Which fashion designer is famous for the "Chelsea" look of the 1960's?	[1] Yves Saint-Laurent [2] Mary Quant [3] Bill Blass [4] Madeleine Vionnet [5] Oscar de la Renta	ANSWER TO Q-1 **[2]** 100,000 people, more than died at Hiroshima, were killed by Allied bombs in Dresden. 69%
2 Cordite is a smokeless:	[1] Tobacco [2] Form of dry ice [3] Revolver [4] Kindling [5] Explosive	ANSWER TO Q-1 **[1]** Djibouti is wedged between Somalia and Ethiopia. 58%
2 With which would you "Rock the baby" or go "Around the world"?	[1] Pool cue [2] Yo-Yo [3] Bag of marbles [4] Golf club [5] Pocket knife	ANSWER TO Q-1 **[3]** It has a fleshy outer layer, or pericarp, and the inner layer hardens in a pit around a seed. 58%
2 Which subject does not involve the study of living things?	[1] Physiology [2] Entomology [3] Acoustics [4] Genetics [5] Ecology	ANSWER TO Q-1 **[4]** In 1983, Sean Connery came out of retirement to play the dashing 007 one last time. 61%

24 Where is your uvula?	[1] Inner ear [2] Mouth [3] Lungs [4] Elbow [5] Intestines	ANSWER TO Q-23 [3] Some of the greatest writers (Shakespeare, for example) were very fond of puns. 89%
24 Where did the Barbary pirates hail from?	[1] North Africa [2] Turkey [3] Greece [4] Spain [5] Balearic Islands	ANSWER TO Q-23 [2] Christie used this name for her romantic fiction novels. 57%
24 The group known as PETA is against the abuse of:	[1] Children [2] Wives [3] Animals [4] The elderly [5] Husbands	ANSWER TO Q-23 [5] "Pixel" is an acronym for picture element. 59%
24 An abnormally fast heartbeat is termed:	[1] Sciatica [2] Thrombosis [3] Phlebitis [4] Tachycardia [5] Myocardial infarction	ANSWER TO Q-23 [2] The popular 1966 movie was followed by a sequel, "Living Free," and a brief TV series. 94%
24 Australia's duck-billed platypus is named after its:	[1] Reproductive method [2] Tiny wings [3] Webbed feet [4] Fish diet [5] Bird-like bill	ANSWER TO Q-23 [4] A doctor inserts the fiberoptic endoscope through a small incision. 76%

3 Which comedian "refused" to age past 39?	[1] Lucille Ball [2] Jack Benny [3] Phyllis Diller [4] George Burns [5] Milton Berle	ANSWER TO Q-2 **[1]** It comes from the Latin word "plumbum," which means lead. 69%
3 Uremia is the result of biochemical disorders due to failure in the:	[1] Lungs [2] Digestive tract [3] Kidneys [4] Liver [5] Thyroid glands	ANSWER TO Q-2 **[2]** Quant has a fashionable boutique in London. 69%
3 All but which are characteristics of amphibians?	[1] Three-chambered heart [2] Four limbs [3] Moist skin [4] Cold-blooded [5] Live births	ANSWER TO Q-2 **[5]** It is made from guncotton, acetone, nitroglycerin and petroleum jelly. 52%
3 Which string instrument is not plucked?	[1] Mandolin [2] Dulcimer [3] Balalaika [4] Lute [5] Zither	ANSWER TO Q-2 **[2]** While you have it in hand, you might as well "Spank the baby" or maybe "Let it sleep." 69%
3 Which country made its first Olympic appearance in 1984?	[1] Turkey [2] China [3] Cuba [4] New Zealand [5] Kenya	ANSWER TO Q-2 **[3]** It is a branch of physics dealing with sound and its transmission. 79%

23 "Lamb stew is much ado about mutton" is an example of a:	[1] Homonym [2] Palindrome [3] Pun [4] Non sequitur [5] Dangling participle	ANSWER TO Q-22 **[3]** In degrees fahrenheit, it would be 68. 43%
23 Which female writer used the pseudonym of Mary Westmacott?	[1] Emily Bronte [2] Agatha Christie [3] Dorothy Parker [4] Lillian Hellman [5] Jackie Collins	ANSWER TO Q-22 **[3]** Serial killer Bianchi terrorized the West Coast in the 1970's. 87%
23 What is the smallest display element on a video display screen?	[1] Meg [2] Byte [3] Tiff [4] Bug [5] Pixel	ANSWER TO Q-22 **[2]** Jeanette Macdonald and Nelson Eddy specialized in musicals based on operettas. 54%
23 Name the lioness raised by Kenya game wardens in the award-winning "Born Free":	[1] Princess [2] Elsa [3] Zaka [4] Louisa [5] Althea	ANSWER TO Q-22 **[1]** A stovepipe is a tall, silk hat, once worn by men for dressy occasions. 89%
23 Arthroscopy is a medical technique to see inside the:	[1] Heart [2] Stomach [3] Lungs [4] Joints [5] Womb	ANSWER TO Q-22 **[2]** It is defined as forgivable behavior meriting no particular punishment. 42%

4 Which country's legendary 14th century hero is William Tell?

[1] Scotland
[2] Normandy
[3] Poland
[4] Finland
[5] Switzerland

ANSWER TO Q-3

[2] Benny's age, stinginess and ineptness at playing the violin were his trademarks.

81%

---

4 If you were visiting the famous Casbah, where would you be?

[1] India
[2] Pakistan
[3] Zanzibar
[4] Morocco
[5] Algeria

ANSWER TO Q-3

[3] Uremia causes a rise in blood urea and other nitrogenous waste products.

82%

---

4 All of these trees are evergreens except the:

[1] Fir
[2] Spruce
[3] Hemlock
[4] Sycamore
[5] Eucalyptus

ANSWER TO Q-3

[5] Most amphibians lay their eggs in the water.

79%

---

4 The world's highest waterfall is in:

[1] Norway
[2] United States
[3] Venezuela
[4] Australia
[5] Canada

ANSWER TO Q-3

[2] It is an instrument with strings stretched over a soundboard and struck with hammers.

69%

---

4 Which city did partici-pants in the Fourth Crusade sack on their way to Jerusalem?

[1] Rome
[2] Constantinople
[3] Damascus
[4] Carthage
[5] Baghdad

ANSWER TO Q-3

[2] Before August 1993, China had never won a world championship in a track event.

57%

22 Which statement fits a day with a temperature of 20 degrees celsius?	[1] Hellishly hot [2] Chilly [3] Mild and lovely [4] Sweltering [5] Freezing cold	ANSWER TO Q-21 **[1]** This diagnostic method makes use of ultrasound pulses that echo off of body organs. 43%
22 Kenneth Bianchi was better known as:	[1] The Nightstalker [2] The Slasher [3] The Hillside Strangler [4] Son of Sam [5] Jack the Ripper	ANSWER TO Q-21 **[4]** Foster co-starred with Scott Baio of "Happy Days" in the 1976 musical gangster spoof. 93%
22 Which team starred in such musicals as "Rose Marie" and "Naughty Marietta"?	[1] Astaire and Rogers [2] Eddy and Macdonald [3] Powell and Keeler [4] Rooney and Garland [5] Burns and Allen	ANSWER TO Q-21 **[4]** Related to kingfishers, they roll over while flying. 54%
22 Which kind of hat is associated with Abraham Lincoln?	[1] Stovepipe [2] Derby [3] Stetson [4] Homburg [5] Coonskin	ANSWER TO Q-21 **[5]** Chagall eventually moved to France. A museum devoted to his work is located in Nice. 67%
22 Which is a good example of venial behavior?	[1] Robbing a home [2] Injuring a mugger [3] Polluting a lake [4] Starting an arson fire [5] Abusing children	ANSWER TO Q-21 **[2]** He saw the world as a constant conflict of wills resulting in pain and frustration. 32%

5 Which is not a Neil Simon play?	[1] Plaza Suite [2] California Suite [3] Only When I Laugh [4] Funny Girl [5] Chapter Two	ANSWER TO Q-4 [5] The legend has him forced to shoot an apple off the head of his son for punishment. 46%
5 The chinook is the largest member of this fish family:	[1] Tuna [2] Ray [3] Salmon [4] Sunfish [5] Marlin	ANSWER TO Q-4 [5] The Casbah is a 16th century fortress in the Muslim quarter of Algiers. 58%
5 "Little boots," "little cords," and "little tongues" are the translated names of:	[1] Danish pastries [2] French wines [3] Russian soups [4] Italian pasta [5] German sausages	ANSWER TO Q-4 [4] Also known as the plane tree and the buttonwood, American species are grown for their wood. 69%
5 These wines are all matched with their native country except:	[1] Champagne - France [2] Riesling - Germany [3] Madeira - portugal [4] Asti Spumante - Italy [5] Tokay - Greece	ANSWER TO Q-4 [3] At 3,212 feet, Angel falls is over twice as tall as the Sears Tower in Chicago. 68%
5 What was the primary use for the Australian aborigine's boomerang?	[1] Hunting [2] Defense [3] Play [4] Skill contests [5] Train kangaroos	ANSWER TO Q-4 [2] The assault discredited the crusade and ruined the goal of uniting the Greek and Latin churches. 35%

21 Echography is a method used by which professional?	[1] Medical doctor [2] Seismologist [3] Astronomer [4] Geologist [5] Meteorologist	ANSWER TO Q-20 **[3]** The long, heavy pole makes it a game of strength rather than skill. 45%
21 Which film stars actress Jodie Foster?	[1] Less Than Zero [2] The Breakfast Club [3] Footloose [4] Bugsy Malone [5] The Lost Boys	ANSWER TO Q-20 **[1]** "Sesqui" means one and a half times; centennial is one hundred. 67%
21 The roller, noted for its aerial acrobatics, is a:	[1] Bat [2] Flying fish [3] Dragonfly [4] Bird [5] Flying squirrel	ANSWER TO Q-20 **[3]** The others are root and tuber vegetables. 89%
21 What Russian-born painter drew on Jewish traditions and folklore for his paintings?	[1] Wassily Kandinsky [2] Mikhail Larionov [3] Kasmir Malevich [4] Mies van der Rohe [5] Marc Chagall	ANSWER TO Q-20 **[5]** All the ponies derive from a Celtic stock of prehistoric work horses. 65%
21 Which German is a philosopher known for his pessimistic world view?	[1] Heinrich Heine [2] Arthur Schopenhauer [3] C. Furst von Metternich [4] Otto von Bismarck [5] Hermann Hesse	ANSWER TO Q-20 **[5]** The heavy-set and shaggy-coated wild ox also occupies barren lands of North America. 43%

6 Which element is not a metal?

[1] Iron
[2] Antimony
[3] Krypton
[4] Iridium
[5] Magnesium

ANSWER TO Q-5

[4] "Funny Girl" was based on a book by Isobel Lennart.

47%

---

6 In the Jewish faith, what is the skullcap called?

[1] Miter
[2] Yarmulke
[3] Biretta
[4] Menorah
[5] Fez

ANSWER TO Q-5

[3] The chinook may reach weights of up to 100 pounds.

47%

---

6 Which children's classic was written by a Canadian writer?

[1] Anne of Green Gables
[2] Black Beauty
[3] Little Women
[4] Winnie the Pooh
[5] The Little Prince

ANSWER TO Q-5

[4] These are the meanings for spaghetti, linguine and a sort of tiny noodle.

68%

---

6 This element is named for the inventor of the periodic table:

[1] Zirconium
[2] Tungsten
[3] Bismuth
[4] Mendelevium
[5] Lawrencium

ANSWER TO Q-5

[5] Tokay is a Hungarian wine.

69%

---

6 Albert II is the king of:

[1] Denmark
[2] Belgium
[3] Norway
[4] Sweden
[5] Saudi Arabia

ANSWER TO Q-5

[1] A boomerang can swoop back and forth and climb to 150 feet at the top of its loop.

69%

20 The caber of the Scottish sport of caber tossing is a/an:

[1] Ball
[2] Iron disk
[3] Heavy pole
[4] Mallet
[5] Racket

ANSWER TO Q-19
[1] More particularly, the concept is associated with the writer, Gustave Flaubert.
53%

---

20 Every 150 years, you have a:

[1] Sesquicentennial
[2] Silver jubilee
[3] Bicentennial
[4] Leap century
[5] Fiscal year

ANSWER TO Q-19
[2] An act of obeisance is a gesture indicating deference, homage or respect.
67%

---

20 Which is a seed vegetable?

[1] Parsnip
[2] Horseradish
[3] Sweetcorn
[4] Turnip
[5] Carrot

ANSWER TO Q-19
[2] Derived from the idea of the Sabbath Day, crops were not sown or reaped in sabbatical years.
42%

---

20 Shetland, Dartmoor and Welsh are types of:

[1] Sheep
[2] Foxes
[3] Wolves
[4] Dogs
[5] Ponies

ANSWER TO Q-19
[5] This classic type of light, clear brew was first made in the town of Pilzen.
78%

---

20 The musk-ox is confined primarily to this country:

[1] Australia
[2] China
[3] East Africa
[4] India
[5] Greenland

ANSWER TO Q-19
[4] He followed up his most famous work with "The Garden of the Prophet."
56%

7 In 1851, Jacob Fussel became the first to manufacturer this treat commercially:	[1] Chewing gum [2] Potato chips [3] Ice cream [4] Soda pop [5] Chocolate bars	ANSWER TO Q-6 **[3]** Krypton is a gaseous element used in electric lamps. 81%
7 In law, what is a tort?	[1] Contract [2] Breach or violation [3] Admission of guilt [4] Accusation [5] Sentence	ANSWER TO Q-6 **[2]** The skullcap is worn by men as a sign of reverence while praying. 81%
7 Lesotho, Gabon and Burkina Faso are:	[1] Venomous snakes [2] Middle Eastern foods [3] African nations [4] Articles of clothing [5] Tropical plants	ANSWER TO Q-6 **[1]** Lucy Montgomery drew on childhood memories of Prince Edward Island for her book. 54%
7 The affliction called "graphospasm" is just another term for:	[1] Athlete's foot [2] Swimmer's ear [3] Dowager's hump [4] Writer's cramp [5] Tennis elbow	ANSWER TO Q-6 **[4]** The table was devised by Dmitri Mendeleev, and revised by Henry Moseley. 58%
7 Which current king came to the throne when his father was deposed due to mental illness?	[1] Albert of Belgium [2] Hassan of Morocco [3] Juan Carlos of Spain [4] Harold V of Norway [5] Hussein of Jordan	ANSWER TO Q-6 **[2]** His brother, Baudouin I, died in July of 1993, leaving him the throne. 71%

19 If you are searching for "le mot juste," you are looking for the:	[1] Right word [2] Headwaiter [3] Lesser of two evils [4] French connection [5] Exit	ANSWER TO Q-18 **[5]** Hippolyta was captured by Theseus, while Achilles fell in love with Penthesilia. 34%
19 Which could be described as an act of obeisance?	[1] Slap [2] Bow [3] Handshake [4] Grin [5] Kiss on the lips	ANSWER TO Q-18 **[4]** There are six Nobel awards; the other two are economics and world peace. 54%
19 The idea of a sabbatical originally came from this cultural source:	[1] US Constitutional Law [2] Mosaic Law [3] English Common Law [4] The Napoleonic Code [5] Imperial China	ANSWER TO Q-18 **[3]** The game became popular during the Civil War and in 1869 Cincinnati paid all players a salary. 45%
19 Which beer type is named for the town in former Czechoslovakia where it was first brewed?	[1] Lager [2] Stout [3] Amber [4] Ale [5] Pilsner	ANSWER TO Q-18 **[2]** The grain, pennyweight, ounce and pound are used in this system of measurement. 78%
19 "The Prophet" is the best known work of this Middle Eastern writer:	[1] Salman Rushdie [2] Tagore [3] Omar Khayyam [4] Kahlil Gibran [5] Saladin	ANSWER TO Q-18 **[4]** The altar is also located in the chancel area and was originally restricted to clergymen. 56%

8 In meteor-ology, ____ is the horizontal movement of a mass of air that warms or chills the air.	[1] Aura [2] Advection [3] Aquarelle [4] Arbitrage [5] Aphasia	ANSWER TO Q-7 [3] Ice cream has been known since ancient times, and reached the U.S. around the 17th century. 43%
8 Which country's freedom fighters are known as the "Mujahideen"?	[1] Libya [2] Israel [3] Syria [4] Palestine [5] Afghanistan	ANSWER TO Q-7 [2] A tort is a violation of civil law other than breach of contract. 81%
8 Which artist is noted for his cartoons in "The New Yorker" magazine?	[1] Al Capp [2] Jim Davis [3] Hank Ketcham [4] Saul Steinberg [5] Walt Kelly	ANSWER TO Q-7 [3] Lesotho is in South Africa. Burkina Faso and Gabon are in West Africa. 81%
8 While at sea, sailors use this instrument to measure time:	[1] Chronometer [2] Anemometer [3] Stroboscope [4] Astrolabe [5] Hygrometer	ANSWER TO Q-7 [4] It often occurs after long periods of writing. 32%
8 "How sharper than a serpent's tooth it is to have a thankless child" is a famous line from a:	[1] Book of the Bible [2] Greek tragedy [3] Shakespeare play [4] Political speech [5] Sermon	ANSWER TO Q-7 [5] King Talal of Jordan was deposed in 1952. 58%

18 In Greek mythology, Hippolyta, Pentheselia and Antiope were all:	[1] Muses [2] Nymphs [3] Fates [4] Furies [5] Amazons	ANSWER TO Q-17 [3] The German physicist's thermometric scale is still used in the U.S. and Canada. 89%
18 Nobel prizes are given in all but one of these categories:	[1] Medicine [2] Physics [3] Literature [4] Music [5] Chemistry	ANSWER TO Q-17 [2] These men pioneered the writing of history in Western civilization. 45%
18 It was the first fully professional baseball team:	[1] New York Yankees [2] Brooklyn Dodgers [3] Cincinnati Red Stockings [4] New York Knickerbockers [5] Columbus Pipers	ANSWER TO Q-17 [2] They were born of necessity, since canned goods and metal were rationed during the war. 56%
18 Troy weight is used to measure:	[1] Medicines [2] Precious metals [3] Liquids [4] Fossil fuels [5] Agricultural products	ANSWER TO Q-17 [5] Known as the lactogenic hormone, prolactin is produced by the anterior pituitary gland. 59%
18 The chancel is the part of the church:	[1] You enter [2] Where the pastor lives [3] Also called a belfry [4] Where the choir sits [5] Congregation sits in	ANSWER TO Q-17 [3] The Black Hand was a lawless secret society engaged in extortion and terrorism. 67%

9 Who won baseball's first World Series?	[1] Brooklyn Dodgers [2] Philadelphia Phillies [3] Pittsburgh Pirates [4] New York Yankees [5] Boston Red Sox	ANSWER TO Q-8 **[2]** Advection may alter other physical properties of the air. 42%
9 Which divinity does not belong to the pantheon of ancient Egyptian gods?	[1] Ganymede [2] Isis [3] Anubis [4] Osiris [5] Thoth	ANSWER TO Q-8 **[5]** The "holy warriors" fiercely resisted the Soviet army after it invaded in 1979. 69%
9 To which body part does the term "brachial" refer?	[1] Ears [2] Chest [3] Lower back [4] Shoulders [5] Arms	ANSWER TO Q-8 **[4]** Steinberg is known for his visual puns and satirical portraits. 57%
9 Who is referred to as the "father of the atomic bomb"?	[1] Albert Einstein [2] Harry Truman [3] Enrico Fermi [4] Niels Bohr [5] Robert Oppenheimer	ANSWER TO Q-8 **[1]** It allowed navigators at sea to determine accurate longitude for the first time. 59%
9 Hamilton, Rochester and Kingston are ports on this Great Lake:	[1] Superior [2] Erie [3] Michigan [4] Huron [5] Ontario	ANSWER TO Q-8 **[3]** King Lear says this line in reference to his cold-hearted daughters, Goneril and Regan. 68%

17 Who invented both the alcohol and mercury thermometers?	[1] Pierre Curie [2] James Watt [3] Daniel Fahrenheit [4] Michael Faraday [5] Louis Pasteur	ANSWER TO Q-16 [3] It later became known that such rings are the basic structure of all aromatic compounds. 34%
17 Who were Herodotus, Tacitus and Suetonius?	[1] Hannibal's adversaries [2] Ancient historians [3] Consorts of Cleopatra [4] Celebrated gladiators [5] Christian martyrs	ANSWER TO Q-16 [1] They lived in Palestine around the time of Christ. 59%
17 Which company gave us the first frozen TV dinners during World War II?	[1] Birdseye [2] Swanson [3] Libby [4] Stouffer [5] Heinz	ANSWER TO Q-16 [3] Remnants of this tongue now survive only in isolated areas of Iraq, Lebanon and Turkey. 89%
17 The hormone prolactin is known to stimulate or increase:	[1] Blood sugar [2] Muscle growth [3] Gastric juices [4] Metabolism [5] Milk production	ANSWER TO Q-16 [5] Lima or white beans are called flageolets. 78%
17 The Black Hand was a ____ terrorist organization.	[1] Palestinian [2] Libyan [3] Sicilian [4] Irish [5] African-American	ANSWER TO Q-16 [3] The comedy was somewhat of a departure from the norm for the late great director. 58%

10 Where are a person's dura mater and pia mater?	[1] Hand [2] Knee [3] Spinal cord [4] Foot [5] Rib cage	ANSWER TO Q-9 [5] The Bosox won the best of 9 series against the Pirates (5-3) in October 1903. 46%
10 Which American military organization is the youngest?	[1] Army [2] Air Force [3] Coast Guard [4] Navy [5] Marine Corps	ANSWER TO Q-9 [1] Ganymede was the cupbearer to the gods in ancient Greek religion. 66%
10 Which word is not synonymous with shy?	[1] Furtive [2] Abashed [3] Diffident [4] Sheepish [5] Timid	ANSWER TO Q-9 [5] The brachium is the part of the arm that extends from the shoulder to the elbow. 43%
10 The last 14 kings of this empire were all named Ptolemy:	[1] Roman [2] Ancient Egypt [3] Babylonians [4] Chinese [5] Russian	ANSWER TO Q-9 [5] Oppenheimer directed the "Manhattan Project," which designed and built the first atomic bombs. 71%
10 The earliest English colony in North America was on Roanoke Island, off the coast of:	[1] Massachusetts [2] Virginia [3] Delaware [4] North Carolina [5] Florida	ANSWER TO Q-9 [5] The smallest of the Great Lakes, Ontario is 193 mi. long, 53 mi. wide and 802 ft. deep. 68%

16 Frederich August Kekule discovered that the structure of benzene is a:

[1] Four-sided box
[2] Figure eight
[3] Closed ring
[4] Square
[5] Rectangle

ANSWER TO Q-15

[3] Cabbage is a "flower" vegetable, like broccoli and the artichoke.
59%

---

16 Today a zealot can be an enthusiastic person or a bigot, but the original zealots were:

[1] Religious fanatics
[2] Gypsies
[3] Bloodthirsty pirates
[4] Clowns
[5] Palace guards

ANSWER TO Q-15

[4] Berkowitz was the serial killer "Son of Sam," who murdered six people in New York in 1978.
92%

---

16 Which famous person would have spoken Aramaic?

[1] Attila the Hun
[2] Shaka Zulu
[3] Jesus of Nazareth
[4] Genghis Khan
[5] Alexander the Great

ANSWER TO Q-15

[5] The poem was written just after Poe married his 13-year old cousin, Virginia Clemm.
84%

---

16 What do you get if you order haricots verte in a French restaurant?

[1] Rabbit
[2] Lamb chops
[3] Fried potatoes
[4] Pastry
[5] String beans

ANSWER TO Q-15

[3] "Oh Captain, My Captain" is another Whitman poem about Lincoln.
52%

---

16 What was the title of Alfred Hitchcock's last film?

[1] The Birds
[2] Frenzy
[3] Family Plot
[4] Vertigo
[5] Topaz

ANSWER TO Q-15

[4] Vena cava: either of two main veins that convey blood from the body to the heart's right atrium.
76%

11 Someone who mends pots and pans is called a:	[1] Haberdasher [2] Tinker [3] Cobbler [4] Milliner [5] Cheapskate	ANSWER TO Q-10 **[3]** They are two of the three membranes that envelop the brain and spinal cord. 57%
11 You would find a dewlap on a:	[1] Mammal [2] Book [3] Computer [4] Leaf [5] Bicycle	ANSWER TO Q-10 **[2]** The Air Force was a part of the Army, and called the Army Air Corps, until 1947. 68%
11 The medical condition of edema is also known as:	[1] Hives [2] Liver spots [3] Narcolepsy [4] Vertigo [5] Dropsy	ANSWER TO Q-10 **[1]** Furtive means to be sly or cunning. 79%
11 The world's highest active volcanoes are found on this continent:	[1] Africa [2] South America [3] Europe [4] Asia [5] Australia	ANSWER TO Q-10 **[2]** The death of Ptolemy XIV placed Cleopatra in power, the last ruler of the Egyptian Empire. 61%
11 Which composer wrote incidental music to Ibsen's "Peer Gynt"?	[1] Frederic Chopin [2] Felix Mendelssohn [3] Edvard Grieg [4] Rimsky-Korsakov [5] Claude Debussy	ANSWER TO Q-10 **[4]** In 1587, a group of Roanoke colonists disappeared without a trace. 69%

15 All of these are considered root vegetables except:	[1] Turnip [2] Parsnip [3] Cabbage [4] Radish [5] Carrot	ANSWER TO Q-14 [2] Inchoate means not yet clearly or completely formed. 78%
15 All of these men assassinated world leaders except:	[1] Lee Harvey Oswald [2] James Earl Ray [3] Leon Czolgosz [4] David Berkowitz [5] John Wilkes Booth	ANSWER TO Q-14 [5] He took the word "atlas" from the figure in Greek myth who was tricked into carrying the earth. 72%
15 Which poetic heroine was created by Edgar Allan Poe?	[1] Lucy Gray [2] The Dark Lady [3] Laura [4] The White Goddess [5] Annabel Lee	ANSWER TO Q-14 [4] Music is usually transposed to accommodate the voice of a singer. 54%
15 The elegy for Abraham Lincoln, "When Lilacs Last in the Dooryard Bloom'd," is by:	[1] Henry W. Longfellow [2] Emily Dickinson [3] Walt Whitman [4] Carl Sandburg [5] Oliver Wendell Holmes	ANSWER TO Q-14 [3] Pinnipeds are seals and walruses. Elephant seals can weigh up to 5,000 lbs. 61%
15 Which would be found traveling through a vena cava?	[1] Fertilized eggs [2] Air traffic [3] Migrating whales [4] Deoxygenated blood [5] Desert caravan	ANSWER TO Q-14 [1] Originally spelled "terreen," it is a deep dish designed for soup. 79%

12 Cortez captured this leader in 1520, ending the Aztec Empire in Mexico:	[1] Montezuma II [2] Quetzelcoatl [3] Amenhotep [4] Geronimo [5] Atahuallpa	ANSWER TO Q-11 [2] Tinkers have gone the way of buggy-whip manufacturers. 58%
12 All but one of the following can be seen among the carved faces on Mt. Rushmore:	[1] Abraham Lincoln [2] Teddy Roosevelt [3] George Washington [4] Woodrow Wilson [5] Thomas Jefferson	ANSWER TO Q-11 [1] This loose flap of skin under the chin is the mammalian equivalent of a wattle. 59%
12 Which is the title of the witty Samuel Butler novel attacking Victorian life?	[1] The Way of All Flesh [2] The Beggar's Opera [3] The Rape of the Lock [4] Bleak House [5] Vanity Fair	ANSWER TO Q-11 [5] It is the excessive accumulation of fluid in the body. 69%
12 Which country does not border the Red Sea?	[1] Egypt [2] Sudan [3] Yemen [4] Ethiopia [5] Turkey	ANSWER TO Q-11 [2] The Andes volcanoes include Ojos del Salado, Lascar and Cotopaxi. 71%
12 A mixed-function gland, it secretes both digestive enzymes and the hormone glucogen:	[1] Pituitary [2] Thyroid [3] Pancreas [4] Hypothalamus [5] Pineal	ANSWER TO Q-11 [3] The suites Grieg fashioned from his music are very popular in the concert hall. 62%

14 All of these words describe a specific shape except:	[1] Ovoid [2] Inchoate [3] Spheroid [4] Globular [5] Rhombic	ANSWER TO Q-13 [5] Zinc is a lustrous bluish-white in color. 64%
14 He published the first atlas, using the word to describe a collection of maps:	[1] Johannes Kepler [2] Henry Cavendish [3] Johannes Gutenberg [4] Archimedes [5] Gerardus Mercator	ANSWER TO Q-13 [3] According to Chinese mythology, the last unicorn seen was at the birth of Confucius. 71%
14 The term for changing the original key of a piece of music is:	[1] Syncopation [2] Augmentation [3] Inversion [4] Transposition [5] Development	ANSWER TO Q-13 [2] Three Dog Night's cover of Randy Newman's "Mama Told Me Not to Come" hit #1 in 1970. 68%
14 The largest of the pinnipeds is the:	[1] Tapeworm [2] Ostrich [3] Elephant seal [4] Siberian tiger [5] Kodiak bear	ANSWER TO Q-13 [5] Herculaneum was destroyed by the same earthquake that shook Pompeii in AD 62. 69%
14 Which food would you serve from a tureen?	[1] Soup [2] Champagne [3] Bacon and eggs [4] Cheese [5] Steaks	ANSWER TO Q-13 [1] The book forced federal meat inspection and passage of the Pure Food and Drug Act. 65%

13 Which movie funny man becomes dictator of "Freedonia" in a classic film comedy?	[1] Woody Allen [2] W.C. Fields [3] Groucho Marx [4] Alan Arkin [5] Charlie Chaplin	ANSWER TO Q-12 **[1]** Although a hostage, he continued as a puppet ruler and was killed by his own subjects. 34%
13 "Island of Despair" and "Speranza" were names this character gave his temporary home:	[1] Prince Valiant [2] Long John Silver [3] The Prisoner of Zenda [4] Captain Nemo [5] Robinson Crusoe	ANSWER TO Q-12 **[4]** The famous monument can be found among the Black Hills of South Dakota. 81%
13 The German and Russian Struves are a noted family of:	[1] Astronomers [2] Physicists [3] Geologists [4] Chemists [5] Zoologists	ANSWER TO Q-12 **[1]** The novel marks the transition from Victorian to Edwardian England. 43%
13 All of these are kinds of crabs except:	[1] Alaska king [2] Razor [3] Spider [4] Blue [5] Hermit	ANSWER TO Q-12 **[5]** The Red Sea is almost landbound; in the north, the Suez Canal links it to the Mediterranean. 47%
13 Three of our names for the days of the week come from ___ gods.	[1] Roman [2] Greek [3] Norse [4] American Indian [5] Egyptian	ANSWER TO Q-12 **[3]** The pancreas belongs to both the endocrine and exocrine systems. 57%

13 Which statement about zinc is untrue?

[1] Metallic element
[2] Used to make brass
[3] Essential for growth
[4] Malleable when heated
[5] Blackish in color

ANSWER TO Q-12

[5] The specialized organs under the abdomen produce the silk threads.
69%

---

13 According to biblical legend, this luckless animal was thrown off Noah's ark and drowned:

[1] Dodo
[2] Griffin
[3] Unicorn
[4] Persian elephant
[5] Phoenix

ANSWER TO Q-12

[5] The inherited disease usually begins with leg weakness before age three, and progresses rapidly.
52%

---

13 Which hit song was not recorded by singer and songwriter James Taylor?

[1] You've Got a Friend
[2] Mama Told Me Not to Come
[3] Steamroller
[4] Shower the People
[5] Fire and Rain

ANSWER TO Q-12

[2] Nymphs were regarded as young, beautiful, musical and amorous.
69%

---

13 With which famous city is the town of Herculaneum associated?

[1] Carthage
[2] Babylon
[3] Sparta
[4] Alexandria
[5] Pompeii

ANSWER TO Q-12

[2] Felix had his "bag of tricks" and his genius friend Poindexter to help him along in life.
63%

---

13 What industry was examined in Upton Sinclair's 1906 book "The Jungle"?

[1] Meatpacking
[2] Oil
[3] Coal mining
[4] Rubber
[5] Automobile

ANSWER TO Q-12

[5] The hard, bony, enamel-covered layer of the tooth is called dentin.
79%

14 When making a traditional Swiss fondue, the cheese is thinned with:	[1] Broth [2] White wine and liqueur [3] Vinegar [4] Sheep's milk [5] Apple cider	ANSWER TO Q-13 [3] In "Duck Soup," Groucho hires Chico and Harpo to spy on his enemies. 58%
14 In the Old Testament, he escaped the evil city of Sodom with his daughters:	[1] Aaron [2] Abraham [3] Joab [4] Lot [5] Zachariah	ANSWER TO Q-13 [5] "Speranza" means hope. Obviously Robinson Crusoe had his good days and his bad days. 58%
14 What does the medical specialty of nosology deal with?	[1] Artificial limbs [2] Plastic surgery [3] Back problems [4] Disease classification [5] Holistic medicine	ANSWER TO Q-13 [1] Otto, the last famous Struve, emigrated to the U.S. to do studies of stellar phenomena. 35%
14 Cy Coleman is known for his contributions to:	[1] Legal theory [2] Musical theater [3] Agriculture [4] Child psychology [5] Sports journalism	ANSWER TO Q-13 [2] "Razor" is a type of clam. 46%
14 Which nerve is located in the human jaw?	[1] Perineal [2] Maxillary [3] Brachial [4] Radial [5] Digital	ANSWER TO Q-13 [3] They are: Tuesday (Tiu, god of war), Thursday (Thor, god of thunder) & Friday (Freya, goddess). 46%

12 What type of bug has spinnerets?

[1] Ant
[2] Bee
[3] Mosquito
[4] Grasshopper
[5] Spider

ANSWER TO Q-11

[3] Mandible is the anatomical term for the lower jawbone.
89%

---

12 Duchenne, which only affects boys, is the most common form of:

[1] Leukemia
[2] Infantile paralysis
[3] Rheumatic fever
[4] Multiple sclerosis
[5] Muscular dystrophy

ANSWER TO Q-11

[5] The others were written by her sister, Charlotte.
73%

---

12 In Greek myth, what were nymphs?

[1] Goddesses of love
[2] Nature spirits
[3] Daughters of Zeus
[4] Messengers of the gods
[5] Winged sisters

ANSWER TO Q-11

[3] Bechamel is a cream sauce.
82%

---

12 Rock Bottom, Poindexter, and the Professor were characters in this cartoon:

[1] George of the Jungle
[2] Felix the Cat
[3] Super Chicken
[4] Mighty Mouse
[5] Huckleberry Hound

ANSWER TO Q-11

[5] The word can also refer to an ordinary, or everyday occurrence.
54%

---

12 An adult mouth contains ___ permanent teeth.

[1] 24
[2] 26
[3] 28
[4] 30
[5] 32

ANSWER TO Q-11

[1] Invented at the end of the Korean War, they are faster, sturdier and more maneuverable.
57%

15 The muskellunge is a member of the ___ family.	[1] Freshwater eel [2] Barracuda [3] Pike [4] Sunfish [5] Carp	ANSWER TO Q-14 **[2]** Some recipes call for white wine and kirsch; others call for white wine and plum brandy. 35%
15 The hero of this book says history is "a nightmare from which I am trying to awake."	[1] Ulysses [2] A Farewell to Arms [3] The Rainbow [4] A Passage to India [5] The Wings of the Dove	ANSWER TO Q-14 **[4]** In legend, his wife changed into a pillar of of salt when she looked back at the doomed city. 79%
15 Which U.S. team has won the most NHL Stanley Cup titles?	[1] Detroit Red Wings [2] Chicago Blackhawks [3] Philadelphia Flyers [4] New York Islanders [5] Boston Bruins	ANSWER TO Q-14 **[4]** Before it designated a branch of medical science, the word meant a list of diseases. 46%
15 All are carnivores except:	[1] Hyena [2] Jaguar [3] Leopard [4] Lynx [5] Warthog	ANSWER TO Q-14 **[2]** "City of Angels" and "Will Rogers" earned Coleman Tonys for best musical. 45%
15 Which famous person is mentioned admiringly in Adolf Hitler's "Mein Kampf"?	[1] Teddy Roosevelt [2] Charles Darwin [3] Bob Mathias [4] Henry Ford [5] Charles Lindbergh	ANSWER TO Q-14 **[2]** The others are in the leg, upper and lower arms and fingers. 47%

<table>
<tr><td>

11 If you are moving your mandible, what are you most likely doing?

[1] Lifting weights
[2] Playing piano
[3] Chewing food
[4] Dreaming
[5] Driving a car

</td><td>

ANSWER TO Q-10

[4] When the dried corn is ground, it becomes hominy grits.

68%

</td></tr>
</table>

11 Which book was written by Emily Bronte?

[1] Shirley
[2] The Professor
[3] Villette
[4] Jane Eyre
[5] Wuthering Heights

ANSWER TO Q-10

[4] This is a hit song by the funky pop group, the B-52's.

59%

11 Which is not a kind of bread?

[1] Brioche
[2] Galette
[3] Bechamel
[4] Croissant
[5] Baguette

ANSWER TO Q-10

[1] "God has given him blood to drink" is the curse Hawthorne placed in the mouth of Matthew Maule.

34%

11 If you are given a quotidian task, how often do you have to do it?

[1] Weekly
[2] Quarterly
[3] Monthly
[4] Annually
[5] Daily

ANSWER TO Q-10

[3] Cavendish was an English physicist who determined the specific heats for numerous substances.

57%

11 Supersonic bombers and fighters became prominent in military aircraft during the:

[1] Vietnam Era
[2] Second World War
[3] Grenada invasion
[4] Somali occupation
[5] Persian Gulf War

ANSWER TO Q-10

[3] Though 124 Americans died when it sank, the the U.S. didn't enter WWI for another two years.

68%

16 Which composer was a contemporary of Johann Sebastian Bach?	[1] Beethoven [2] Mendelssohn [3] Wagner [4] Handel [5] Brahms	ANSWER TO Q-15 **[3]** Like the other members of this fish family, it is known for its fighting abilities. 34%
16 The early Russian socialists split into two branches, the Bolsheviks and the:	[1] Marxists [2] Czarists [3] Leninists [4] Mensheviks [5] Partizans	ANSWER TO Q-15 **[1]** Joyce's Stephen Dedalus is referring to the horrors of Ireland's bloody history. 48%
16 What is blackstrap?	[1] Licorice [2] Strong coffee [3] Root beer [4] Molasses [5] Beef jerky	ANSWER TO Q-15 **[1]** The Red Wings have won seven Stanley Cup titles with the Bruins next at five. 52%
16 Judy Blume, S.E. Hinton and Robert Cormier are known for their books about:	[1] New Age spirituality [2] Ethnic cuisine [3] Political scandals [4] Virtual reality [5] Adolescent problems	ANSWER TO Q-15 **[5]** The hideous warthog eats grass and other vegetation. 44%
16 All of these musicals are by Lerner and Loewe except:	[1] Brigadoon [2] Paint Your Wagon [3] Carousel [4] My Fair Lady [5] Camelot	ANSWER TO Q-15 **[4]** Ford gave millions to the Nazis, viewing his contribution as a way of defeating communism. 56%

10 Hominy, a favorite dish in the southern United States, is made from:	[1] Okra [2] Lima beans [3] Sweet potatoes [4] Corn [5] Black-eyed peas	ANSWER TO Q-9 [2] His work in reproductive biology led to the development of the oral contraceptive. 45%
10 Which is not a hit song by the Talking Heads?	[1] Once in a Lifetime [2] Take Me to the River [3] Burning Down the House [4] Rock Lobster [5] Psycho Killer	ANSWER TO Q-9 [4] By using the password, he entered the treasure cave of the 40 thieves. 75%
10 Maule's curse affected the inhabitants of:	[1] House of Seven Gables [2] Baskerville Manor [3] Amityville, Long Island [4] Northanger Abbey [5] Castle Dracula	ANSWER TO Q-9 [3] A climate treaty, a biodiversity treaty and a forest agreement were other results of Rio. 42%
10 Who was not a famous pirate?	[1] William Kidd [2] Edward Teach [3] Henry Cavendish [4] Jean Lafitte [5] Sir Henry Morgan	ANSWER TO Q-9 [2] People never tire of this famous recitation piece. 84%
10 What caused the ocean liner "Lusitania" to sink, sending 1198 people to their deaths?	[1] Ran into iceberg [2] Typhoon [3] German torpedo [4] Boilers blew up [5] Time-bombed luggage	ANSWER TO Q-9 [5] It is based on Celtic legends as old as those of King Arthur. 23%

17 A circumspect person is very:

[1] Argumentative
[2] Sneaky
[3] Vulgar
[4] Prudent
[5] Ill-tempered

ANSWER TO Q-16

[4] Both Bach and Handel were born in 1685. The others lived primarily in the 19th century.

44%

---

17 The Capulets and the Montagues are the feuding families in:

[1] Romeo and Juliet
[2] Rigoletto
[3] War of the Roses
[4] Arsenic and Old Lace
[5] The Little Foxes

ANSWER TO Q-16

[4] Led by Plekhanov, the Mensheviks favored developing a bourgeois-democratic state.

49%

---

17 Which city provides the setting for most of the "Dirty Harry" films?

[1] Boston
[2] New York
[3] Los Angeles
[4] Philadelphia
[5] San Francisco

ANSWER TO Q-16

[4] The dark color of molasses is due to carmelization of the remaining sugars.

58%

---

17 Which animal is found only on the islands of Borneo and Sumatra?

[1] Koala
[2] Komodo dragon
[3] Orangutan
[4] Vampire bat
[5] Pangolin

ANSWER TO Q-16

[5] They deal with sex and identity problems, as well as child-parent conflicts.

71%

---

17 Hair is made of keratin. Which of the following is not made of keratin?

[1] Foot of a camel
[2] Ostrich feathers
[3] Rhinoceros horn
[4] Penguin's beak
[5] Elephant tusk

ANSWER TO Q-16

[3] The team of Rodgers and Hammerstein gave us "Carousel."

45%

9 20th century scientist Gregory Pincus made important discoveries in this field:	[1] Astronomy [2] Biology [3] Meteorology [4] Anthropology [5] Physics	ANSWER TO Q-8 **[1]** This novel by Robert Penn Warren won the Pulitzer in 1947, and an Oscar in 1949. 54%
9 In Arabian mythology, who said "Open sesame"?	[1] Aladdin [2] Genie [3] Scheherazade [4] Ali Baba [5] Sinbad	ANSWER TO Q-8 **[5]** "Satchmo" was 63 when his rendition of "Hello, Dolly" reached number one on the charts. 68%
9 Agenda 21 was a document that resulted from:	[1] SALT talks [2] Geneva convention [3] Rio Earth Summit [4] Camp David accords [5] Yalta conference	ANSWER TO Q-8 **[3]** Fred Macmurray discovers flubber in this 1961 Disney flick, and flies to prove its worth. 69%
9 In what town was mighty Casey playing when he struck out at bat?	[1] Hooterville [2] Mudville [3] Hadleyville [4] Birchwood [5] Lynchburg	ANSWER TO Q-8 **[5]** Tel Aviv was not founded until 1909; it is now Israel's second-largest city. 82%
9 What Wagner opera takes place in Brittany and Cornwall?	[1] Parsifal [2] Tannhauser [3] Lohengrin [4] The Rheingold [5] Tristan und Isolde	ANSWER TO Q-8 **[2]** An emetic induces vomiting and should be used in cases of non-caustic poisoning. 69%

HOW ARE THE QUESTIONS CREATED?

We wrote 'em, one at a time. Do that day in day out, year after year, and the questions start adding up. We employ a large staff of talented writers and editors who spend their days trying to intrigue you. We store the questions in a number of large databases that enable us to organize our collection into some kind of meaningful whole. For example, we can find all the material we have about Elvis or look at all the questions we have about oceans.

When we were designing our game, we decided to explain ourselves after each question, to give some supporting information about why our answer is indeed correct, or why one of the other choices is incorrect. Sometimes we just make a humorous comment or do a little editorializing. It's this feature that we feel makes our game not only unique, but highly credible. Every question we have contains source information. If there's ever a question about a question from our players, we can easily go back to the original reference used to create the question and take a second look at it. We also attempt to verify most of our material against second or, sometimes, third sources. We maintain a large in-house reference library, subscribe to a wide variety of publications, and use materials available to us on CD-ROM and out in cyberspace.

When deciding what kinds of questions to create, we ask ourselves the following: Does this test knowledge? Is this something people may know from their public school education? Has this been covered by major media? Is this fun, creative, or interesting? Does anyone care about this? While some of our players would disagree, it's not our intention to ask trick questions. We want to challenge you to use your own powers of deduction to figure out the correct answer. When you finally see the answer, our goal is to elicit one of these comments from you:

Yay! I knew that!
Geez, I used to know that!
Darn, I should have known that!
Wow, that's interesting; I didn't know that!

We have also created a game that is written entirely by our players. It's called Viewer's Revue and it's played every Tuesday night. All contributors get credit during the show after their question appears. If you get the urge to try your hand at writing a few questions, feel free to send for our Writer's Guidelines by sending a self-addressed, stamped envelope to:

Viewer's Revue Guidelines
NTN Communications, Inc.
2121 Palomar Airport Road, Second Floor
Carlsbad, CA 92009

You can also fax us at 619-438-3505 (address your fax to Viewer's Revue) and request the guidelines.

We'd love to hear from you!

PLAYER QUOTES AND ANECDOTES ...

"My significant other wanted to get married on Valentine's day, but I told him it would interfere with Trivia and to pick another day."—ALARIC, Cincinnati, OH

"When me and my boyfriend have a rift in our relationship, the first thing we do is designate establishments where one can play NTN Trivia without having to run into the other!" —DESSIE, referring to boyfriend ABETV, New York, NY

"I won the big prize in Showdown several years ago. I won it on a day when I knew very few NTN sites would be open. Even though I didn't have a very impressive score, it was enough to win the big prize. It was Christmas Day, 1990." —SEKA, Sacramento, CA

"NTN Trivia is a great opportunity to meet girls. You have to use your mind, for once." —COOK, Cape Coral, FL

"I found out pretty early that we need to check guns at the door so people don't get out of hand." —Rick Hunt, Owner of Rick's American Grill, Denton, TX, only half joking when referring to the competition level in his establishment.

18 Which is not the name of an individual star?	[1] Orion [2] Sirius [3] Betelgeuse [4] Rigel [5] Vega	ANSWER TO Q-17 **[4]** It is the prudent person who considers all the angles before acting. 79%
18 Shoe, drum and lining are parts of a:	[1] Telephone line [2] Boot [3] Pneumatic tire [4] Train wheel [5] Brake	ANSWER TO Q-17 **[1]** "China Girl" and "West Side Story" are two latter-day versions of the same story. 88%
18 "Power tends to corrupt; absolute power corrupts absolutely" was said by this nobleman:	[1] Lord Nelson [2] Marquis de Lafayette [3] Lord Byron [4] Lord Acton [5] Marquis de Sade	ANSWER TO Q-17 **[5]** Clint Eastwood plays the rogue crimefighter in 6 movies, 5 of which are in San Francisco. 79%
18 This woman outlaw, the Bandit Queen, consorted with Cole Younger and Jesse James:	[1] Annie Oakley [2] Mother Jones [3] Calamity Jane [4] Lizzie Borden [5] Belle Starr	ANSWER TO Q-17 **[3]** Fossil remains tell that a giant species of orangutans existed in China 500,000 years ago. 68%
18 Who played the "Six Million Dollar Man" in the TV movie and long-running TV series?	[1] Charles Bronson [2] Leslie Nielsen [3] Robert Culp [4] Burt Reynolds [5] Lee Majors	ANSWER TO Q-17 **[5]** Elephant tusks are elongated teeth, while rhino horns are made of dense layers of hair. 58%

8 Which Pulitzer Prize-winning novel also won an Oscar for best picture?	[1] All the King's Men [2] To Kill a Mockingbird [3] The Old Man and the Sea [4] The Grapes of Wrath [5] The Caine Mutiny	ANSWER TO Q-7 [4] The fine glass-making in the French tradition dates from the late 19th century. 78%
8 In 1964, with this song, musician Louis Armstrong became the oldest artist to hit #1:	[1] What a Wonderful World [2] California, Here I Come [3] Saints Go Marching In [4] Ain't Misbehavin' [5] Hello, Dolly	ANSWER TO Q-7 [3] When a dam burst in Pennsylvania on May 31, 1889, 2200 people died in the flood. 61%
8 A Model-T Ford drove airborne over Washington in this fantasy movie:	[1] Love Bug [2] Chitty Chitty Bang Bang [3] Absent-Minded Professor [4] Bedknobs & Broomsticks [5] Mary Poppins	ANSWER TO Q-7 [1] Waugh was noted for his snobbery and his satirical novels. 72%
8 Which city is not mentioned in the Bible?	[1] Jerusalem [2] Bethany [3] Emmaus [4] Nazareth [5] Tel Aviv	ANSWER TO Q-7 [1] He started hosting it in 1953, when it was still a local show on WNBC-TV in New York. 69%
8 You'd employ an emetic as a first-aid treatment for which malady?	[1] Foreign body in eye [2] Poisoning [3] Electric shock [4] Compound fracture [5] Convulsions	ANSWER TO Q-7 [2] She came to power after the premature deaths of her two brothers, ruling from 1482 to 1503 B.C. 76%

19 Which was discovered in the 18th century?	[1] Blood groups [2] Cosmic rays [3] Smallpox vaccine [4] Pluto [5] Penicillin	ANSWER TO Q-18 **[1]** Orion is the name of the constellation in which Rigel appears. 71%
19 Which is not identified with the collection of tales, "1001 Nights" or "Arabian Nights"?	[1] Aladdin [2] Prince Genjo [3] Samarkand [4] Sinbad [5] Ali Baba	ANSWER TO Q-18 **[5]** The shoe is a metal protective plate. 81%
19 What liqueur is used in a margarita?	[1] Triple Sec [2] Grand Marnier [3] Benedictine [4] Cointreau [5] Creme de Menthe	ANSWER TO Q-18 **[4]** Acton is considered to be the first philosopher of resistance to the evils of the state. 32%
19 "Good to the last drop" was an advertisement for:	[1] Beer [2] Soda [3] Coffee [4] Motor oil [5] Eye drops	ANSWER TO Q-18 **[5]** Her Oklahoma home became notorious as an outlaw refuge. 31%
19 The "con" in con man is short for:	[1] Conniving [2] Contrary [3] Confidence [4] Concerned [5] Consternation	ANSWER TO Q-18 **[5]** The movie also generated the series "Bionic Woman" starring Lindsey Wagner. 92%

7 Emile Galle, Louis Comfort Tiffany and Rene Lalique are all noted:	[1] Leaders of French Canada [2] Pioneers of the cinema [3] World War II spies [4] Makers of glassware [5] Composers	ANSWER TO Q-6 [5] The effects on human health of long term exposure to dioxin are still being disputed. 58%
7 All of these events took place in the 20th century except:	[1] Russian Revolution [2] Wright Brothers flight [3] Johnstown Flood [4] Mt. Everest climbed [5] Titanic sinking	ANSWER TO Q-6 [4] The city of Stockholm is built on several peninsulas and islands. 58%
7 Which novelist was not a woman?	[1] Evelyn Waugh [2] George Eliot [3] Charlotte Bronte [4] Jane Austen [5] George Sand	ANSWER TO Q-6 [3] It is the earliest edition of Shakespeare's collected works. 78%
7 Who was the original host of "The Tonight Show"?	[1] Steve Allen [2] Jack Paar [3] Ernie Kovacs [4] Phil Silvers [5] Mike Douglas	ANSWER TO Q-6 [2] Even though he protects Bess, she leaves town with a rival in this sentimental musical. 58%
7 Pick out the queen among the Egyptian kings:	[1] Ramses [2] Hatshepsut [3] Tutankhamen [4] Amenhotep [5] Cheops	ANSWER TO Q-6 [3] The age of volcanic rock is determined by the decay rate of its radioactive elements. 69%

20 Which famous character is both a princess and a slave?	[1] Topsy [2] Aida [3] Rebecca [4] Lolita [5] Ophelia	ANSWER TO Q-19 **[3]** The others were 20th century discoveries. 68%
20 If you're counting, "one-two-three, one-two three," you're learning to do this dance:	[1] Waltz [2] Jitterbug [3] Rumba [4] Foxtrot [5] Two-step	ANSWER TO Q-19 **[2]** Prince Genjo is the hero of Japan's first great work of literature. 69%
20 Which of these famous books was published first?	[1] Fahrenheit 451 [2] Animal Farm [3] Catch-22 [4] A Clockwork Orange [5] Slaughterhouse-Five	ANSWER TO Q-19 **[1]** It is made with three parts of tequila to one part triple sec. 77%
20 All of these words express negative feelings except:	[1] Anger [2] Affinity [3] Antipathy [4] Asperity [5] Animus	ANSWER TO Q-19 **[3]** This was a slogan for Maxwell House coffee. 92%
20 Which NBA star made the "sky hook" famous?	[1] Wilt Chamberlain [2] Bill Russell [3] Kareem Abdul-Jabbar [4] Julius Erving [5] John Havlicek	ANSWER TO Q-19 **[3]** The term is short for "confidence game," one of the famed early scams con men used to pull. 58%

6 Agent Orange contains this chemical compound:	[1] Arsenic [2] Cyanide [3] Mercury [4] Thallium [5] Dioxin	ANSWER TO Q-5 [2] The term can be used figuratively or literally. 79%
6 This city lies on the coast of the Baltic Sea:	[1] Reykjavik [2] Oslo [3] Amsterdam [4] Stockholm [5] Hamburg	ANSWER TO Q-5 [4] Zoology is a life science. 53%
6 Which author is associated with "The First Folio"?	[1] Charles Dickens [2] George Bernard Shaw [3] William Shakespeare [4] Cervantes [5] Homer	ANSWER TO Q-5 [3] Their 1966 "Tell It Like It Is" was adopted as the anthem of the Black Power movement. 65%
6 In the Gershwin opera "Porgy and Bess," Porgy is a:	[1] Railroad conductor [2] Beggar [3] Criminal [4] Store clerk [5] Minister	ANSWER TO Q-5 [5] The others empty into the Mediterranean or Adriatic Seas. 62%
6 Which discovery made it possible to accurately calculate the Earth's age?	[1] Continental drift [2] Carbon dating [3] Radioactivity [4] The greenhouse effect [5] Fossils	ANSWER TO Q-5 [5] An adze is an ax-like tool for trimming and smoothing wood. 53%

21
Which Greek philosopher sought an honest man?

[1] Socrates
[2] Diogenes
[3] Plato
[4] Aristotle
[5] Epicurus

ANSWER TO Q-20

[2] The daughter of the king of Ethiopia, she was captured and enslaved by the Egyptians.

54%

21
What was the magic phrase Ali Baba used to open the cave of the forty thieves?

[1] Mumbo Jumbo
[2] Abracadabra
[3] Shazam
[4] Alakazam
[5] Open Sesame

ANSWER TO Q-20

[1] All the rest of the dances are based on counts of two or four.

79%

21
Which is not a space on which you can land when playing Monopoly?

[1] Free Parking
[2] Go to Jail
[3] Community Chest
[4] Park Place
[5] Red Line Railroad

ANSWER TO Q-20

[2] Orwell's book dates from 1945, while the others were published after 1950.

57%

21
The nickname of former heavyweight champion James Douglas is:

[1] Bonecrusher
[2] Pops
[3] Buster
[4] Tank
[5] Razor

ANSWER TO Q-20

[2] Affinity is a natural liking or sympathy toward someone or something.

81%

21
What drink do you make with red wine, fruit slices, sugar and a little brandy?

[1] Sangria
[2] Spritzer
[3] Black Velvet
[4] Tom and Jerry
[5] Planter's Punch

ANSWER TO Q-20

[3] Jabbar used his patented shot in becoming the all-time leading scorer in NBA history.

82%

5 A veneer is a:	[1] Mammal [2] Covering [3] Lamp [4] Automobile [5] Fruit	ANSWER TO Q-4 **[1]** The capital of Iceland lies roughly 200 miles below the Arctic Circle. 57%
5 Which is not an earth science?	[1] Oceanography [2] Geology [3] Paleontology [4] Zoology [5] Meteorology	ANSWER TO Q-4 **[4]** "Buddenbrooks" concerns a once-prosperous family in the midst of decay. 42%
5 Aaron, Art, Charles and Cyril are the _____ brothers.	[1] Flying Burrito [2] Righteous [3] Neville [4] Everly [5] Isley	ANSWER TO Q-4 **[4]** An intense gambler, the Earl created it so he could eat while he played at the tables. 68%
5 Which river empties into the North Sea?	[1] Ebro [2] Rhone [3] Po [4] Nile [5] Elbe	ANSWER TO Q-4 **[3]** They all decided while still at Cambridge in the 1930's to become Soviet spies. 65%
5 What type of person would use an adze?	[1] Plumber [2] Electrician [3] Appliance repair [4] Roofer [5] Carpenter	ANSWER TO Q-4 **[1]** The assassination of Archduke Francis Ferdinand in Sarajevo led to European war. 62%

22 The Parsees are a religious community located in:	[1] India [2] Libya [3] Armenia [4] Ethiopia [5] Mongolia	ANSWER TO Q-21 **[2]** He lived in a tub to dramatize his motto that the virtuous life is the simple life. 69%
22 A butterfly's proboscis is its:	[1] Antenna [2] Tongue [3] Wing [4] Body [5] Chrysalis	ANSWER TO Q-21 **[5]** Ali's slave, Morgiana, killed the thieves by pouring boiling oil into the jars where they hid. 75%
22 What kind of creature is the caterpillar hunter?	[1] Bird [2] Amphibian [3] Beetle [4] Reptile [5] Rodent	ANSWER TO Q-21 **[5]** Monopoly's 4 railroads are Reading, B&O, Pennsylvania and Short Line. 91%
22 A red wine made from gamay grapes grown in the Lyon region of France is:	[1] Amontillado [2] Beaujolais [3] Asti spumante [4] Hock [5] Moselle	ANSWER TO Q-21 **[3]** His knockout of Mike Tyson in 1990 ranks among the biggest upsets in boxing history. 86%
22 In "Peanuts," Snoopy's fantasy antagonist is this legendary figure:	[1] The Desert Fox [2] Sheriff of Nottingham [3] The Great Khan [4] Red Baron [5] Attila the Hun	ANSWER TO Q-21 **[1]** There is a "blond" variation made with white wine. 81%

4 Which capital lies closest to the Arctic Circle?	[1] Reykjavik [2] Stockholm [3] Oslo [4] Helsinki [5] Warsaw	ANSWER TO Q-3 **[1]** The scuffle in question took place at Boston's North Bridge. 67%
4 Johann Buddenbrooks is the patriarch in a classic novel by:	[1] James Joyce [2] George Eliot [3] D.H. Lawrence [4] Thomas Mann [5] Henry James	ANSWER TO Q-3 **[2]** Calgary is located in the Canadian Rockies. 89%
4 The sandwich was invented by:	[1] Count of Monte Cristo [2] Sandwich Islanders [3] Reuben Laudkins [4] Earl of Sandwich [5] Corny la Beuf	ANSWER TO Q-3 **[2]** Cephalalgia is just a big word for a headache. 78%
4 Which person was not a notorious spy?	[1] Sir Anthony Blunt [2] Guy Burgess [3] Sydney Carton [4] Donald Maclean [5] Kim Philby	ANSWER TO Q-3 **[4]** The acclaimed film stars Snipes as a drug lord who wants out of the business. 68%
4 The assassination of this country's Archduke led to World War I:	[1] Austria [2] Belgium [3] Holland [4] Germany [5] Britain	ANSWER TO Q-3 **[1]** Von Zipper was Frankie Avalon and Annette Funicello's nemesis in the film "Beach Party." 65%

23 Gasoline vaporizes in the ____ before it enters the cylinder of an engine.

[1] Carburetor
[2] Solenoid
[3] Alternator
[4] Starter
[5] Distributor

ANSWER TO Q-22
[1] The economically important group left Iran to escape Muslim persecution.
65%

23 The first _____ was formed in 1792 and a second was formed in 1871.

[1] French monarchy
[2] Commune of Paris
[3] Vichy government
[4] Franco-American entente
[5] French academy

ANSWER TO Q-22
[2] Butterflies feed mainly on nectar which they suck from flowers with the proboscis.
69%

23 Which writer wrote his plays in French and then translated them into English?

[1] Vladimir Nabokov
[2] Joseph Conrad
[3] Sir Richard Burton
[4] Samuel Beckett
[5] Jerzy Kosinski

ANSWER TO Q-22
[3] They eat large quantities of butterfly larvae, even climbing trees to hunt them.
43%

23 Whoopi Goldberg stars in all these films except:

[1] Sister Act
[2] The Color Purple
[3] Boomerang
[4] Ghost
[5] Sarafina

ANSWER TO Q-22
[2] The others listed are neither red wines nor French wines.
45%

23 Which is not one of the four basic golf clubs?

[1] Driver
[2] Iron
[3] Putter
[4] Wedge
[5] Hook

ANSWER TO Q-22
[4] With his scarf flapping in the breeze, the fearless beagle bravely faces the German ace in Charles Schulz's comic strip.
95%

3 Emerson's "Shot heard 'round the world" was the gunfire at the start of the:	[1] American Revolution [2] Little Bighorn [3] First World War [4] California Gold Rush [5] Spanish American War	ANSWER TO Q-2 [4] The Brotherhood is a Communist-party-like organization in "Invisible Man." 54%
3 Where does the spectacular rodeo known as "The Stampede" take place?	[1] Houston [2] Calgary [3] Denver [4] Regina [5] Phoenix	ANSWER TO Q-2 [3] "The Run for the Roses" is considered by some to be the most exciting two minutes in sports. 89%
3 If you are suffering from cephalalgia, what should you do?	[1] Take a brisk walk [2] Swallow some aspirin [3] Hold your breath [4] Call 911 [5] Rinse your eye in water	ANSWER TO Q-2 [5] Banana peels contain dopamine and were smoked in the 1960's as a potential "high." 79%
3 Who stars in the movie, "Sugar Hill"?	[1] Denzel Washington [2] Giancarlo Esposito [3] Larry Fishburne [4] Wesley Snipes [5] Eddie Murphy	ANSWER TO Q-2 [3] After shooting President Lincoln, Booth leaped from the balcony to the stage and injured himself. 76%
3 Of these oddly named people, which one is entirely fictional?	[1] Eric von Zipper [2] Johnny Rotten [3] Moon Unit Zappa [4] Mata Hari [5] Niccolo Machiavelli	ANSWER TO Q-2 [1] Mrs. Malaprop, from the 1775 play "The Rivals," habitually misused words that sounded alike. 45%

24 Every 10 years, since 1634, the villagers of Oberammergau, Germany, have performed:	[1] Faust [2] The Passion Play [3] Boris Godunov [4] Don Juan [5] Madam Butterfly	ANSWER TO Q-23 **[1]** The carburetor mixes the vapor with air for efficient combustion. 68%
24 Miles Davis was a jazz musician known for playing the:	[1] Stand-up bass [2] Piano [3] Guitar [4] Trumpet [5] Drums	ANSWER TO Q-23 **[2]** Radical alternative governments, both communes exerted major political influence. 21%
24 What is the purpose of an auger?	[1] Measuring distances [2] Signaling ships [3] Cutting steel [4] Mixing chemicals [5] Boring holes	ANSWER TO Q-23 **[4]** Irishman Beckett felt the French language curbed a tendency toward verbosity. 32%
24 "The Sound of Music" starred Mary Martin on Broadway; the movie starred:	[1] Carol Burnett [2] Sally Field [3] Loretta Young [4] Tammy Grimes [5] Julie Andrews	ANSWER TO Q-23 **[3]** Whoopi Goldberg has surprised many by becoming one of the most bankable female film stars. 91%
24 "The House of the Spirits" is a novel by:	[1] Toni Morrison [2] Margaret Atwood [3] Isabel Allende [4] Alice Walker [5] Adrienne Rich	ANSWER TO Q-23 **[5]** Each is shaped for a different purpose; for example, the wedge is for short, high shots. 75%

2 Which organization is not found in Orwell's "1984"?	[1] Ministry of truth [2] Thought police [3] Anti-sex league [4] The Brotherhood [5] Inner party	ANSWER TO Q-1 [5] Roland is the most famous of Charlemagne's paladins, or knights. 69%
2 What are the official flowers of the Kentucky Derby?	[1] Black-eyed Susans [2] Queen Anne's Lace [3] Roses [4] Gardenias [5] White carnations	ANSWER TO Q-1 [1] Grandpa was a character on "The Munsters." 91%
2 The banana is notable for its high content of which mineral nutrient?	[1] Zinc [2] Iron [3] Calcium [4] Niacin [5] Potassium	ANSWER TO Q-1 [5] Charlie Chaplin made a movie and Bela Bartok composed an opera about this gruesome murderer. 64%
2 John Wilkes Booth was injured in this way as he fled the scene of Lincoln's assassination:	[1] Burned his face [2] Shot himself in hand [3] Broke his leg [4] Lost an eye [5] Dislocated his shoulder	ANSWER TO Q-1 [1] Many consider Macdonald to be the best writer of American mysteries. 43%
2 The term "malapropism" was derived from a:	[1] Literary character [2] Famous politician [3] City in France [4] European fermented drink [5] Silent film	ANSWER TO Q-1 [4] The Alien and Sedition Acts were passed by the U.S. Congress after the American Revolution. 42%

25 Which Russian leader held power for the longest time?

[1] Stalin
[2] Lenin
[3] Brezhnev
[4] Khrushchev
[5] Molotov

ANSWER TO Q-24

[2] The villagers pledged to perform the play after being spared from the plague.

58%

---

25 Which sort of gemstone would be called a chatoyant?

[1] Paste
[2] Solitaire
[3] Cat's eye
[4] Turquoise
[5] Doublet

ANSWER TO Q-24

[4] He was a catalyst of "cool" jazz in the 50's and led influential bands through the 60's.

79%

---

25 To which language group does modern Arabic belong?

[1] Romance
[2] Semitic
[3] Dravidian
[4] Slavic
[5] Nordic

ANSWER TO Q-24

[5] The three types of augers used for boring holes in wood are the screw, ship and lip-ring.

69%

---

25 What is the primary ingredient of coq au vin?

[1] Duck
[2] Cod
[3] Chicken
[4] Lamb
[5] Lobster

ANSWER TO Q-24

[5] She played Maria, governess and then mother to the Von Trapp family.

98%

---

25 The Latin translation of the Bible is known as the:

[1] Authorized version
[2] Septuagint
[3] Vulgate
[4] Pentateuch
[5] Apocrypha

ANSWER TO Q-24

[3] The Chilean writer's book is the basis of a film starring Meryl Streep and Glenn Close.

42%

1 Who was not a knight of the round table?	[1] Lancelot [2] Galahad [3] Percival [4] Gawain [5] Roland	Turn to the top frame on the next left hand page for the correct answer and the next question.
1 Which was not a character on TV's "The Addams Family"?	[1] Grandpa [2] Lurch [3] Morticia [4] Pugsley [5] Cousin It	Turn to the second frame on the next left hand page for the correct answer and the next question.
1 Which legendary figure had the reputation of being a notorious wife killer?	[1] Don Juan [2] Jack the Ripper [3] Count Dracula [4] Ivan the Terrible [5] Bluebeard	Turn to the middle frame on the next left hand page for the correct answer and the next question.
1 "The Galton Case," "The Chill" and "The Underground Man" are mystery novels by:	[1] Ross Macdonald [2] Raymond Chandler [3] Dashiell Hammett [4] Mickey Spillane [5] Agatha Christie	Turn to the fourth frame on the next left hand page for the correct answer and the next question.
1 Which was not passed by the British Parliament during the colonial era?	[1] Stamp Act [2] Sugar Act [3] Tea Act [4] Alien and Sedition Acts [5] Intolerable Acts	Turn to the bottom frame on the next left hand page for the correct answer and the next question.

26 They are composed of dense bundles of collagenous fibers known as fibroblasts:	[1] Plastics [2] Igneous rocks [3] Telephone wires [4] Tree trunks [5] Ligaments	ANSWER TO Q-25 **[1]** Stalin unofficially came to power in 1924 after the death of Lenin and ruled until 1953. 71%
26 Dickens' Mr. Micawber has come to symbolize the:	[1] Perfect butler [2] Cruel taskmaster [3] Eternal optimist [4] Typical philistine [5] Philandering husband	ANSWER TO Q-25 **[3]** A chatoyant is a stone with a changing luster or twinkling surface. 32%
26 Jimmy Cagney played George M. Cohan on film. Who played "George M!" on stage?	[1] Buddy Ebsen [2] Sid Caesar [3] Joel Grey [4] Ray Bolger [5] David Carradine	ANSWER TO Q-25 **[2]** The Semitic languages are spoken mostly in western Asia. 53%
26 Which alcoholic beverage is fermented twice?	[1] Ale [2] Vodka [3] Tequila [4] Port [5] Champagne	ANSWER TO Q-25 **[3]** This classic French chicken dish is made with red wine and mushrooms. 69%
26 Which film did not earn a black performer an acting Oscar?	[1] In the Heat of the Night [2] An Officer & a Gentleman [3] Gone with the Wind [4] Glory [5] Ghost	ANSWER TO Q-25 **[3]** The Vulgate is the translation of the bible still used by Roman Catholic priests. 32%

GAME NUMBER 12

ANSWER TO Q-15

[5] Chervil is an herb in the parsley family.

72%

GAME NUMBER 30

ANSWER TO Q-15

[4] The others chummed around with the Lone Ranger, Cisco Kid, Tonto and Roy Rogers.

57%

GAME NUMBER 48

ANSWER TO Q-15

[4] The Inuit, or Eskimos, had been on the large island for several thousand years.

76%

GAME NUMBER 66

ANSWER TO Q-15

[1] Neptune was discovered in 1846; the rest were known from ancient times.

59%

GAME NUMBER 84

ANSWER TO Q-15

[3] An official judgment of the Catholic Church, an anathema is pronounced by the Pope.

72%

330

27 This disciple's name was Simon, but Jesus renamed him:	[1] Paul [2] Peter [3] James [4] John [5] Luke	ANSWER TO Q-26 **[5]** Ligaments come in two varieties: yellow and white. 21%
27 A lathe is used to:	[1] Mix chemicals [2] Till soil [3] Measure distances [4] Study stars [5] Shape wood or metal	ANSWER TO Q-26 **[3]** This "David Copperfield"' character always seeks a fortune to turn up to save him from debt. 32%
27 Alvy Singer is a Woody Allen character from which of his films?	[1] Purple Rose of Cairo [2] Annie Hall [3] Manhattan [4] Sleeper [5] Stardust Memories	ANSWER TO Q-26 **[3]** The role followed Grey's award-winning master of ceremonies role in "Cabaret." 43%
27 Which of these cartoon characters could not fly?	[1] Mighty Mouse [2] Rocky the Squirrel [3] Speedy Gonzalez [4] Woodstock [5] Tweety Bird	ANSWER TO Q-26 **[5]** The carbon dioxide produced by the second fermentation is retained to make the bubbles. 42%
27 Which statement about Marco Polo is false?	[1] Never returned to Italy [2] Visited Kublai Khan [3] Traveled with his father [4] Served the Khan in India [5] Citizen of Venice	ANSWER TO Q-26 **[1]** Sidney Poitier won his Oscar for "The Lilies of the Field." 44%

15 Which is not a type of hat?	[1] Toque [2] Fedora [3] Tricorne [4] Fez [5] Chervil	ANSWER TO Q-14 **[5]** It was named for the hero of a Robert Burns poem. 65%
15 Which equine actor was Gene Autry's favorite mount?	[1] Silver [2] Diablo [3] Scout [4] Champion [5] Trigger	ANSWER TO Q-14 **[2]** It is slightly less pungent than the more popular white variety. 67%
15 Until the arrival of Europeans, this area was inhabited solely by the Inuit:	[1] Brazil [2] Japan [3] Australia [4] Greenland [5] Hawaii	ANSWER TO Q-14 **[5]** Norway voted itself independent of Sweden in 1905. 43%
15 Which planet on this list was the most recently discovered?	[1] Neptune [2] Mercury [3] Mars [4] Jupiter [5] Saturn	ANSWER TO Q-14 **[5]** Since Mercury is closely aligned with the sun, it cannot be observed at night. 45%
15 Which term is out of place in that it has nothing to do with the occult?	[1] Medium [2] Seance [3] Anathema [4] Ouija board [5] Ectoplasm	ANSWER TO Q-14 **[3]** Hollywood was quick to employ the UFO scare as a metaphor for the 1950's "Red Scare." 68%

28 Myology is a branch of anatomy which deals with:	[1] Bones [2] Vital organs [3] Muscle tissue [4] Digestive system [5] Circulation	ANSWER TO Q-27 **[2]** Peter means "rock" in Greek and Jesus said, "Upon this rock I will build my church." 79%
28 Saffron has been used for all these purposes except:	[1] Flavor food [2] Coloring dye [3] Medicine [4] Preservative [5] Perfume	ANSWER TO Q-27 **[5]** A lathe shapes a piece of wood by holding and turning it against the edge of a cutting tool. 81%
28 What is the real family name of Martin and Charlie Sheen?	[1] Caine [2] Estevez [3] Lewis [4] Finney [5] Turner	ANSWER TO Q-27 **[2]** Allen's Alvy Singer is a neurotic, romantic New York stand-up comic. 82%
28 The firmament is an archaic word for the earth's:	[1] Skies [2] Flora [3] Oceans [4] Fauna [5] Subterranean regions	ANSWER TO Q-27 **[3]** Speedy was a small, hyper mouse who used his great land speed to escape impending danger. 85%
28 "Great God! This is an awful place," wrote explorer Robert Scott upon reaching the:	[1] Mouth of the Amazon [2] Interior of Australia [3] Belgian Congo [4] Siberian Tundra [5] South Pole	ANSWER TO Q-27 **[1]** Marco Polo returned to Venice in 1275, where he published an account of his travels. 47%

14 A soft, flat, knitted wool hat with a pompom on top is a:	[1] Fedora [2] Chaperon [3] Breton [4] Castor [5] Tam-o'-shanter	ANSWER TO Q-13 **[2]** The hat's purpose was to cushion the rider's head if he happened to fall from his horse. 56%
14 What is added to red horseradish to give it its color?	[1] Food dye [2] Beet juice [3] Tomato sauce [4] Rhubarb [5] Red pepper puree	ANSWER TO Q-13 **[2]** One could say that "horse" users have no horse sense. 97%
14 Which country voted to become independent in the 20th century?	[1] Italy [2] Switzerland [3] Mexico [4] Liberia [5] Norway	ANSWER TO Q-13 **[2]** Members of General MacArthur's staff drew up the document after Japan's defeat in WWII. 54%
14 Which planet is always seen during early morning or twilight?	[1] Pluto [2] Saturn [3] Neptune [4] Uranus [5] Mercury	ANSWER TO Q-13 **[4]** However, the temperature drops to an icy 190° below zero at night. 53%
14 Which unusual trend flared up in the 1950's?	[1] Housewife prostitutes [2] Celebrity seances [3] UFO sightings [4] Satanic cults [5] Bigfoot hunts	ANSWER TO Q-13 **[4]** Amulets are passive and need only be worn, but a talisman must be kissed, touched, or waved about. 45%

29 Which famous TV show aired first?	[1] I Married Joan [2] The Real McCoys [3] I Love Lucy [4] Father Knows Best [5] Ozzie & Harriet	ANSWER TO Q-28 **[3]** It comes from the greek word "mys" which means muscle. 52%
29 Which of these famous musicians died as a teenager?	[1] Sid Vicious [2] Sam Cooke [3] Ritchie Valens [4] Buddy Holly [5] Brian Jones	ANSWER TO Q-28 **[4]** A very expensive cooking spice, it is used to dye the robes of Buddhist monks. 57%
29 In which Italian city did pizza originate?	[1] Turin [2] Milan [3] Rome [4] Venice [5] Naples	ANSWER TO Q-28 **[2]** Emilio kept the family name when he went into show business. 82%
29 Reggie Jackson never played for this team during his major league career:	[1] California Angels [2] Kansas City Royals [3] Oakland A's [4] New York Yankees [5] Baltimore Orioles	ANSWER TO Q-28 **[1]** The sky was poetically viewed as a solid, arched vault. 53%
29 The subclavian vein carries blood from the _____ to the heart:	[1] Foot [2] Arm [3] Pelvis [4] Stomach [5] Throat	ANSWER TO Q-28 **[5]** Capt. Robert F. Scott reached the South Pole a month after Norwegian Roald Amundsen. 64%

13 The top hat, now associated with black-tie dress, was originally used during:	[1] Chimney cleaning [2] Fox hunts [3] Ice skating [4] Infantry assaults [5] Tennis matches	ANSWER TO Q-12 [3] A shift is a shapeless dress. 76%
13 "Horse" is slang for which drug?	[1] Amphetamines [2] Heroin [3] Cocaine [4] Marijuana [5] Valium	ANSWER TO Q-12 [5] It's the oblong-shaped object gynasts vault over. With handles, it's called a pommel horse. 91%
13 Members of the United States Armed Forces helped write this country's constitution:	[1] Russia [2] Japan [3] Mexico [4] China [5] Vietnam	ANSWER TO Q-12 [2] Chiang Kai Shek fled to Taiwan after Mao took over the mainland in 1949. 67%
13 On which planet will you find comfortable afternoon temperatures of around 80°?	[1] Mercury [2] Venus [3] Neptune [4] Mars [5] Jupiter	ANSWER TO Q-12 [2] "Just one of those days" on Venus is equal to 117 days on Earth. 65%
13 The difference between a talisman and an amulet is that a talisman:	[1] Is a religious figure [2] Can only do evil deeds [3] Is just a love charm [4] Must be actively used [5] Brings bad luck	ANSWER TO Q-12 [2] The idea was that you would hit the evil spirit in the eye so he would leave you alone. 53%

30 All of these words are associated with the word "green" except:	[1] Verdant [2] Malachite [3] Corundum [4] Inexperienced [5] Emerald	ANSWER TO Q-29 **[3]** The television show "I Love Lucy" was first aired on October 15, 1951. 68%
30 Gold occurs in all these forms except:	[1] Dust [2] Nuggets [3] Grains [4] Flakes [5] Crystals	ANSWER TO Q-29 **[3]** Ritchie Valens was only 17 years old when he died in a plane crash with Buddy Holly in 1955. 79%
30 A book in the Bible, it is an exchange among a chorus of young women, a girl and a king:	[1] Exodus [2] Ruth [3] The Song of Solomon [4] Job [5] The Revelation	ANSWER TO Q-29 **[5]** Sailors from the famous harbor spread the basic Neapolitan pizza to ports worldwide. 57%
30 This legendary dragon slayer is the patron saint of England:	[1] George [2] Patrick [3] Boniface [4] Joan of Arc [5] Stephen	ANSWER TO Q-29 **[2]** Jackson played for the A's when they were in Kansas City (1968), but never for the Royals. 54%
30 Six of the twenty highest waterfalls in the world are in this U.S. national park:	[1] Yosemite [2] Yellowstone [3] Zion [4] Grand Canyon [5] Redwood	ANSWER TO Q-29 **[2]** It is one of two veins which carry blood from the arm; the brachial vein is the other. 67%

12 Which item is not worn on the head?	[1] Mantilla [2] Fez [3] Shift [4] Bowler [5] Babushka	ANSWER TO Q-11 **[3]** They are often worn by soldiers or as badges. 45%
12 In which sport is a "horse" used by participants?	[1] Water polo [2] Wrestling [3] Ice hockey [4] Skiing [5] Gymnastics	ANSWER TO Q-11 **[5]** Horsehair is stiff fabric made from horse's hair. 79%
12 Which Chinese leader established the Nationalist Republic of China in Taiwan?	[1] Sun Yat Sen [2] Chiang Kai Shek [3] Chou En Lai [4] Deng Xiaping [5] Mao Zedong	ANSWER TO Q-11 **[3]** After four years of heavy fighting, the Dutch granted sovereignty in 1949. 56%
12 Which planet has the longest day, from sunrise to sunrise?	[1] Mercury [2] Venus [3] Jupiter [4] Uranus [5] Pluto	ANSWER TO Q-11 **[3]** The second largest planet in the solar system, it would float in an ocean. 79%
12 Why should you throw spilled salt over your left shoulder?	[1] To cleanse the air [2] Eliminate evil spirits [3] It's good for your rugs [4] Beckon good spirits [5] Feed the spirits	ANSWER TO Q-11 **[2]** Libra is represented by scales; the rest of the zodiac consists of four human and seven animal houses. 89%

BRAIN BUSTER

GAME NUMBER 8

ANSWER TO Q-30

[3] A corundum is a mineral associated with rubies and sapphires.

79%

BRAIN BUSTER

GAME NUMBER 26

ANSWER TO Q-30

[5] Gold occurs in quartz veins or lodes and in alluvial placer deposits.

81%

BRAIN BUSTER

GAME NUMBER 44

ANSWER TO Q-30

[3] King Solomon and the unnamed girl exchange expressions of love as the young women comment.

77%

BRAIN BUSTER

GAME NUMBER 62

ANSWER TO Q-30

[1] The others are patron saints of Ireland, Germany, France and Hungary.

85%

BRAIN BUSTER

GAME NUMBER 80

ANSWER TO Q-30

[1] Yosemite Falls, which drops 2425 feet, is the highest in North America.

75%

11 Ribbons, feathers and rosettes on hats are called:	[1] Homburgs [2] Coronas [3] Cockades [4] Tercels [5] Rubrics	ANSWER TO Q-10 **[3]** In the 1920's, the toque was easily worn over bobbed hair, pulled down to the penciled brow. 59%
11 All of these are plants except:	[1] Horse-tail [2] Horse-weed [3] Horse-nettle [4] Horse-mint [5] Horse-hair	ANSWER TO Q-10 **[2]** The former western star Allan "Rocky" Lane was the voice of Mr. Ed. 68%
11 Indonesia gained its independence from this nation in 1949:	[1] France [2] England [3] The Netherlands [4] Spain [5] Russia	ANSWER TO Q-10 **[2]** Westerners used the name Persia until 1935, when the Iranians asked that the name be changed. 89%
11 This is the least dense planet in our solar system:	[1] Venus [2] Mars [3] Saturn [4] Uranus [5] Pluto	ANSWER TO Q-10 **[4]** Its four largest moons, Callistro, Ganymede, Europa and Amalthea, were discovered by Galileo in 1610. 71%
11 What is the one sign of the zodiac that is an object, rather than a person or animal?	[1] Gemini [2] Libra [3] Aries [4] Leo [5] Taurus	ANSWER TO Q-10 **[3]** Some things have got to be believed to be seen. 81%

1 Cantons play a large role in life in Switzerland. What are they?	[1] Miniature cheese snacks [2] Alpine rescue dogs [3] Governmental units [4] Subsidized housing [5] Weekly festivals	Turn to the top frame on the next right hand page for the correct answer and the next question.
1 Which term does not refer to a type of wind?	[1] Sirocco [2] Mistral [3] El Nino [4] Chinook [5] Papagayo	Turn to the second frame on the next right hand page for the correct answer and the next question.
1 In 1993, a peace accord between Tutsi rebels and this nation's government was signed:	[1] Sri Lanka [2] Madagascar [3] Tibet [4] The Philippines [5] Rwanda	Turn to the middle frame on the next right hand page for the correct answer and the next question.
1 Modern man evolved in this geologic epoch, which ended just 10,000 years ago:	[1] Pleistocene [2] Mesozoic [3] Cambrian [4] Holocene [5] Jurassic	Turn to the fourth frame on the next right hand page for the correct answer and the next question.
1 The Treaty of Verdun divided this emperor's empire among his heirs:	[1] Octavian [2] Louis XIV [3] William of Orange [4] King Arthur [5] Charlemagne	Turn to the bottom frame on the next right hand page for the correct answer and the next question.

10 Name the tight-fitting wool hat worn by women:	[1] Cornet [2] Dolly Varden [3] Toque [4] Mobcap [5] Tarboosh	ANSWER TO Q-9 **[5]** Sold at an auction for $29,471, Napoleon's cap became the most expensive hat ever. 79%
10 Who starred as the man who could talk with his horse in the TV sitcom "Mr. Ed"?	[1] Tim Conway [2] Alan Young [3] John McIntire [4] Eddie Albert [5] Dick York	ANSWER TO Q-9 **[5]** Pedicabs are three wheeled vehicles that are ridden like a bicycle. 67%
10 Which country was once known as Persia?	[1] Iraq [2] Iran [3] Saudi Arabia [4] Yemen [5] Egypt	ANSWER TO Q-9 **[1]** Bolshevik workers captured government buildings and the Winter Palace in October 1917. 54%
10 Its four largest moons are referred to as the "Galilean Moons":	[1] Uranus [2] Venus [3] Pluto [4] Jupiter [5] Saturn	ANSWER TO Q-9 **[1]** The spot may be the vortex of a hurricane that has been whirling for seven centuries. 81%
10 The raising of an object into the air using supernatural power is called:	[1] Ghostly erection [2] Pandering [3] Levitation [4] Grafting [5] Hyperkinesis	ANSWER TO Q-9 **[2]** These beings were first described by Paracelsus, a 15th-century alchemist and physician. 57%

2 This analytic technique makes use of differences in density:	[1] Filtration [2] Centrifugation [3] Distillation [4] Electrophoresis [5] Chromatography	ANSWER TO Q-1 **[3]** Each of the 23 cantons has more power to govern itself than the federal Swiss government does. 79%
2 Who was not one of the original Twelve Apostles of Christ?	[1] Andrew [2] Thomas [3] Peter [4] Paul [5] Matthew	ANSWER TO Q-1 **[3]** El Nino is the term used for the periodic warming of the Earth's equatorial waters. 69%
2 What famous structure did Frank Lloyd Wright design in Bear Run, Pennsylvania?	[1] Larkin Building [2] Unity Temple [3] Fallingwater [4] Trinity College Library [5] Century Club	ANSWER TO Q-1 **[5]** The Tutsi, known for being extremely tall, were exiled to Rwanda from Uganda in 1980. 68%
2 In physics, the capital letter W is the symbol for:	[1] Energy [2] Weight [3] Planck's Constant [4] Entropy [5] Impedance	ANSWER TO Q-1 **[1]** That epoch began 1.8 million years ago; we are now in the Holocene, or recent, epoch. 57%
2 Where would you find Tobit, Judith, Wisdom, and Baruch?	[1] In Frank Zappa's family [2] Indiana [3] CIA code book [4] Jerusalem Bible [5] A music glossary	ANSWER TO Q-1 **[5]** Charlemagne's empire included a western part (France), an eastern part (Germany), and a middle kingdom. 46%

9 Napoleon did all his masterminding in which type of cap?

[1] Zuccheto
[2] Slouch hat
[3] Babushka
[4] Forage cap
[5] Tricorne

ANSWER TO Q-8

[3] A havelock is a cloth cap, a Stetson a cowboy hat and a bowler a felt hat.
46%

---

9 All of these are kinds of horse-drawn carriages except:

[1] Four-in-hand
[2] Trap
[3] Hackney
[4] Fly
[5] Pedicab

ANSWER TO Q-8

[1] The Indianapolis Colts are originally from Baltimore and play in the Hoosier Dome.
68%

---

9 The Bolshevik Revolt is also known as the _____ Revolution.

[1] October
[2] May
[3] December
[4] January
[5] November

ANSWER TO Q-8

[3] These famous words were written by Henry Lee.
62%

---

9 Which planet has a "great red spot" on its surface that is 25,000 miles wide?

[1] Jupiter
[2] Uranus
[3] Saturn
[4] Neptune
[5] Venus

ANSWER TO Q-8

[4] Of the planet's 16 known moons, Io is closest to Jupiter and is the most geologically active.
65%

---

9 These little, imaginary, mis-shapen people live in the bowels of the earth guarding metals:

[1] Troll
[2] Gnome
[3] Sprite
[4] Brownie
[5] Ogre

ANSWER TO Q-8

[2] It stems from the belief that the sign of the cross will ward off evil.
45%

344

3 Crossing the Khyber Pass, you go from the Valley of Pakistan to the high plateau of:	[1] Iraq [2] Afghanistan [3] Morocco [4] Turkey [5] Nepal	ANSWER TO Q-2 [2] In a centrifuge, higher density material separates itself from less dense material. 35%
3 In the book of Daniel, this ruler is said to have grazed like an ox after going insane:	[1] Herod [2] Attila [3] Solomon [4] Caesar [5] Nebuchadnezzar	ANSWER TO Q-2 [4] Paul came later, and was known as an apostle for his work in spreading the Gospel. 69%
3 Which of these famous structures is oldest?	[1] Angkor Wat [2] The Alhambra [3] Notre Dame de Paris [4] Taj Mahal [5] Hagia Sophia	ANSWER TO Q-2 [3] Built in 1936, the building is cantilevered over a waterfall. 42%
3 What Arabic number is represented by the Roman numeral MDCCLXVII?	[1] 1972 [2] 1066 [3] 1557 [4] 1767 [5] 1917	ANSWER TO Q-2 [1] Energy is the ability of matter or radiation to do work. 68%
3 Spanish poet Federico Garcia Lorca achieved his first successes with poetic explorations of:	[1] The Parisian streets [2] Spain's gypsy culture [3] The Spanish civil war [4] Ancient Greece [5] Musical rhythms	ANSWER TO Q-2 [4] Though considered part of the Apocrypha by some scholars, the books have yet to gain wide acceptance. 43%

8 A flat-topped, stiff straw hat with a round, flat brim is a:	[1] Havelock [2] Cloche [3] Boater [4] Stetson [5] Bowler	ANSWER TO Q-7 **[2]** The milliner originated in Milan, Italy, in the 16th century. 81%
8 Which NFL football team has a "horsey" name?	[1] Indianapolis [2] Atlanta [3] Cincinnati [4] Seattle [5] Phoenix	ANSWER TO Q-7 **[1]** A horse must be trained to pace (trot with the legs moving in lateral pairs). 57%
8 Who was "First in war, first in peace, and first in the hearts of his countrymen"?	[1] John F. Kennedy [2] Winston Churchill [3] George Washington [4] Napoleon Bonaparte [5] Vladimir Lenin	ANSWER TO Q-7 **[2]** Called Canada Day or Dominion Day, it celebrates the founding of Canada in 1867. 46%
8 One of its moons, Io, has active volcanoes:	[1] Saturn [2] Uranus [3] Neptune [4] Jupiter [5] Pluto	ANSWER TO Q-7 **[2]** Temperatures on Venus have measured up to 984 degrees. 35%
8 Crossing your fingers evolved from a symbol representing:	[1] Devil horns [2] The cross [3] Submission to emperor [4] Holy Trinity [5] The Star of David	ANSWER TO Q-7 **[2]** The "I Ching," which means "Book of Changes," is based on the teachings of Confucius. 79%

4 The number of protons and neutrons contained in the nucleus of an atom is the:	[1] Atomic number [2] Isotope [3] Electron configuration [4] Mass number [5] Atomic weight	ANSWER TO Q-3 **[2]** The ancient land highway to India, it was used by the conquerors Alexander the Great and Tamerlane. 66%
4 American general Philip Schuyler was blamed for, but later acquitted of, abandoning this fort:	[1] The Alamo [2] West Point [3] Fort Ticonderoga [4] Fort Knox [5] Fort Sumter	ANSWER TO Q-3 **[5]** There is no historical confirmation of the biblical story about the Assyrian king. 65%
4 Which famous man is not best remembered for being a great statesman?	[1] Alexander Dubcek [2] Sir Anthony Eden [3] Henry Clay [4] Robert Walpole [5] William Herschel	ANSWER TO Q-3 **[5]** The Hagia Sophia was built as a Christian church in Constantinople in the sixth century. 57%
4 He wrote "The Compleat Angler," the 1653 essay on fishing, peace and virtue in man:	[1] Rene Descartes [2] Henry David Thoreau [3] William Shakespeare [4] Benjamin Franklin [5] Izaak Walton	ANSWER TO Q-3 **[4]** M=1000, D=500, C=100, L=50, X=10, V=5 and I=1. 79%
4 This emperor ruled from 1867-1912, and transformed Japan into a modern industrial state:	[1] Tokugawa [2] Meiji [3] Chou En-lai [4] Hirohito I [5] Yamamoto	ANSWER TO Q-3 **[2]** His exploration of music and poetry ended with his assassination during the Spanish civil war. 21%

7 If you make hats, you are a:	[1] Jongleur [2] Milliner [3] Tonsure [4] Torsade [5] Dredge	ANSWER TO Q-6 [2] The "coolie hat" of China is worn by one-third of the people on earth. 69%
7 Which is not one of a horse's four natural gaits?	[1] Pace [2] Walk [3] Canter [4] Gallop [5] Trot	ANSWER TO Q-6 [2] The horsemen, from Revelation, are thought to represent Christ, war, famine and death. 67%
7 This country celebrates its founding every July 1st:	[1] Spain [2] Canada [3] Ireland [4] New Zealand [5] Australia	ANSWER TO Q-6 [3] West African military forces divided the country into two zones after a 1990 rebellion. 57%
7 The hottest temperature in the solar system was recorded on this planet:	[1] Mercury [2] Venus [3] Mars [4] Jupiter [5] Saturn	ANSWER TO Q-6 [3] Surface winds on Saturn can reach 1100 miles per hour, compared to 250 mph on Jupiter. 45%
7 To make predictions by using the "I Ching," one must do this:	[1] Play cat's cradle [2] Throw coins or bones [3] Read tea leaves [4] Use tarot cards [5] Drop pebbles in wells	ANSWER TO Q-6 [5] European vampire lore originates in the Balkan region but the belief in vampires is universal. 35%

5 Hands are known for their chiral property. What does "chiral" mean?	[1] Not used for propulsion [2] Sensitive to touch [3] Having mirror-image form [4] Being unique to humans [5] Able to grasp	ANSWER TO Q-4 [4] The number of protons (atomic number) defines the elements and orders the periodic table. 45%
5 The Duke of Medina Sidonia commanded this famous military force:	[1] Spanish Armada [2] Roughriders [3] French Foreign Legion [4] Light Brigade [5] Brown Shirts	ANSWER TO Q-4 [3] During the Revolution, George Washington removed him from command after he surrendered the fort. 32%
5 In which country did the Piast Dynasty rule?	[1] Hungary [2] Poland [3] France [4] Italy [5] Vietnam	ANSWER TO Q-4 [5] William Herschel was the British astronomer who discovered Uranus. 43%
5 Who did Ramon Mercador Del Rio assassinate?	[1] Leon Trotsky [2] Pope Paul I [3] Huey Long [4] Indira Gandhi [5] Lord Louis Mountbatten	ANSWER TO Q-4 [5] He also did biographies of his close friends John Donne and George Herbert. 21%
5 The Alfold is a great, fertile plain in the eastern portion of this country:	[1] France [2] Sweden [3] Scotland [4] Belgium [5] Hungary	ANSWER TO Q-4 [2] Although he was 15 years old when he gained the throne, his power was more symbolic than actual. 21%

6 The most common hat in the world today is made of:	[1] Straw [2] Bamboo [3] Felt [4] Fur [5] Fabric	ANSWER TO Q-5 [3] The famous cowboy hats were expensive but guaranteed to last a lifetime. 45%
6 Where can you find the first reference to the "Four Horsemen of the Apocalypse"?	[1] Shakespeare [2] The Bible [3] Aesop's fables [4] Greek mythology [5] Icelandic sagas	ANSWER TO Q-5 [4] Henry Fonda starred in the 1976 TV remake of the 1946 classic film version of the story. 79%
6 In 1822, Liberia was founded by:	[1] The East India Company [2] Pirates [3] Freed slaves [4] A French expedition [5] A Dutch gold mining co.	ANSWER TO Q-5 [4] France's support was based on its hatred for England rather than love of popular democracy. 79%
6 Which planet has the highest winds?	[1] Earth [2] Jupiter [3] Saturn [4] Uranus [5] Mercury	ANSWER TO Q-5 [3] It travels at 107,000 mph. The closer planets must travel faster to escape the Sun's pull. 81%
6 According to gypsy lore, vampires return from the dead for all these reasons except:	[1] Revenge [2] Restlessness [3] Sexual hunger [4] Improper burial [5] To warn the living	ANSWER TO Q-5 [1] For example, lines that slant upward indicate optimism and a downward slant shows caution. 79%

6 In Ireland, the word "lough" means:	[1] Lazy, slovenly person [2] Impassable obstruction [3] Lake, or ocean inlet [4] Boiled potatoes [5] Overweight	ANSWER TO Q-5 **[3]** Gloves are chiral, but socks are achiral, because a sock can be worn on either foot. 31%
6 What musical instrument has a "frog" in the U.S. and a "nut" in Great Britain?	[1] Trombone [2] Organ [3] Guitar [4] Saxophone [5] Violin	ANSWER TO Q-5 **[1]** The Spanish duke lost 70 ships and some 10,000 men in the 1588 defeat by the English. 33%
6 In the Bible, Abaddon is the angel who presides over:	[1] A bottomless pit [2] The Garden of Eden [3] Jacob's Ladder [4] The Gates of Heaven [5] The Walls of Jericho	ANSWER TO Q-5 **[2]** The first dynasty of Polish dukes and kings ruled from 962 to 1370. 15%
6 Which historical figure nailed the famous "Ninety-five Theses" to a church door?	[1] Joan of Arc [2] Oliver Cromwell [3] Martin Luther [4] Napoleon Bonaparte [5] Thomas Jefferson	ANSWER TO Q-5 **[1]** Leon Trotsky was murdered while exiled in Mexico, probably on orders from Josef Stalin. 25%
6 Englishman Alfred R. Wallace is noted for developing theories similar to those of:	[1] Sigmund Freud [2] Karl Marx [3] Adam Smith [4] Charles Darwin [5] Niccolo Machiavelli	ANSWER TO Q-5 **[5]** Hungary's main exports are grains, fruits and grapes grown in the fertile plain. 32%

5 When this hat first came out, it cost almost a month's wages to buy:	[1] Pillbox hat [2] Fez [3] Stetson [4] Top hat [5] Bowler	ANSWER TO Q-4 **[4]** A bearskin is the type of hat seen on the guards at Buckingham Palace. 46%
5 The title of John Steinbeck's novel about a young boy's love for his horse is:	[1] Black Beauty [2] My Friend Flicka [3] Black Stallion [4] The Red Pony [5] The Yearling	ANSWER TO Q-4 **[4]** The king crab's exoskeleton has a broad, horseshoe-shaped front part. 54%
5 Which European country was the prime ally of the U.S. in the Revolutionary War?	[1] England [2] Spain [3] Italy [4] France [5] Portugal	ANSWER TO Q-4 **[3]** It continued under a monarch until 1889, when a bloodless revolution established a republic. 67%
5 Which planet orbits the sun at the fastest speed?	[1] Mars [2] Venus [3] Mercury [4] Saturn [5] Uranus	ANSWER TO Q-4 **[2]** The Earth's diameter is only 220 miles longer than that of Venus. 68%
5 Analysis of character through handwriting is called:	[1] Graphology [2] Divination [3] Lithomancy [4] Phrenology [5] Palmistry	ANSWER TO Q-4 **[2]** The swords in a tarot card deck correspond to spades, wands to clubs, cups to hearts, and pentacles to diamonds. 25%

7 Who wrote about the encounters of American heroines with European culture?	[1] Ezra Pound [2] Henry Miller [3] Thomas Wolfe [4] Henry James [5] Richard Wright	ANSWER TO Q-6 [3] In Scotland, the term of reference is "loch." 33%
7 Sedimentary rock is formed from sediment in a process called:	[1] Diagenesis [2] Induration [3] Leaching [4] Infibulation [5] Abiogenesis	ANSWER TO Q-6 [5] It is the part of the bow that is used to tighten the hair. 21%
7 Which famous city is set along the banks of the Dnieper River?	[1] Oslo [2] Amsterdam [3] Nice [4] Kiev [5] Teheran	ANSWER TO Q-6 [1] The description of this place of death is found in the book of Revelation. 44%
7 Quito is the capital of which nation?	[1] Sudan [2] Thailand [3] Ecuador [4] Dominican Republic [5] Bulgaria	ANSWER TO Q-6 [3] He attacked the Catholic Church's practice of selling indulgences to the wealthy. 57%
7 Which Michelangelo sculpture is in Rome's St. Peter's Cathedral?	[1] David [2] Last Judgment [3] Conversion of Paul [4] Martyrdom of Peter [5] Pieta	ANSWER TO Q-6 [4] A naturalist, his work in Brazil led to a concept of evolution very much like Darwin's. 43%

4 The wide-brimmed fedora hat that Harrison Ford made popular in "Indiana Jones" is called:	[1] Kaffiyeh [2] Shako [3] Bearskin [4] Borsalino [5] Sombrero	ANSWER TO Q-3 **[4]** The term is used when a player scores three goals in one game. 91%
4 The horseshoe crab is also called the ____ crab.	[1] Hermit [2] Blue [3] Soft-shell [4] King [5] Dungeness	ANSWER TO Q-3 **[2]** The tree got its name because the seeds were used to treat equine respiratory illnesses. 53%
4 This Latin American nation was a colony of Portugal until 1822:	[1] Colombia [2] Venezuela [3] Brazil [4] Panama [5] Mexico	ANSWER TO Q-3 **[5]** The native Aborigines are thought to have migrated from Southeast Asia 20,000 years ago. 89%
4 Which two planets are almost identical in size?	[1] Saturn - Jupiter [2] Earth - Venus [3] Uranus - Saturn [4] Mars - Mercury [5] Pluto - Neptune	ANSWER TO Q-3 **[3]** The four terrestrials, made of solid material, are Mercury, Earth, Venus and Mars. 79%
4 Which is not one of the four suits found in a tarot card deck?	[1] Swords [2] Crowns [3] Wands [4] Cups [5] Pentacles	ANSWER TO Q-3 **[2]** Burying an animal upside down behind a barn will have the same effect. 24%

8 The ancient Roman province of Cappadocia occupied the land that is modern-day:	[1] France [2] Greece [3] England [4] Turkey [5] India	ANSWER TO Q-7 [4] Brother of psychologist William James, his most famous work is "Portrait of a Lady." 41%
8 In the Old Testament, Nebuchadnez-zar had all but ____ cast into the fiery furnace.	[1] Meshach [2] Daniel [3] Samuel [4] Shadrach [5] Abednego	ANSWER TO Q-7 [1] Abiogenesis is a theory that living things can develop from nonliving matter. 22%
8 What is the main tool used by the U.S. Federal Reserve Board to control the money supply?	[1] The gold standard [2] Reserve requirements [3] The stock exchange [4] The bond market [5] Inflation	ANSWER TO Q-7 [4] Kiev is the capital of Ukraine. 22%
8 The aver-age distance a molecule or atom can travel before colliding is called:	[1] Atomic distance [2] Perigee [3] Mach number [4] Diffusion constant [5] Mean free path	ANSWER TO Q-7 [3] However, Guayaquil is the country's largest city and chief port of trade. 35%
8 Which ac-tress starred in "Wings," the first film to win the Oscar for Best Picture?	[1] Mary Pickford [2] Clara Bow [3] Claudette Colbert [4] Helen Hayes [5] Gloria Swanson	ANSWER TO Q-7 [5] The others are in Florence, the Sistine Chapel and the Pauline Chapel respectively. 44%

3 "Hat trick" is a term from this sport:	[1] Swimming [2] Basketball [3] Track [4] Hockey [5] Baseball	ANSWER TO Q-2 **[4]** The nickname comes from the hatmaker's real name: John Batterson Stetson. 43%
3 Horsechestnuts were once used as:	[1] Money [2] Horse medicine [3] Cattle food [4] Good luck charms [5] Glue ingredient	ANSWER TO Q-2 **[5]** "The Horse's Mouth" is a classic Alec Guinness comedy based on the Joyce Cary novel. 88%
3 What country was founded as a British penal colony?	[1] Bahamas [2] Honduras [3] Kenya [4] Tanzania [5] Australia	ANSWER TO Q-2 **[1]** The February revolution in France marked the beginning of unrest throughout Europe. 24%
3 Which is the largest of the four terrestrial planets?	[1] Mercury [2] Venus [3] Earth [4] Mars [5] Jupiter	ANSWER TO Q-2 **[3]** Scientists believe they are the remnants of planets that exploded in other galaxies. 43%
3 If you are a witch, what will tying a knot in a cow's tail do?	[1] Produce good offspring [2] Keep milk from curdling [3] Cure hoof and mouth disease [4] Cause a good harvest [5] Remove a curse	ANSWER TO Q-2 **[5]** 56 cards make up the Minor Acaana; 22 cards, the Major. 43%

9 If a "kachina" is your ancestor spirit, you are a member of this small-scale society:	[1] Maori of New Zealand [2] Djuka of Suriname [3] Pueblo Indians of U.S. [4] Abelam of New Guinea [5] Yoruba of Nigeria	ANSWER TO Q-8 **[4]** At various times, Turkey has been Hittite, Roman, Persian, Ottoman and Byzantine property. 11%
9 Russian musician Sviatoslav Richter is known in the world of music as a:	[1] Gypsy violinist [2] Orchestra conductor [3] Classical pianist [4] Avant-garde composer [5] Opera baritone	ANSWER TO Q-8 **[3]** After they were unharmed, Nebuchadnezzar decreed that the God of the Hebrews be respected. 34%
9 Fashion plate Beau Brummel was a friend and contemporary of this famous figure:	[1] Mark Twain [2] English King George IV [3] Sarah Bernhardt [4] Mozart [5] Socrates	ANSWER TO Q-8 **[2]** The agency controls the supply by requiring banks to keep deposits on reserve. 45%
9 In this ancient religion, Horus was the sky god of light and goodness:	[1] Greek [2] Druidic [3] Roman [4] Egyptian [5] Chinese	ANSWER TO Q-8 **[5]** The figure is only an average, and scientists don't know what the particles collide with. 55%
9 Jean Paul Marat was a famous French ____.	[1] Spy novelist [2] World War I general [3] Serial killer [4] Fashion designer [5] Revolutionary leader	ANSWER TO Q-8 **[2]** The 1927 Academy Award winner also features spectacular WWI aerial combat footage. 51%

2 A "John B." is the nick-name for a:	[1] Panama hat [2] Tam-o'-shanter [3] Bowler [4] Stetson hat [5] Busby hat	ANSWER TO Q-1 **[1]** The hat is named for a strong wind from the southwest. 89%
2 All of these movies were about horses except:	[1] National Velvet [2] Hot to Trot [3] My Friend Flicka [4] Equus [5] The Horse's Mouth	ANSWER TO Q-1 **[1]** Cows and deer are "even-toed" because they have two hooves on each foot. 54%
2 The revolutions of 1848 took place in all but which country?	[1] Ireland [2] France [3] Germany [4] Austria [5] Italy	ANSWER TO Q-1 **[4]** The revolution might not have gotten very far if King Louis had agreed to abide by a constitution. 81%
2 What celestial bodies are also known as "Minor Planets"?	[1] Moons [2] Comets [3] Asteroids [4] Novas [5] White dwarfs	ANSWER TO Q-1 **[2]** The second farthest planet from the sun was discovered in 1846 by astronomer Johann Galle. 79%
2 Where are Minor Arcana and Major Arcana found?	[1] Blood relatives [2] The zodiac [3] Mars [4] Human brain [5] Tarot deck	ANSWER TO Q-1 **[4]** In ancient times, disease and the like were thought to come from roaming evil. 88%

10 Cannae was the site of a remarkable victory by which military leader?	[1] Alexander the Great [2] Hannibal [3] Napoleon [4] Patton [5] Rommel	ANSWER TO Q-9 [3] Kachinas are symbolized by various sculptures and sacred masks. 55%
10 The Treaty of Kiel in 1814 gave Norway its independence from:	[1] Sweden [2] Denmark [3] Portugal [4] France [5] England	ANSWER TO Q-9 [3] Richter is noted for the warmth of his interpretations of 19th-century classics. 22%
10 Dido, the tragic Queen of Carthage, was the sister of this famous figure of mythology:	[1] Hercules [2] Pygmalion [3] Odysseus [4] Jason [5] Agamemnon	ANSWER TO Q-9 [2] The arbiter of fashion fled to France to escape his creditors in 1816. 21%
10 He discovered the "red shift," laying the foundation for the Big Bang theory:	[1] Carl Sagan [2] J. Allen Hynek [3] Werner Heisenberg [4] Linus Pauling [5] Edwin Hubble	ANSWER TO Q-9 [4] He defeated Set, the god of evil and darkness, avenging his father Osiris's murder. 11%
10 After the American Revolution, a soldier named Daniel Shays led a revolt on behalf of:	[1] Southern slaves [2] New England farmers [3] Irish immigrants [4] Local Indian tribes [5] Coal miners	ANSWER TO Q-9 [5] A supporter of the Reign of Terror, he was knifed to death in his bath by Charlotte Corday. 35%

1 Who would wear a sou'wester?	[1] A sailor [2] Someone in the tropics [3] A jockey [4] Palace guards [5] The Pope	Turn to the top frame on the next left hand page for the correct answer and the next question.
1 Why are horses called odd-toed animals?	[1] One hoof on each foot [2] Feathered feet [3] Toe at back of leg [4] Five gaited [5] Ability to prance	Turn to the second frame on the next left hand page for the correct answer and the next question.
1 Which event marked the beginning of the French Revolution?	[1] Beheading of Louis XVI [2] The defeat at Waterloo [3] Marie Antoinette's hoax [4] Storming of the Bastille [5] Reign of Terror	Turn to the middle frame on the next left hand page for the correct answer and the next question.
1 Which planet is normally between Uranus and Pluto?	[1] Mercury [2] Neptune [3] Saturn [4] Mars [5] Jupiter	Turn to the fourth frame on the next left hand page for the correct answer and the next question.
1 An amulet is something that is worn to protect against:	[1] Pregnancy [2] Ultraviolet rays [3] Rain [4] Evil [5] Animal attacks	Turn to the bottom frame on the next left hand page for the correct answer and the next question.

GAME NUMBER 9

ANSWER TO Q-10

[2] To this day, historians use the victory as a point of reference for a very decisive victory.

33%

GAME NUMBER 27

ANSWER TO Q-10

[2] Norway then spent the next century freeing itself from its union with Sweden.

31%

GAME NUMBER 45

ANSWER TO Q-10

[2] In Vergil's drama "Aeneid," Pygmalion murders Dido's husband to get his wealth.

35%

GAME NUMBER 63

ANSWER TO Q-10

[5] He was also the first to prove the existence of galaxies beyond our Milky Way.

45%

GAME NUMBER 81

ANSWER TO Q-10

[2] Shays' rebellion is one of the earliest American examples of a working class uprising.

52%

Hat's Off

GAME NUMBER 11

ANSWER TO Q-30

[1] "Yond Cassius has a lean and hungry look, he thinks too much: such men are dangerous."

43%

Horse Sense

GAME NUMBER 29

ANSWER TO Q-30

[1] The stories all focus on uncanny events and personalities.

43%

Nations

GAME NUMBER 47

ANSWER TO Q-30

[3] "Tyger, tyger, burning bright..." is from William Blake's "Songs of Experience."

42%

Planetarium

GAME NUMBER 65

ANSWER TO Q-30

[3] They are dwarfed by a system of pruning roots and branches. Branches are also trained by tying.

67%

The Occult

GAME NUMBER 83

ANSWER TO Q-30

[1] It was first described by English chemist and physicist John Dalton.

52%

1 Which is not a type of shoe?	[1] Galosh [2] Mukluk [3] Loafer [4] Dickey [5] Wellington	Turn to the top frame on the next right hand page for the correct answer and the next question.
1 Which actor received seven Oscar nominations, but never won the award?	[1] Laurence Harvey [2] Paul Newman [3] Richard Burton [4] Jack Lemmon [5] John Wayne	Turn to the second frame on the next right hand page for the correct answer and the next question.
1 "Tales of Ordinary Madness" and "Hollywood" are books by this controversial author:	[1] Allen Ginsburg [2] Charles Bukowski [3] Norman Mailer [4] Henry Miller [5] William Burroughs	Turn to the middle frame on the next right hand page for the correct answer and the next question.
1 In "The Jungle Book," Mowgli's surrogate mother is a:	[1] Wolf [2] Monkey [3] Bear [4] Snake [5] Panther	Turn to the fourth frame on the next right hand page for the correct answer and the next question.
1 Which statement about John the Baptist is not accurate?	[1] Swallowed by a whale [2] Birth foretold by angel [3] Imprisoned by Herod [4] Mother was Mary's cousin [5] Baptized Jesus	Turn to the bottom frame on the next right hand page for the correct answer and the next question.

30 Who noticed that Cassius had "A lean and hungry look" in Shakespeare's play?	[1] Caesar [2] Brutus [3] Hamlet [4] Lady Macbeth [5] Marc Antony	ANSWER TO Q-29 [4] Belarus is a republic that was created after the fall of the Soviet Union. 76%
30 "Twice Told Tales" is a famous collection of short stories by:	[1] Nathaniel Hawthorne [2] Washington Irving [3] Katherine Mansfield [4] Henry Miller [5] Isak Dinesen	ANSWER TO Q-29 [2] Leveraged buyouts have been used to combat hostile takeover bids. 79%
30 Which visionary poem is incorrectly paired with the poet who wrote it?	[1] The Drunken Boat - Rimbaud [2] Kubla Khan - Coleridge [3] The Tyger - Shelley [4] The Raven - Poe [5] The Twelve - Blok	ANSWER TO Q-29 [5] Paris, Prince of Troy, abducted Helen, the Queen of Sparta, and started the Trojan War. 54%
30 Bonsai trees are tiny because they are:	[1] Burned at the tip [2] Naturally mini [3] Pruned in a special way [4] Never watered [5] Grown in the dark	ANSWER TO Q-29 [4] The champion of workers' rights founded the American Federation of Labor in 1886. 54%
30 If you suffer from daltonism, you are:	[1] Color blind [2] Mute [3] Deaf [4] A dwarf [5] Schizophrenic	ANSWER TO Q-29 [2] Less academic cave exploration is called spelunking. 53%

2 On his famous seven voyages, Sinbad encountered all of these except:	[1] A giant bird, the roc [2] An enormous whale [3] Seven wise men [4] The old man of the sea [5] Cannibal giants	ANSWER TO Q-1 [4] A dickey is an insert worn to fill in the neckline. 75%
2 Genuine Waterford crystal comes from:	[1] China [2] Canada [3] Italy [4] Ireland [5] India	ANSWER TO Q-1 [3] Actor Peter O'Toole shares this dubious distinction with Richard Burton, but still has a chance to win one. 66%
2 Which TV show was set at the Ponderosa ranch?	[1] Gunsmoke [2] Big Valley [3] Bonanza [4] Dallas [5] Beverly Hillbillies	ANSWER TO Q-1 [2] The specialist in the lives and loves of down and outers, he died in March of 1994. 65%
2 Which city in South America is not a seaport?	[1] Georgetown [2] Valparaiso [3] Cayenne [4] Montevideo [5] Bogota	ANSWER TO Q-1 [1] Walt Disney adapted Rudyard Kipling's tales into an animated musical in 1967. 71%
2 To take umbrage is to:	[1] Take offense [2] Show loyalty [3] Offer an apology [4] Incite envy [5] Seek vengeance	ANSWER TO Q-1 [1] It was Old Testament figure Jonah who was swallowed by a "great fish." 81%

29 Which is not a republic born out of the old Yugoslavia?	[1] Croatia [2] Slovenia [3] Bosnia and Herzegovina [4] Belarus [5] Macedonia	ANSWER TO Q-28 **[5]** This is not to say that there isn't room for one more! 71%
29 In business terms, a leveraged buyout is the purchase of a company by:	[1] A competing firm [2] An employee group [3] The U.S. government [4] A national bank [5] Foreign interests	ANSWER TO Q-28 **[2]** Lot was a survivor of the destruction of Sodom and Gomorrah. 78%
29 In Greek myth, they represented the handsomest man and most beautiful woman:	[1] Abelard and Heloise [2] Tristan and Isolde [3] Aeneas and Dido [4] Lancelot and Guinevere [5] Paris and Helen	ANSWER TO Q-28 **[2]** Frank L. Baum wrote the long series of Oz books. 98%
29 Samuel Gompers' name is associated with this aspect of U.S. history:	[1] Western expansion [2] Civil War [3] Louisiana purchase [4] Growth of labor unions [5] Slavery	ANSWER TO Q-28 **[4]** The others mean post office, fountain, highway and avenue, respectively. 34%
29 What would you study if you were a speleologist?	[1] Water sources [2] Caves [3] Mineral deposits [4] Trees [5] Mountains	ANSWER TO Q-28 **[3]** The "Splendid Splinter" was Ted Williams, whose fame came with the Boston Red Sox. 54%

3 The Enola Gay is the name of a famous:	[1] Cruise ship [2] Submarine [3] Bomber [4] Battleship [5] Tank	ANSWER TO Q-2 **[3]** Sinbad's stories are to be found in the tales collected as "The Arabian Nights." 57%
3 A numismatist is one who:	[1] Likes stamps [2] Catches butterflies [3] Explores caves [4] Donates funds [5] Collects coins	ANSWER TO Q-2 **[4]** Stains in your crystal may often be removed by soaking the glass with denture tablets. 71%
3 The Kamchatka peninsula is part of this country:	[1] Turkey [2] Russia [3] India [4] Indonesia [5] Saudi Arabia	ANSWER TO Q-2 **[3]** The 600,000-acre ranch was owned by the Cartwrights of Virginia City. 99%
3 Jonathan Demme's 1980 film "Melvin and Howard" was about this subject:	[1] Watergate's Howard Hunt [2] Minor league baseball [3] Howard Hughes' will [4] Siamese twins [5] Drug smuggling	ANSWER TO Q-2 **[5]** The Colombian capital is found inland and boasts a population of over 4.8 million. 57%
3 If you read a book on mnemonics, you must be trying to improve your:	[1] Vocabulary [2] Speaking voice [3] Health [4] Posture [5] Memory	ANSWER TO Q-2 **[1]** The word is derived from the Latin "umbra," meaning "shadow." 68%

28 Which of these literary names has not come to mean "a seductive male"?	[1] Lovelace [2] Casanova [3] Lothario [4] Don Juan [5] Antonio	ANSWER TO Q-27 [3] Mongrels and alloys are mixtures. Collies and iron are pure. 53%
28 Lot was the nephew of this Old Testament figure:	[1] Noah [2] Abraham [3] Moses [4] Joshua [5] Jacob	ANSWER TO Q-27 [1] The political struggle between capitalists and communists included nuclear stockpiling. 76%
28 The ___ city is found in the land of Oz.	[1] Topaz [2] Emerald [3] Opal [4] Turquoise [5] Zircon	ANSWER TO Q-27 [3] The clown on the Howdy Doody Show communicated by horn. 46%
28 If you want to visit a palace in South America, look for a sign saying:	[1] Correro [2] Fuente [3] Camino Real [4] Alcazar [5] Alameda	ANSWER TO Q-27 [5] "The Bald Soprano" and "Rhinoceros" are his most celebrated plays. 67%
28 Which baseball nickname does not refer to past members of the New York Yankees club?	[1] The Bambino [2] "Joltin" Joe [3] Splendid Splinter [4] Mr. October [5] Murderer's Row	ANSWER TO Q-27 [5] The 1967 classic, "King of Hearts," starred Alan Bates. 68%

4 Which writer was a native English speaker?	[1] Isak Dinesen [2] Vladimir Nabokov [3] Joseph Conrad [4] James Joyce [5] Jerzy Kosinski	ANSWER TO Q-3 **[3]** The Enola Gay dropped the bomb on Hiroshima toward the end of the Second World War. 78%
4 "Moon River" is the signature song of this middle-of-the-road balladeer:	[1] Andy Williams [2] Engelbert Humperdinck [3] Perry Como [4] Frank Sinatra [5] Tony Bennett	ANSWER TO Q-3 **[5]** The term is derived from the latin "numisma," meaning coin. 77%
4 Which kind of whale could be called the unicorn of the sea?	[1] Sperm [2] Beluga [3] Humpback [4] Narwhal [5] Great white	ANSWER TO Q-3 **[2]** This Siberian land mass is known for its prodigious wildlife. 79%
4 Where is the pelagic zone located?	[1] Open sea [2] Polar ice cap [3] Pelvic girdle [4] Serengeti plains [5] Cerebral cortex	ANSWER TO Q-3 **[3]** Melvin Dummar claimed Hughes had left him $156 million for loaning him a quarter. 75%
4 Which is not true of the film "Annie Hall"?	[1] Set in New York City [2] Centers on talent agency [3] Directed by Woody Allen [4] Stars Diane Keaton [5] Won Best Picture	ANSWER TO Q-3 **[5]** Mnemonics are techniques for improving the memory by using certain formulas. 81%

27 Mongrel is to collie as ___ is to ___.	[1] Man - god [2] Man - angel [3] Alloy - iron [4] Anger - piety [5] Varied - motley	ANSWER TO Q-26 **[4]** The scheming Englishwoman is beheaded near the end of the book. 63%
27 Bernard Baruch used the term "Cold War" to describe the period in history following:	[1] World War II [2] Great Depression [3] Spanish American War [4] 1929 stock market crash [5] Korean War	ANSWER TO Q-26 **[2]** Guacamole is a Mexican dip of mashed avocado, lemon juice, garlic and olive oil. 71%
27 Which TV character never spoke?	[1] Mr. Greenjeans [2] Big Bird [3] Clarabell the Clown [4] Kukla [5] Mr. Hooper	ANSWER TO Q-26 **[5]** An enigma is something puzzling. 89%
27 Eugene Ionesco was closely associated with this school of drama:	[1] Theater of Cruelty [2] Kitchen Sink [3] Happenings [4] Southern Gothic [5] Theater of the Absurd	ANSWER TO Q-26 **[5]** The two famous arches are west and east of the Forum. 69%
27 Which "king" film does not exist?	[1] King Kong [2] King of Kings [3] King of Comedy [4] King Rat [5] King of Diamonds	ANSWER TO Q-26 **[2]** Her work has greatly influenced the humane treatment of terminally ill patients. 78%

5 This is a statement by a stockholder that appoints another person to vote in his place:	[1] Codicil [2] Mandamus [3] Proxy [4] Underwriter [5] Dower	ANSWER TO Q-4 **[4]** James Joyce was Irish; the others wrote in English although it was their second language. 75%
5 Which system in the body includes lymphocytes and phagocytes?	[1] Respiratory [2] Immune [3] Reproductive [4] Hormonal [5] Circulatory	ANSWER TO Q-4 **[1]** The song is sung by Audrey Hepburn in the film, "Breakfast at Tiffany's." 82%
5 The autobiographical drama "After the Fall" was written by:	[1] Eugene O'Neill [2] Arthur Miller [3] Harold Pinter [4] Lillian Hellman [5] William Inge	ANSWER TO Q-4 **[4]** The mature narwhal loses all but one tooth which then grows into a long, protruding spike. 68%
5 Who was the first baseball player to make one million dollars in a single season?	[1] Babe Ruth [2] Ty Cobb [3] Nolan Ryan [4] Willie Mays [5] Jose Canseco	ANSWER TO Q-4 **[1]** It extends from the ocean's surface to the continental slope above the deep-sea floor. 54%
5 Which term refers to a shrub, a gemstone and a color?	[1] Hemophilia [2] Hemoglobin [3] Halitosis [4] Heresy [5] Heliotrope	ANSWER TO Q-4 **[2]** Woody Allen plays a comedian who falls in love with a woman who hopes to become a singer. 82%

26 The Lady de Winter is the villainess in what great adventure novel?	[1] The Scarlet Pimpernel [2] Count of Monte Cristo [3] 20,000 Leagues Under the Sea [4] The Three Musketeers [5] Treasure Island	ANSWER TO Q-25 **[2]** It is believed that Aesop was a slave in ancient Greece but nobody knows for sure. 85%
26 Where did guacamole originate?	[1] Brazil [2] Mexico [3] United States [4] Spain [5] Italy	ANSWER TO Q-25 **[5]** Louie DePalma was the pint-sized tyrant played by Danny Devito on the TV show "Taxi." 91%
26 Which term does not refer to a bias of some sort?	[1] Partiality [2] Bigotry [3] Predisposition [4] Prejudice [5] Enigma	ANSWER TO Q-25 **[4]** "A Horse With No Name" reached number one in 1972 and "Sister Golden Hair" in 1975. 82%
26 Which city boasts the Arches of Tiberius and Titus?	[1] Athens [2] London [3] Milan [4] Jerusalem [5] Rome	ANSWER TO Q-25 **[3]** Frances H. Burnett was an English-born American author of romances for children. 56%
26 Elizabeth Kubler-Ross wrote this best selling book:	[1] The Healing Heart [2] On Death and Dying [3] Learning to Love Again [4] The Sensuous Woman [5] The Hite Report	ANSWER TO Q-25 **[4]** In Greek legend, he fell in love with his statue of a nymph, so Aphrodite brought it to life. 23%

6 Which conifer is native to the swampy areas of North America?	[1] Ginkgo tree [2] Dogwood [3] Bald cypress [4] Joshua tree [5] Magnolia	ANSWER TO Q-5 [3] The term "proxy" is derived from the word "procuratia," meaning "to come for." 82%
6 After his abdication, King Edward VIII became the Duke of Windsor and governor of:	[1] India [2] Hong Kong [3] Zanzibar [4] Gibraltar [5] The Bahamas	ANSWER TO Q-5 [2] Lymphocytes fight bacteria and other invaders; phagocytes eat disruptive cells. 72%
6 Which familiar word is not used to designate a part of the ear?	[1] Stirrup [2] Anvil [3] Iris [4] Hammer [5] Drum	ANSWER TO Q-5 [2] The play caused controversy because of the way Arthur Miller portrayed former wife Marilyn Monroe. 65%
6 Which of these animals has a four-chambered heart?	[1] Shark [2] Polar bear [3] Squid [4] Rattlesnake [5] Penguin	ANSWER TO Q-5 [3] In 1979, pitcher Ryan signed a four-year contract with the Astros, earning $1 million per year. 53%
6 There are twelve pitches in this musical scale:	[1] Whole tone scale [2] Gregorian scale [3] Chromatic scale [4] Diatonic scale [5] Pentatonic scale	ANSWER TO Q-5 [5] Besides being another name for bloodstone, heliotrope refers to a reddish purple color. 57%

25 Aesop is best known for writing:	[1] Erotica [2] Fables [3] Epics [4] Jokes [5] Political speeches	ANSWER TO Q-24 [4] Brazil's business center has a population of 19 million. 65%
25 Which classic TV character has an office behind a wire cage?	[1] Lou Grant [2] Arthur Fonzerelli [3] Oscar Madison [4] Fred Sanford [5] Louie DePalma	ANSWER TO Q-24 [3] Before his election in 1968, Suharto had led the army in crushing a communist coup. 35%
25 Which group had the number one hits "Horse with No Name" and "Sister Golden Hair"?	[1] The Association [2] Jan and Dean [3] The Turtles [4] America [5] The Guess Who	ANSWER TO Q-24 [2] Originally known as baggatway, lacrosse was invented by North American Indians. 82%
25 The author of "Little Lord Fauntleroy" is also the author of:	[1] The Wind in the Willows [2] The Wizard of Oz [3] The Secret Garden [4] National Velvet [5] Black Beauty	ANSWER TO Q-24 [3] There were two previous King Charleses, both of the house of Stuart. 46%
25 George Bernard Shaw named one of his plays after the original Pygmalion, who was a:	[1] Greek god [2] School teacher [3] Christian saint [4] Sculptor [5] Nordic she-warrior	ANSWER TO Q-24 [2] Other animals of the Chinese new year are tiger, hare, sheep and dragon. 68%

7 The bluepoint is a highly prized:	[1] Scallop [2] Prawn [3] Squid [4] Oyster [5] Snail	ANSWER TO Q-6 [3] They are easily recognized from their woody projections above the waterline. 32%
7 Which city is not located in South Africa?	[1] Johannesburg [2] Cape Town [3] Pretoria [4] Durban [5] Freetown	ANSWER TO Q-6 [5] Edward and his wife, Wallis Simpson, were the Bahamas' first couple from 1940 to 1945. 42%
7 This TV manufacturer's brand name is a synonym for apex:	[1] Sony [2] Magnavox [3] Sharp [4] Zenith [5] Monsanto	ANSWER TO Q-6 [3] The iris is the pigmented circular area in the front of the eye. 81%
7 Which of these famous female celebrities died at the youngest age?	[1] Carole Lombard [2] Jayne Mansfield [3] Mama "Cass" Elliot [4] Jean Harlow [5] Marilyn Monroe	ANSWER TO Q-6 [2] A polar bear is a mammal and all mammals have four-chambered hearts. 32%
7 Which of these is not an aviation term?	[1] Wingover [2] Stall [3] Torque [4] Flying jib [5] Lift-off	ANSWER TO Q-6 [3] On the piano, the chromatic scale is composed of the seven white keys and the five black keys. 59%

24 The third most populated city in the world, after Tokyo and Mexico City, is:	[1] New York [2] Rio de Janeiro [3] Bombay [4] Sao Paulo [5] Calcutta	ANSWER TO Q-23 **[2]** Reeves is noted for appearing in both popular and esoteric films. 81%
24 In 1993, Suharto was elected to serve his 6th consecutive term as president of:	[1] Peru [2] Bangledesh [3] Indonesia [4] Malaysia [5] Guyana	ANSWER TO Q-23 **[2]** Most recipes for squash can be applied to pumpkins as well. 78%
24 Which sport is not an Olympic event?	[1] Shooting [2] Lacrosse [3] Archery [4] Yacht racing [5] Judo	ANSWER TO Q-23 **[5]** His bloody rebellion was committed to wiping out Marxism; he resigned in 1990, after 16 years. 65%
24 When the Prince of Wales is crowned king of England, he will be:	[1] Charles I [2] Charles II [3] Charles III [4] Charles IV [5] Charles V	ANSWER TO Q-23 **[3]** The spicy chickpea patties are deep fried. 62%
24 Which animal is not used to a represent a year in the Chinese cycle of years?	[1] Pig [2] Frog [3] Monkey [4] Ox [5] Snake	ANSWER TO Q-23 **[1]** This new element, number 106, is named for Nobel laureate Glenn Seaborg. 23%

8 Which TV show was not set in Boston?	[1] Family Ties [2] St. Elsewhere [3] Spenser: For Hire [4] Cheers [5] Goodnight, Beantown	ANSWER TO Q-7 **[4]** If you order oysters on the half shell, it is likely you will be served bluepoints. 69%
8 Which epic hero tells the story of his adventures to a court of listeners?	[1] Ulysses [2] Roland [3] El Cid [4] Aeneas [5] Sinbad	ANSWER TO Q-7 **[5]** Freetown is the capital of the African republic of Sierra Leone. 52%
8 Henry Deringer is remembered for having invented a:	[1] Firearm [2] Submarine [3] Typewriter [4] Stove [5] Dictaphone	ANSWER TO Q-7 **[4]** They both mean the highest point, peak or climax. 69%
8 Who played the lovable maid on the TV sitcom "Hazel"?	[1] Ann B. Davis [2] Ethel Waters [3] Imogene Coca [4] Shirley Booth [5] Eve Arden	ANSWER TO Q-7 **[4]** The silent screen legend died at age 26 in 1937; the others died in their thirties. 59%
8 Tampere and Turku are major cities in this European country:	[1] Portugal [2] Greece [3] Finland [4] Ireland [5] Turkey	ANSWER TO Q-7 **[4]** A flying jib is a small triangular sail placed in front of a sailboat's jib sail. 68%

23 Keanu Reeves appears in all of these movies except:	[1] Much Ado About Nothing [2] Benny and Joon [3] Bram Stoker's Dracula [4] Little Buddha [5] Speed	ANSWER TO Q-22 **[2]** Pronghorns belong to a family of their own. Antelopes are native to Africa. 76%
23 Take an edible gourd, cook it and serve it as a vegetable. What do you have?	[1] Turnip [2] Squash [3] Rutabaga [4] Parsnip [5] Spinach	ANSWER TO Q-22 **[4]** The meniscuses are two crescent-shaped pieces of cartilage found in the knee. 46%
23 Augusto Pinochet led the coup that overthrew:	[1] Marcos [2] Somoza [3] Franco [4] Batista [5] Allende	ANSWER TO Q-22 **[2]** Polly Holiday played Flo, the wise-cracking waitress who worked with Alice in Mel's diner. 82%
23 What is the primary ingredient in the Middle Eastern dish of falafel?	[1] Lamb [2] Eggs [3] Chickpeas [4] Spinach [5] Codfish	ANSWER TO Q-22 **[4]** Mantegna plays a cop who deals with racial tensions while investigating a murder. 74%
23 What is seaborgium?	[1] New trans-uranium element [2] Nuclear submarine [3] Variety of plankton [4] Capital city of Atlantis [5] Asteroid	ANSWER TO Q-22 **[5]** Bartolomeo Columbus, Christopher's brother, founded Santo Domingo in 1496. 57%

9 All of these songs are national anthems except:	[1] La Paloma [2] God Save the King [3] The Star-Spangled Banner [4] La Marseillaise [5] O Canada	ANSWER TO Q-8 **[1]** This family series starred Michael J. Fox was set in a suburb of Columbus, Ohio. 88%
9 What is the motto of the Three Musketeers?	[1] The pen is mightier [2] Live long and prosper [3] All for one, one for all [4] Stab first, ask later [5] Liberty for all	ANSWER TO Q-8 **[1]** Homer's was the earliest known use of the flashback in Western literature. 44%
9 Which is not a fairy tale by the Brothers Grimm?	[1] Jack and the Beanstalk [2] Rapunzel [3] Red Riding Hood [4] Hansel and Gretel [5] Rumpelstiltskin	ANSWER TO Q-8 **[1]** Even though Deringer spelled his name with one "r," the gun's name is spelled with two r's. 79%
9 Which "Smith" was not a famous jazz performer?	[1] Bessie Smith [2] Jimmy Smith [3] Kate Smith [4] Tommy Smith [5] Willie Smith	ANSWER TO Q-8 **[4]** Booth won an Oscar for the movie "Come Back Little Sheba" before starring in the series. 68%
9 Which of these was the first situation comedy featuring police officers?	[1] Highway Patrol [2] Barney Miller [3] Adam-12 [4] Car 54, Where Are You? [5] Police Squad	ANSWER TO Q-8 **[3]** Tampere and Turku are the two largest cities in Finland, after the capital, Helsinki. 25%

22 Although the term is incorrectly used, the pronghorn is usually called an:	[1] Eagle [2] Antelope [3] Otter [4] Iguana [5] Elk	ANSWER TO Q-21 **[2]** With six plants making them, Glens Falls, NY is called the catheter capital of the world. 81%
22 The lateral meniscus and medial meniscus are parts of the:	[1] Brain [2] Eye [3] Heart [4] Knee [5] Foot	ANSWER TO Q-21 **[5]** It was David, not Samson, who killed the giant Philistine Goliath. 78%
22 On which 1970's TV show would you have heard the classic line "Kiss my Grits"?	[1] All in the Family [2] Alice [3] Sanford and Son [4] Dukes of Hazzard [5] Good Times	ANSWER TO Q-21 **[4]** The intellectual group made London's Bloomsbury Square its center. 23%
22 Joe Mantegna plays a Jewish police detective in which David Mamet film?	[1] House of Games [2] Suspect [3] Glengarry Glenn Ross [4] Homicide [5] Rush	ANSWER TO Q-21 **[5]** Alfred Nobel was a Swedish chemist and inventor. 57%
22 The oldest European settlement in the Americas is found here:	[1] Roanoke Island [2] Newfoundland [3] Venezuela [4] Uruguay [5] Dominican Republic	ANSWER TO Q-21 **[2]** Ives was the artist and Currier the technician who made everyday life lithos of the 1800's. 79%

10 Which is not a type of animal?	[1] Caracara [2] Osiris [3] Phoebe [4] Narwhal [5] Quetzal	ANSWER TO Q-9 **[1]** This popular Mexican song is about a dove. 79%
10 In what American satirical novel does the character "Major Major Major" appear?	[1] Catch-22 [2] Slaughterhouse Five [3] M*A*S*H [4] Player Piano [5] Day of the Locust	ANSWER TO Q-9 **[3]** "The Three Musketeers" was the first story adapted by Classic Comics in October 1941. 82%
10 This word, also the title of a Sir Thomas More classic, means "nowhere" in Greek:	[1] Earth [2] Heaven [3] Exodus [4] Inferno [5] Utopia	ANSWER TO Q-9 **[1]** Jack and the Beanstalk is a folk tale, known by various societies from Zulus to Icelanders. 69%
10 What is a bight?	[1] Steep mountain slope [2] Body of water [3] Type of geyser [4] Narrow canyon [5] Area of land	ANSWER TO Q-9 **[3]** Kate Smith was a singer best known for her rendition of "God Bless America." 79%
10 Which film is not set during prehistoric times?	[1] Iceman [2] One Million Years B.C. [3] Clan of the Cave Bear [4] Caveman [5] Quest for Fire	ANSWER TO Q-9 **[4]** This early sixties series starred Nipsy Russell, Fred Gwynne and Charlotte Rae. 68%

21 A catheter is used to:	[1] Euthanize animals [2] Inject or withdraw fluid [3] Repair appliances [4] Make cappuccino [5] Cook donuts	ANSWER TO Q-20 [2] He is also the only person to ever serve as general in both the Army and the Air Force. 24%
21 Which statement is not true of the biblical hero Samson?	[1] Famous for his strength [2] Pulled down a temple [3] Was blinded by enemies [4] Deceived by Delilah [5] Killed Goliath	ANSWER TO Q-20 [1] Until the 17th century, Gascony was a partly independent area of southwest France. 68%
21 All of these were members of the famed Bloomsbury group except:	[1] John Maynard Keynes [2] Virginia Woolf [3] Roger Fry [4] H.G. Wells [5] Clive Bell	ANSWER TO Q-20 [1] They are map lines which join places with like characteristics, such as temperature. 71%
21 Which famous Scandinavian is not Norwegian?	[1] Edvard Grieg [2] Thor Heyerdahl [3] Henrik Ibsen [4] Sonja Henie [5] Alfred Nobel	ANSWER TO Q-20 [2] The Shah was forced into exile by the Ayatollah Khomeini in 1979. 62%
21 American artists Currier and Ives are famous for:	[1] Mobiles [2] Lithographs [3] Figurines [4] Plates [5] Sculpture	ANSWER TO Q-20 [4] Located north of the zodiac, the Little Dipper is also Ursa Minor (little bear). 78%

11 Large versions of this insect are able to eat frogs, lizards and nesting birds:	[1] Praying mantis [2] Giant water bug [3] Dragonfly [4] Locusts [5] Silverfish	ANSWER TO Q-10 [2] Osiris was a deity in ancient Egypt. 79%
11 The novel "A Room with a View" was written by this author:	[1] D.H. Lawrence [2] George Orwell [3] E.M. Forster [4] John Galsworthy [5] Kingsley Amis	ANSWER TO Q-10 [1] The reluctant commander was portrayed by Bob Newhart in the film adaptation. 55%
11 Which book was not published in the 1950's?	[1] The Lonely Crowd [2] The Organization Man [3] Catcher in the Rye [4] A Farewell to Arms [5] On the Road	ANSWER TO Q-10 [5] More set his ideal society on a mythical South Pacific island. 68%
11 The following works are all matched with their authors except:	[1] Absalom, Absalom-Tolstoy [2] East of Eden-Steinbeck [3] The Waste Land-Eliot [4] The Good Earth-Buck [5] Jane Eyre-Bronte	ANSWER TO Q-10 [2] A bight is a bay formed by a bend in the coastline. 45%
11 British writer Jan Morris describes her _____ in the 1972 book, "Conundrum."	[1] Trip to Vietnam [2] Sex change operation [3] Ascent of Mt. Everest [4] Out-of-body experience [5] Previous lives	ANSWER TO Q-10 [1] Timothy Hutton stars in this film about a group of archaeologists who discover an ancient man. 81%

20 Hap Arnold is known as the father of the U.S.:	[1] Militia [2] Air Force [3] Coast Guard [4] Navy [5] Marines	ANSWER TO Q-19 **[3]** The canal, acquired by the British in 1875, was nationalized by Egypt in 1956. 60%
20 Gascony is a historic region of:	[1] France [2] Italy [3] Germany [4] Romania [5] Spain	ANSWER TO Q-19 **[4]** "Places in the Heart," a moving story of a widowed mother, starred Sally Field. 58%
20 Where would you find an isobar, isobath, isohyet and isotherm?	[1] Map [2] Calendar [3] Bar chart [4] Meat scale [5] Barometer	ANSWER TO Q-19 **[2]** Kennedy's plan would eventually become "The Great Society" plan of Lyndon Johnson. 68%
20 All of these headline events happened between 1985 and 1990 except:	[1] Gorbachev is Soviet head [2] Shah of Iran deposed [3] Bush elected president [4] Armenian quake [5] Chernobyl blows	ANSWER TO Q-19 **[3]** He is known for his essays on world culture as well as his highly regarded poetry. 57%
20 The North Star is found in what constellation?	[1] Big Bear [2] Aquarius [3] Southern Cross [4] Little Dipper [5] Orion the Hunter	ANSWER TO Q-19 **[2]** Augustus was the adopted son of Julius Caesar and also the first Roman emperor. 47%

12 "Food, Glorious Food," is a song from this Broadway musical:	[1] The King and I [2] Oliver! [3] Fiddler on the Roof [4] Annie [5] The Wiz	ANSWER TO Q-11 [1] The Asian varieties of this insect are much larger than North American types. 65%
12 He wrote "Fifteen men on the dead man's chest . . . yo-ho-ho, and a bottle of rum!":	[1] Mark Twain [2] James M. Barrie [3] Robert Browning [4] William S. Gilbert [5] Robert Louis Stevenson	ANSWER TO Q-11 [3] It was made into a critically acclaimed film, as was his novel "Howards End." 55%
12 If you are drinking darjeeling, you are drinking:	[1] Tea [2] Fruit juice [3] Coffee [4] Chocolate [5] Rum	ANSWER TO Q-11 [4] Hemingway's "A Farewell to Arms" was published in 1929. 43%
12 What TV show ended with a pair of hands clapping forcibly until a station break took over?	[1] The Flip Wilson Show [2] The Carol Burnett Show [3] Laugh-In [4] The Beverly Hillbillies [5] Hee-Haw	ANSWER TO Q-11 [1] The novel "Absalom, Absalom" by William Faulkner is about the Southern experience. 68%
12 After "I Love Lucy," this was the most popular TV show of 1950's television:	[1] Gunsmoke [2] Dragnet [3] Topper [4] Burns & Allen [5] Hopalong Cassidy	ANSWER TO Q-11 [2] Morris is regarded as one of the few authentic stylists in English journalism. 43%

19 Which was not a headline in 1961?	[1] JFK inaugurated [2] Bay of Pigs invasion [3] Egypt takes Suez Canal [4] Berlin Wall erected [5] First man in orbit	ANSWER TO Q-18 **[2]** "Goodtime Charlie" and "party animal" are the less elegant American equivalents. 75%
19 Which of these movies didn't feature the versatile Meryl Streep?	[1] Heartburn [2] Sophie's Choice [3] Falling in Love [4] Places in the Heart [5] Manhattan	ANSWER TO Q-18 **[1]** Merlin was advisor and wizard to both father and son. 46%
19 The economic program known as "The New Frontier" was a project of this president:	[1] Richard M. Nixon [2] John F. Kennedy [3] Gerald Ford [4] Harry Truman [5] Lyndon Johnson	ANSWER TO Q-18 **[4]** A figure of the Age of Reason, Swift died in 1745. 58%
19 Octavio Paz is a noted Mexican:	[1] Painter [2] Soldier [3] Poet [4] Composer [5] Athlete	ANSWER TO Q-18 **[3]** He was forced to retire in 1964 after backing down to the U.S. and removing the missiles. 72%
19 Who was the Roman emperor at the time of Christ's birth?	[1] Julius Caesar [2] Augustus Caesar [3] Cassius [4] Claudius [5] Caligula	ANSWER TO Q-18 **[4]** "The Fortune Cookie" has Jack Lemmon and Walter Matthau involved in an insurance scam. 79%

13 Which is a type of igneous rock?	[1] Glare [2] Porphyry [3] Budgie [4] Toltec [5] Ivory	ANSWER TO Q-12 **[2]** "I'd Do Anything" and "As Long as He Needs Me" are from the same production. 78%
13 Which film does not center on a horse?	[1] National Velvet [2] Big Red [3] Phar Lap [4] Casey's Shadow [5] Black Beauty	ANSWER TO Q-12 **[5]** You can find this little verse in "Treasure Island." 61%
13 Which of these writers is not associated with literature of the absurd?	[1] Edward Albee [2] George Orwell [3] Samuel Beckett [4] Harold Pinter [5] Eugene Ionesco	ANSWER TO Q-12 **[1]** It is a fine variety of aromatic black tea, grown in the Darjeeling region of India. 81%
13 What type of animal is a kingfisher?	[1] Bird [2] Mammal [3] Fish [4] Reptile [5] Insect	ANSWER TO Q-12 **[3]** Remember Richard Nixon solemnly declaring, "Sock it to me"? 74%
13 Printers use this measurement:	[1] Bolt [2] Chain [3] Point [4] Gauge [5] Hand	ANSWER TO Q-12 **[2]** It first aired in 1951, shot to number 2 and stayed popular for 11 years. 56%

18 A bon vivant is one who has a:	[1] Neurotic obsession [2] Very active social life [3] Connection with the mob [4] Healthy appetite [5] Steady job	ANSWER TO Q-17 [2] In Latin, spurious means bastard. 79%
18 Uther Pendragon was King Arthur's:	[1] Father [2] Page [3] Nephew [4] Wizard [5] Enemy	ANSWER TO Q-17 [2] His slapstick comedies starring the likes of Keaton and Chaplin were all shot at Keystone. 57%
18 Which influential figure did not live during the 19th century?	[1] Karl Marx [2] Alfred Lord Tennyson [3] Harriet Beecher Stowe [4] Jonathan Swift [5] Herman Melville	ANSWER TO Q-17 [3] She was one of Flip Wilson's many regular characters on his one-hour variety show. 68%
18 Which Soviet leader's downfall stemmed from the Cuban Missile Crisis?	[1] Yuri Andropov [2] Leonid Brezhnev [3] Nikita Khrushchev [4] Konstantin Chernenko [5] Aleksei Rykov	ANSWER TO Q-17 [2] During his distinguished career, the ice hockey legend showed he was quite well versed in both. 35%
18 Which film is not set in the Far East?	[1] The Last Emperor [2] The Lover [3] Indochine [4] The Fortune Cookie [5] King Rat	ANSWER TO Q-17 [4] This resort city is on the Pacific Coast. 47%

14 Gastronomy is the art of:	[1] Fortune telling [2] Creating exotic perfumes [3] Observing the stars [4] Enjoying fine food [5] Sand painting	ANSWER TO Q-13 **[2]** Porphyry is an igneous rock with large crystals embedded in a groundmass. 32%
14 What is a dashiki?	[1] Japanese vice-emperor [2] Coral atoll [3] Hindu sage [4] Indonesian lion [5] African garment	ANSWER TO Q-13 **[2]** This film centers on a boy's special relationship with an Irish setter. 68%
14 What movie features Diane Keaton, Jessica Lange & Sissy Spacek as three eccentric sisters?	[1] Hannah and Her Sisters [2] Violets Are Blue [3] Fried Green Tomatoes [4] Crimes of the Heart [5] Manhattan	ANSWER TO Q-13 **[2]** Orwell is an allegorist; absurdists broke from an ordered world view to one of senselessness. 58%
14 Which film is about 1960's radicals coping with life as middle-aged yuppies?	[1] The Right Stuff [2] Tender Mercies [3] Lean on Me [4] The Big Chill [5] Body Heat	ANSWER TO Q-13 **[1]** Kingfishers frequent sandbanks near freshwater streams around the world. 46%
14 The world's largest flesh-eating fish is the:	[1] Great white shark [2] Giant barracuda [3] Whale shark [4] White-tipped shark [5] Giant grouper	ANSWER TO Q-13 **[3]** Picas and ems are other units of measure used by printers. 59%

17 Spurious means:	[1] Alert [2] Inauthentic [3] Unlucky [4] Hostile [5] Obsolete	ANSWER TO Q-16 **[3]** "Pride and Prejudice" deals with Mrs. Bennet's aim in life: to marry off her three daughters. 65%
17 Film director Mack Sennett is known for his work with Buster Keaton at this studio:	[1] MGM [2] Keystone [3] RKO [4] Universal [5] Paramount	ANSWER TO Q-16 **[1]** Parnassus is the name of a mountain in Greece. 57%
17 "What you see is what you get" was the catch-phrase of this TV comedy character:	[1] Dick Van Dyke [2] Florence Johnston [3] Geraldine Jones [4] Alice Kramden [5] Carol Brady	ANSWER TO Q-16 **[2]** He endures cyclops and slavery, and is rewarded in the end. 71%
17 Which sports great said, "All pro athletes are bilingual. They speak English and profanity"?	[1] Billy Martin [2] Gordie Howe [3] Howard Cosell [4] Joe Namath [5] Casey Stengel	ANSWER TO Q-16 **[2]** South Carolina slaves mounted the Stono Rebellion in 1739. 24%
17 All these Mexican cities are on the Yucatan Peninsula except:	[1] Merida [2] Cozumel [3] Cancun [4] Mazatlan [5] Campeche	ANSWER TO Q-16 **[5]** "Moll" was once a common nickname for Mary. 67%

15 Artifacts from the Olmec, Maya, Toltec and Aztec cultures are considered ____ art.	[1] Pre-Columbian [2] Feudalistic [3] Third World [4] Art Nouveau [5] Pre-Raphaelite	ANSWER TO Q-14 [4] Prehistoric man took a giant step toward gastronomy when he used fire to cook his food. 79%
15 In cooking, arrowroot is used as a:	[1] Seasoning [2] Garnish [3] Thickener [4] Vegetable side dish [5] Condiment	ANSWER TO Q-14 [5] Loose and colorful, they became popular with the rise of the Black Power movement. 59%
15 Which literary character encounters a monarch known as the "Red Queen"?	[1] Dorothy [2] Bilbo Baggins [3] Alice [4] Long John Silver [5] The Little Prince	ANSWER TO Q-14 [4] Their idiosyncrasies and family secrets are exposed at an ill-fated reunion. 71%
15 All these musical terms relate to tempo except:	[1] Allegro [2] Adagio [3] Andante [4] Presto [5] Mezzo forte	ANSWER TO Q-14 [4] The film starred Tom Berenger, Glenn Close and William Hurt. 88%
15 What game or sport is played in a bonspiel match?	[1] Water polo [2] Chess [3] Horseshoes [4] Bowling [5] Curling	ANSWER TO Q-14 [1] Great white sharks may measure over 30 feet and are considered the most dangerous shark of all. 57%

16 Which of these classic novels was not about an adulterous woman?	[1] The Scarlet Letter [2] Madame Bovary [3] Pride and Prejudice [4] Lady Chatterley's Lover [5] Anna Karenina	ANSWER TO Q-15 [3] Mercury's diameter is 3100 miles while Pluto's is 1430 miles. 58%
16 Which name listed is not the designation of a famous dam?	[1] Parnassus [2] Aswan [3] Glen Canyon [4] Boulder [5] Owen Falls	ANSWER TO Q-15 [2] Bond wins the match after catching baddie Auric Goldfinger trying to cheat. 59%
16 This well-known person figures in stories about his seven voyages:	[1] Lemuel Gulliver [2] Sinbad the Sailor [3] Marco Polo [4] Phineas Fogg [5] Robinson Crusoe	ANSWER TO Q-15 [2] The movie's songs explore differences in heritage within African-American culture. 79%
16 Which conflict of the colonial period was a slave uprising?	[1] Pequot Wars [2] Stono Rebellion [3] King Philip's War [4] Bacon's Rebellion [5] War of Jenkins' Ear	ANSWER TO Q-15 [1] The missing regular is Gertie, the receptionist that no one ever saw. 61%
16 In the slang of the thirties, a moll was a:	[1] Gambler [2] Starlet [3] Machine gun [4] Bookie [5] Gangster's mistress	ANSWER TO Q-15 [3] Lake Michigan separates the upper and lower sections of the state. 79%

16 What was Sydney Barrow's celebrated criminal monicker?	[1] Boston Strangler [2] Mayflower Madam [3] The Nightstalker [4] The Zodiac Killer [5] Son of Sam	ANSWER TO Q-15 [1] Mexico had 2500 years of Indian civilizations before the first Europeans arrived. 56%
16 Fore-seeing some future event or the unknown by means of an omen or oracle is:	[1] Transcendence [2] Psychokinesis [3] Hedonism [4] Divination [5] Pantheism	ANSWER TO Q-15 [3] It is the name given to starches removed from roots and used to thicken sauces. 65%
16 "Beware of Greeks bearing gifts," refers to:	[1] Pegasus [2] Aristotle Onassis [3] The Parthenon [4] Trojan horse [5] A Sappho poem	ANSWER TO Q-15 [3] In Carroll's "Through the Looking-Glass" the Red Queen is a walking, talking chess piece. 72%
16 Which Academy Award-winning film was not based on a novel?	[1] The Godfather [2] Dances with Wolves [3] The Silence of the Lambs [4] Reversal of Fortune [5] Ordinary People	ANSWER TO Q-15 [5] Mezzo forte is a term relating to volume and means "sort of loud." 49%
16 Which of the following Monopoly properties commands the most rent?	[1] North Carolina [2] Pennsylvania [3] Atlantic [4] Marvin Gardens [5] Ventnor	ANSWER TO Q-15 [5] A bonspiel is a curling match between two clubs or towns. 35%

15 In diameter, this planet is about twice the size of Pluto:	[1] Venus [2] Earth [3] Mercury [4] Mars [5] Neptune	ANSWER TO Q-14 [3] Her poems brought her to the attention of Thomas Jefferson. 51%
15 In which Bond film does 007 play golf against the villain?	[1] Moonraker [2] Goldfinger [3] Live and Let Die [4] Man with the Golden Gun [5] You Only Live Twice	ANSWER TO Q-14 [1] Omaha was the bloodiest. The others were Gold, Juno, Utah and Sword. 28%
15 Director Spike Lee's second film, "School Daze," is different from his other films in that:	[1] Lee doesn't act in it [2] It is a musical [3] It's a documentary [5] It's about Latinos [4] It's in 3-D	ANSWER TO Q-14 [5] The Stephen King musical closed almost immediately after opening. "Big River" was the title of the musical based on Huck Finn. 61%
15 Which character was not a regular on "Perry Mason"?	[1] Dale Purner [2] Lt. Tragg [3] Paul Drake [4] Della Street [5] Hamilton Burger	ANSWER TO Q-14 [1] This rodeo, which goes back several centuries, is controversial due to its purported cruelty. 49%
15 The only U.S. state that is divided into two separate parts by a large body of water is:	[1] Hawaii [2] Washington [3] Michigan [4] Alaska [5] Florida	ANSWER TO Q-14 [3] The duodenum is the upper part of the small intestine and belongs to the digestive system. 73%

17 The brontosaurus, the diplodocus and the brachiosaurus are all dinosaurs which had:	[1] Tiny forelimbs [2] Spikes [3] Wings [4] Crests [5] Long necks	ANSWER TO Q-16 **[2]** Sydney Biddle Barrow was convicted of pandering – running a high-class house of prostitution. 78%
17 Which legendary hero successfully fought the human monster, Grendel?	[1] David [2] Hercules [3] Ulysses [4] Beowulf [5] Gulliver	ANSWER TO Q-16 **[4]** Present-day forms of divination include crystal balls, palmistry and astrology. 59%
17 Bernard Malamud is the author of this baseball story that was made into a major film:	[1] The Natural [2] Damn Yankees [3] Pride of the Yankees [4] Bull Durham [5] The Boys of Spring	ANSWER TO Q-16 **[4]** The wooden horse filled with soldiers was a most unwelcome gift. 65%
17 The glomeruli and hilum are parts of the:	[1] Kidney [2] Liver [3] Eye [4] Ear [5] Lung	ANSWER TO Q-16 **[4]** "Reversal of Fortune," with Jeremy Irons and Glenn Close, is adapted from Alan Dershowitz's book about the Von Bulow trial. 68%
17 Grog, once standard issue in Britain's Royal Navy, is a mixture of honey, lemon, rum and:	[1] Eggnog [2] Goat's milk [3] Boiling water [4] Coffee [5] Fruit juice	ANSWER TO Q-16 **[2]** Pennsylvania Avenue gets $320, North Carolina $300, Marvin Gardens $280, and Ventnor and Atlantic Avenues $260. 81%

14 Phyllis Wheatley is known as the first African-American:	[1] Teacher [2] Lawyer [3] Woman poet [4] Opera singer [5] Medical doctor	ANSWER TO Q-13 **[4]** Lady Bracknell is one of the main characters in "The Importance of Being Earnest." 35%
14 Which was one of the five landing sites of the Normandy Invasion?	[1] Omaha Beach [2] Portsmouth [3] Dunkirk [4] Anzio [5] Somme	ANSWER TO Q-13 **[1]** Davis began his jazz career playing with Charlie Parker. 46%
14 This book-turned-Broadway musical was a notorious flop:	[1] Oliver Twist [2] Les Miserables [3] Huckleberry Finn [4] Phantom of the Opera [5] Carrie	ANSWER TO Q-13 **[1]** The heroine of the tale is the last wife, who escapes from her murderous husband. 35%
14 The Charreada is Mexico's national:	[1] Sport [2] Dish [3] Bird [4] Newspaper [5] Parliament	ANSWER TO Q-13 **[1]** The chase was filmed on location in San Francisco in 1968. 68%
14 Which is not part of the body's respiratory system?	[1] Diaphragm [2] Lungs [3] Duodenum [4] Trachea [5] Larynx	ANSWER TO Q-13 **[5]** Kenyatta, who died in 1978, was imprisoned by the British for a time in the fifties. 79%

18 Which is an example of a cetacean?	[1] Chimpanzee [2] Right whale [3] Abalone [4] Turkey vulture [5] Amoeba	ANSWER TO Q-17 [5] The brontosaurus or apatosaurus once inhabited all the continents. 59%
18 White rose and russet are two common varieties of:	[1] Onion [2] Pepper [3] Potato [4] Eggplant [5] Radish	ANSWER TO Q-17 [4] He's the hero of England's oldest epic, named for him and penned by an unknown author. 55%
18 Cervical, thoracic, and lumbar are bones of the:	[1] Chest [2] Spine [3] Leg [4] Arm [5] Foot	ANSWER TO Q-17 [1] Robert Redford plays the mysterious old rookie who leads his team to unlikely triumph. 62%
18 In literature, when a serious tone is applied to a trivial subject, the result is:	[1] Satire [2] Burlesque [3] Comedy of manners [4] Farce [5] Grotesquerie	ANSWER TO Q-17 [1] The function of the kidneys is the excretion of the body's urine. 46%
18 The Lumière brothers were pioneers in the field of:	[1] Medicine [2] Flight [3] Psychology [4] Photography [5] Computers	ANSWER TO Q-17 [3] It is named for Admiral Edward Vernon, who always wore a grogram hat. 49%

13 Which titled person is fictional?	[1] King Wenceslas [2] Edward the Black Prince [3] Queen Nefertiti [4] Lady Bracknell [5] Earl of Sandwich	ANSWER TO Q-12 **[4]** Bellamy wrote the Pledge to commemorate Columbus Day in 1892. 46%
13 John Coltrane rose to prominence while playing saxophone with the ____.	[1] Miles Davis Quintet [2] Duke Ellington Band [3] Count Basie Band [4] Nat King Cole Trio [5] Blakey's jazz messengers	ANSWER TO Q-12 **[3]** Jim Backus was also the voice of cartoon character "Mr. Magoo." 85%
13 Which fairy tale has the heroine discover that her husband has murdered previous wives?	[1] Bluebeard [2] Beauty and the Beast [3] Puss in Boots [4] Sleeping Beauty [5] Eros and Psyche	ANSWER TO Q-12 **[2]** Only recently have Nin's diaries and Harris' "My Life and Loves" been published unexpurgated. 67%
13 The car chase scene from this Steve McQueen film is considered one of Hollywood's best:	[1] Bullitt [2] The Getaway [3] Papillon [4] The Magnificent Seven [5] The Great Escape	ANSWER TO Q-12 **[4]** Russia declared war on Turkey while France and Great Britain aided Greece indirectly. 45%
13 Which African leader was president of Kenya?	[1] Kwame Nkrumah [2] Haile Selassie [3] Idi Amin [4] Julius Nyerere [5] Jomo Kenyatta	ANSWER TO Q-12 **[5]** In 1969, U.S. troops seized this hill after ten unsuccessful attempts. 57%

19 The Triton is a celebrated:	[1] Destroyer [2] Airplane [3] Submarine [4] Hydrogen bomb [5] Aircraft carrier	ANSWER TO Q-18 **[2]** Taxonomically speaking, whales are classified under the order Cetacea, hence the name. 58%
19 The arachnids classified as the "harvestmen" are better known as:	[1] Black widows [2] Chiggers [3] Horseshoe crabs [4] Daddy longlegs [5] Ticks	ANSWER TO Q-18 **[3]** The lighter, waxier skin easily distinguishes the white rose from the russet. 79%
19 Young and Rubicam is the world's largest firm in this industry:	[1] Insurance [2] Publishing [3] Advertising [4] Retail [5] Securities	ANSWER TO Q-18 **[2]** Cartilage disks separate and cushion the bones and protect the spinal cord. 70%
19 Cotswold, Merino and Lincoln are breeds of:	[1] Ponies [2] Cows [3] Sheep [4] Dogs [5] Chickens	ANSWER TO Q-18 **[2]** An example would be writing about a flea's adventures in the style of Homer. 34%
19 Which would best cool a mouth on fire from eating hot chili peppers?	[1] Beer [2] Chewing gum [3] Yogurt [4] Rice [5] Water	ANSWER TO Q-18 **[4]** The French inventors made the first machine for photographing and projecting film. 68%

12 Francis Bellamy is known for writing:

[1] Standard wedding vows
[2] Boy Scout pledge
[3] The president's oath
[4] Pledge of Allegiance
[5] Hippocratic oath

ANSWER TO Q-11

[3] In the early centuries after Christ, it was the center of the opulent Byzantine Empire.

68%

---

12 Which actor played millionaire Thurston Howell III on "Gilligan's Island"?

[1] Fred Gwynne
[2] Larry Hagman
[3] Jim Backus
[4] Alan Hale
[5] Bob Denver

ANSWER TO Q-11

[1] These various types of burial mounds have been uncovered during archaeological digs.

57%

---

12 Frank Harris and Anais Nin are writers known for their:

[1] Social criticism
[2] Erotic frankness
[3] Use of local color
[4] Political biographies
[5] Books about wildlife

ANSWER TO Q-11

[2] The queen says his name after she overhears him muttering his name to himself.

72%

---

12 When Greece declared its independence in 1822, it was invaded by:

[1] France
[2] Russia
[3] Britain
[4] Turkey
[5] Germany

ANSWER TO Q-11

[5] His rule saw the final transformation of Byzantine Constantinople to Turkish Istanbul.

57%

---

12 During the Vietnam War, Hill 937 became better known as ___ Hill.

[1] Bunker
[2] My Lai
[3] Blueberry
[4] Pork Chop
[5] Hamburger

ANSWER TO Q-11

[1] For centuries, raids took place across the Cheviot until James I unified the countries.

69%

20 Cartoonist Chester Gould is known for creating this classic character:	[1] Dick Tracy [2] Alley Oop [3] Superman [4] Woody Woodpecker [5] Heathcliff the Cat	ANSWER TO Q-19 **[3]** The U.S. Navy sub made the first around-the-world voyage without surfacing. 69%
20 Which term refers to the action of water carrying minerals as it drains through soil?	[1] Induration [2] Diagenesis [3] Convection [4] Leaching [5] Tropism	ANSWER TO Q-19 **[4]** They have eight long, slender legs extending from a small body. 54%
20 Who is the only player to hit 50 home runs for two different teams?	[1] Hank Greenberg [2] Frank Robinson [3] Dave Kingman [4] Jimmie Foxx [5] Babe Ruth	ANSWER TO Q-19 **[3]** This New York-based company has an annual worldwide income of $994 million. 69%
20 They live in an apiary:	[1] Ants [2] Bees [3] Birds [4] Termites [5] Field mice	ANSWER TO Q-19 **[3]** Sheep are bred for their wool, meat, skins and milk. 68%
20 Which cooking term means to pickle in vinegar or brine?	[1] Force [2] Score [3] Render [4] Souse [5] Mask	ANSWER TO Q-19 **[3]** Casein, found in dairy products, combats the capsaicin that is the pepper's heat source. 43%

11 Istanbul was formerly called Constantinople; before that it had yet another name:	[1] Bengal Nation [2] Estonia [3] Byzantium [4] Atlantis [5] Marrakesh	ANSWER TO Q-10 **[5]** "Lord of the Flies" was written by William Golding in 1954. It was his first novel. 56%
11 Cairns, barrows, and tumuluses are all types of:	[1] Burial mounds [2] Hardware [3] Legal documents [4] Stuffed pastries [5] Horse-drawn carriages	ANSWER TO Q-10 **[1]** Mismatched country twins meet their city counterparts in the 1988 release. 89%
11 Which fairy tale figure is destroyed after his name is mentioned?	[1] Tom Thumb [2] Rumpelstiltskin [3] Iron Hans [4] The Robber Bridegroom [5] The Frog Prince	ANSWER TO Q-10 **[2]** Elevated levels of phenylketonuria (pku) can cause retardation if not treated. 59%
11 Suleyman the Magnificent ruled over:	[1] Siam [2] Gothic tribes [3] Angkor Wat [4] Ancient Babylon [5] Ottoman Empire	ANSWER TO Q-10 **[3]** A cameo is a relief carving on certain gems or shells. 74%
11 The Cheviot Hills separate which two countries?	[1] England - Scotland [2] Portugal - Spain [3] Austria - Poland [4] France - Germany [5] Norway - Denmark	ANSWER TO Q-10 **[5]** Derived from the root of a plant related to the ginger plant, it is used in curry powder. 79%

21 The black cavalry-men known as the Buffalo Soldiers were given that name by:	[1] Confederate soldiers [2] Ulysses S. Grant [3] American Indians [4] Marcus Garvey [5] Sheep ranchers	ANSWER TO Q-20 **[1]** It was called the first "realistic" police strip upon its release in 1931. 64%
21 The q.t. in the expression "on the q.t." is derived from this word:	[1] Quarantine [2] Quilt [3] Quiet [4] Quality [5] Quintessential	ANSWER TO Q-20 **[4]** Soils become acidic since leaching tends to remove alkaline substances. 71%
21 What will you get if you order saltimbocca in an Italian restaurant?	[1] Pasta with cheese [2] Fish stew [3] Hard salami [4] Veal and ham [5] Fruity custard	ANSWER TO Q-20 **[4]** Foxx hit 58 for the A's in 1932 and 50 for the Red Sox in 1938. 54%
21 Which is not a term in mathematics?	[1] Homunculus [2] Calculus [3] Integer [4] Secant [5] Trigonometry	ANSWER TO Q-20 **[2]** The word comes from the Latin, "apis," meaning bee. 67%
21 To use a fricative, you would have to:	[1] Drive a car [2] Speak [3] Attend a formal dinner [4] Fall asleep [5] Fire a gun	ANSWER TO Q-20 **[4]** The others mean to stuff, cut, remove fat and cover with sauce. 43%

10 Author Graham Greene wrote all these novels except:	[1] **The Power and the Glory** [2] **The Quiet American** [3] **Our Man in Havana** [4] **The Honorary Consul** [5] **Lord of the Flies**	ANSWER TO Q-9 [1] The instrument had been little used since the days of Sidney Bechet, a pioneer of jazz. 45%
10 Bette Midler and _____ played two pairs of twins in the comedy film "Big Business."	[1] **Lily Tomlin** [2] **Goldie Hawn** [3] **Shelley Long** [4] **Whoopi Goldberg** [5] **Steve Martin**	ANSWER TO Q-9 [5] Pumpernickel's darker color comes from added caramel or molasses. 67%
10 The PKU test, given to infants soon after birth, tests for:	[1] **Diabetes** [2] **Enzyme deficiency** [3] **Calcium deficiency** [4] **Fetal alcohol syndrome** [5] **Anemia**	ANSWER TO Q-9 [4] Both of these terms refer to the spasm of the jaw muscles symptomatic of tetanus. 23%
10 Which does not refer to a factor that helps determine a diamond's value?	[1] **Clarity** [2] **Color** [3] **Cameo** [4] **Carat** [5] **Cut**	ANSWER TO Q-9 [2] For example, the apocryphal books of the Bible are left out due to their doubtful origin. 45%
10 Turmeric is a:	[1] **Garment** [2] **Painting** [3] **Weapon** [4] **Drug** [5] **Spice**	ANSWER TO Q-9 [1] A bevel consists of a rule with an adjustable arm. 79%

22 What fruit flavor is in framboise liqueur?	[1] Cherry [2] Raspberry [3] Plum [4] Orange [5] Peach	ANSWER TO Q-21 **[3]** From 1867 to 1898, they had the highest number of Congressional Medals of Honor of any unit. 21%
22 Which international organization is the oldest?	[1] WTO [2] OPEC [3] OAU [4] EFTA [5] NATO	ANSWER TO Q-21 **[3]** To do something "on the q.t." means to do it surreptitiously. 55%
22 All these songs come from "West Side Story" except:	[1] Tonight [2] Sunrise, Sunset [3] I Feel Pretty [4] Somewhere [5] Maria	ANSWER TO Q-21 **[4]** Thin slices of veal and ham are rolled together and sauteed in butter seasoned with sage. 57%
22 The Verrazano-Narrows Bridge is located at the entrance of this city's harbor:	[1] Naples [2] New York [3] Havana [4] Panama City [5] Miami	ANSWER TO Q-21 **[1]** A homunculus is a manikin (i.e., miniature man), especially one used to study anatomy. 68%
22 Who played the role of Miss Daisy's son in the film "Driving Miss Daisy"?	[1] Dan Aykroyd [2] Jeff Bridges [3] Ken Russell [4] Jeff Goldblum [5] Kevin Kline	ANSWER TO Q-21 **[2]** Fricatives are consonant sounds such as the "f" and "v" in English. 45%

9 Who revived the soprano saxophone as a jazz instrument?	[1] John Coltrane [2] Coleman Hawkins [3] Lester Young [4] Art Blakey [5] Miles Davis	ANSWER TO Q-8 **[1]** Lewis Carroll wrote "Through the Looking-Glass and What Alice Found There." 65%
9 Pumpernickel is a form of ____ bread.	[1] White [2] Sourdough [3] Whole wheat [4] Multi-grain [5] Rye	ANSWER TO Q-8 **[5]** The picture, which co-starred Dabney Coleman as their boss, was Dolly Parton's acting debut. 81%
9 Trismus is the same symptom as:	[1] Excessive sleeping [2] Flatulence [3] Depression [4] Lockjaw [5] Sciatica	ANSWER TO Q-8 **[3]** The lilac belongs to a genus of shrubs that does not bear edible fruit. 35%
9 The term "apocryphal" alludes to writings of:	[1] Professional criminals [2] Questionable authority [3] Explicit sexuality [4] Religious fanatics [5] Athletic figures	ANSWER TO Q-8 **[5]** Traditionally, it's consumed in a single gulp. 91%
9 A carpenter would use a _____ to measure or mark angles.	[1] Bevel [2] Behemoth [3] Brogan [4] Bore [5] Bromine	ANSWER TO Q-8 **[5]** Bouillon is a fish or meat broth. 89%

23 Which adjective does not connote some type of stability?	[1] Immutable [2] Steadfast [3] Latent [4] Staunch [5] Fixed	ANSWER TO Q-22 **[2]** Framboise comes from the Alsace region in France. 61%
23 What flavors the liqueur creme de noisette?	[1] Bitter almonds [2] Violets [3] Pineapple [4] Hazelnuts [5] Black currants	ANSWER TO Q-22 **[5]** NATO was formed in 1949. The others were formed in the 50's, 60's or 90's. 59%
23 New Mexico's White Sands is noted as the site of the:	[1] Painted Desert [2] Legendary cities of gold [3] Last stand of Geronimo [4] First A-bomb explosion [5] Grand Canyon	ANSWER TO Q-22 **[2]** "Sunrise, Sunset" is from "Fiddler on the Roof." 72%
23 "Knowledge is Good" is the motto of the college in which youth-oriented film?	[1] Animal House [2] The Graduate [3] The Sure Thing [4] Revenge of the Nerds [5] St. Elmo's Fire	ANSWER TO Q-22 **[2]** It is the longest vehicular suspension bridge in the U.S. 74%
23 A word whose letters can be rearranged to form an entirely different word is a/an:	[1] Palindrome [2] Rebus [3] Anagram [4] Spoonerism [5] Homonym	ANSWER TO Q-22 **[1]** "Driving Miss Daisy" won an Oscar for Best Picture in 1989. 81%

8 Where is Jabberwocky wood found?	[1] Looking-Glass land [2] Shangri-La [3] Freedonia [4] Penguin Island [5] Ruritania	ANSWER TO Q-7 [4] It is the sap of the cell, excluding the nucleus. 81%
8 The secretaries in "9 to 5" were played by Dolly Parton, Lily Tomlin and:	[1] Sally Field [2] Michelle Pfeiffer [3] Melanie Griffith [4] Cher [5] Jane Fonda	ANSWER TO Q-7 [4] Victims often have hallucinations of insects or other creatures. 88%
8 All these plants are related except:	[1] Almond [2] Peach [3] Lilac [4] Apricot [5] Nectarine	ANSWER TO Q-7 [3] He appears in "The Hunt for Red October" and "Patriot Games," among other books. 79%
8 If you order a whiskey neat, how will it be served?	[1] Mixed with fruit juice [2] Heated with lemon peel [3] Poured over crushed ice [4] Mixed with club soda [5] Straight shot	ANSWER TO Q-7 [5] "Tis the prettiest little parlour that you ever did spy," says the spider. 71%
8 Which is not a term for appetizers?	[1] Dim sum [2] Antipasto [3] Tapas [4] Starters [5] Bouillon	ANSWER TO Q-7 [1] This 956-mile river flows northerly from the Andes mountains in S.W. Colombia up to the sea. 43%

24 Which metal works best as an electrical conductor?	[1] Brass [2] Nickel [3] Silver [4] Copper [5] Tin	ANSWER TO Q-23 **[3]** Latent refers to something that is hidden or undeveloped. 68%
24 Which Nazi leader's widely read memoirs were titled "Inside the Third Reich"?	[1] Rudolf Hess [2] Adolf Hitler [3] Joseph Goebbels [4] Albert Speer [5] Adolf Eichmann	ANSWER TO Q-23 **[4]** The others flavor cremes de noyaux, yvette, D'anana and cassis, respectively. 57%
24 Maltose is a type of sugar used in making:	[1] Beer [2] Preserves [3] Bread [4] Taffy [5] Ice cream	ANSWER TO Q-23 **[4]** The area includes a missile testing range, a national monument and a wildlife refuge. 68%
24 The first televised ___ occurred in 1960.	[1] Product advertisement [2] U.S. Presidential debate [3] Oscar ceremonies [4] World Series [5] Moon landing	ANSWER TO Q-23 **[1]** Lovely Faber College, home of Delta House, is the proud owner of this appropriate motto. 81%
24 Which famed animal of Calaveras County did Mark Twain write about?	[1] Rin Tin Tin [2] Wiley Coyote [3] Jumping frog [4] Calico cat [5] Blue ox	ANSWER TO Q-23 **[3]** For example, the word "supersonic" can be rearranged to form the word "percussion." 61%

7 Which is part of a cell?	[1] Cytogene [2] Cyberne [3] Cyclotron [4] Cytoplasm [5] Cytology	ANSWER TO Q-6 **[1]** The noted English historian served in Parliament from 1774 to 1783. 57%
7 Delirium tremens is a condition caused by:	[1] Diabetes [2] A heart attack [3] Pregnancy [4] Alcohol withdrawal [5] Quitting smoking	ANSWER TO Q-6 **[4]** A harlequin is a masked comic player in a pantomime. 75%
7 Which popular writer's hero is a history professor named Jack Ryan?	[1] John Grisham [2] Robert B. Parker [3] Tom Clancy [4] Mary Higgins Clark [5] Dean Koontz	ANSWER TO Q-6 **[2]** His companies built the Bay Bridge in Northern California, and both the Hoover and Grand Coulee dams. 46%
7 "Will you walk into my parlour?" said the ____ to the ____.	[1] Lion - lamb [2] Fox - hen [3] Wolf - sheep [4] Cat - mouse [5] Spider - fly	ANSWER TO Q-6 **[2]** The showman ran his own lottery as a child in Connecticut, and started his circus at age 60. 81%
7 The Magdalena is a river that empties into the:	[1] Caribbean Sea [2] Black Sea [3] Mediterranean Sea [4] Caspian Sea [5] North Sea	ANSWER TO Q-6 **[3]** The title comes from Miranda's line: "O brave new world that hath such creatures in it." 35%

25 All of these films were based on plays except:	[1] Shirley Valentine [2] Salem's Lot [3] Agnes of God [4] Driving Miss Daisy [5] Crimes of the Heart	ANSWER TO Q-24 **[3]** Although silver is preferred, copper is used more often because it is less expensive. 71%
25 By heating limestone and clay, then grinding it into a fine powder, you are making a typical:	[1] Hydraulic cement [2] Asphalt [3] Blackboard chalk [4] Plaster of Paris [5] Bone china	ANSWER TO Q-24 **[4]** The Nazi Minister of Armaments was sentenced to 20 years in prison as a war criminal. 75%
25 Tycoon Rupert Murdoch founded this U.S. television network:	[1] ABC [2] CBS [3] ESPN [4] FOX [5] NBC	ANSWER TO Q-24 **[1]** From starch, maltose is converted into glucose and then fermented to make ethanol. 72%
25 The star of the movie "Doc Hollywood" was:	[1] Woody Allen [2] Michael Caine [3] Michael J. Fox [4] Dudley Moore [5] Steve Martin	ANSWER TO Q-24 **[2]** John Kennedy and Richard Nixon squared off in what proved to be a big part of JFK's election. 79%
25 He won a Pulitzer Prize for his novel "Humboldt's Gift":	[1] Saul Bellow [2] John Updike [3] Philip Roth [4] John Barth [5] Thomas Pynchon	ANSWER TO Q-24 **[3]** The story started a craze of jumping frog contests that continue to this day. 75%

6 Who wrote "The History of the Decline and Fall of the Roman Empire"?	[1] Edward Gibbon [2] Thomas Carlyle [3] H.G. Wells [4] Thomas Macaulay [5] Arnold Toynbee	ANSWER TO Q-5 [4] Discovered by George Vancouver, it was named in honor of a son of King George III. 67%
6 Which word does not refer to a person who sings?	[1] Diva [2] Minstrel [3] Prima donna [4] Harlequin [5] Troubadour	ANSWER TO Q-5 [1] An ell is equal to 45 inches or 1/32nd of a bolt. 71%
6 American business mogul Henry J. Kaiser amassed his wealth in this industry:	[1] Oil [2] Construction [3] Auto manufacturing [4] Publishing [5] Filmmaking	ANSWER TO Q-5 [2] Cab Calloway made his mark at Harlem's famous Cotton Club during the 1930's. 69%
6 Who is famous for saying "There's a sucker born every minute"?	[1] Bob Hope [2] P.T. Barnum [3] Groucho Marx [4] J.P. Morgan [5] W.C. Fields	ANSWER TO Q-5 [4] The mineral, which is also used as a pigment, is mined in California, Italy and Spain. 54%
6 Which novel takes its title from Shakespeare's play "The Tempest"?	[1] Wuthering Heights [2] Paradise Lost [3] Brave New World [4] The Once and Future King [5] Canterbury Tales	ANSWER TO Q-5 [1] The after-dinner drink is a concoction of brandy, creme de cacao and cream. 54%

26 This is an instrument used for measuring the altitude of a celestial body:

[1] Lithograph
[2] Stroboscope
[3] Anemometer
[4] Sextant
[5] Heliotrope

ANSWER TO Q-25
[2] "Salem's Lot" was based on a novel by Stephen King.
71%

---

26 Which vegetable plant is a perennial?

[1] Asparagus
[2] Radish
[3] Carrot
[4] Green pea
[5] Bell pepper

ANSWER TO Q-25
[1] Some forms of cement add gypsum during the grinding process.
57%

---

26 Who is the swash-buckling hero in "King Solomon's Mines"?

[1] Indiana Jones
[2] Beau Geste
[3] Dirk Beauregard
[4] Panama Red
[5] Allan Quartermain

ANSWER TO Q-25
[4] The Australian started the network by buying 20th Century Fox and six television stations.
79%

---

26 Which thing listed could be labeled prolix?

[1] Automobile
[2] Liquid
[3] Vegetable
[4] Statement
[5] Houseplant

ANSWER TO Q-25
[3] Fox plays a big city physician who is forced to tend to the ills of a small, rural town.
82%

---

26 The 33 vertebrae in the human spine are divided into all these types except:

[1] Cervical
[2] Lumbar
[3] Sacral
[4] Coccygeal
[5] Thoracic

ANSWER TO Q-25
[1] Bellow won the Nobel prize for literature a year after this novel's publication in 1975.
59%

5 Which body of water is not named after the explorer who discovered it?	[1] Hudson River [2] Frobisher's Bay [3] Lake Champlain [4] Prince William Sound [5] Strait of Magellan	ANSWER TO Q-4 **[3]** The term forte commands a loud, or forceful, volume. 58%
5 The ell and the bolt are units of length used to measure:	[1] Cloth [2] Land [3] Firewood [4] Rainfall [5] Fruit	ANSWER TO Q-4 **[3]** The coccyx, at the base of the spine, is commonly called the tail bone. 69%
5 Which jazz artist was dubbed "The Highness of Hi-De-Ho"?	[1] Charlie Byrd [2] Cab Calloway [3] Count Basie [4] Ray Charles [5] Quincy Jones	ANSWER TO Q-4 **[4]** Often called a gizzard, a bird's crop is an enlargement of the gullet for food storage. 68%
5 The red mineral cinnabar is the chief source of:	[1] Cinnamon [2] Table salt [3] Ethanol [4] Mercury [5] Clay	ANSWER TO Q-4 **[3]** Cecil Rhodes instituted the scholarship for U.S., German and British commonwealth students. 79%
5 What is the other ingredient in a Brandy Alexander?	[1] Creme de cacao [2] Vodka [3] Applejack [4] Kahlua [5] Gin	ANSWER TO Q-4 **[1]** The original Arabian Nights tale is a bit different from the animated Disney version! 78%

27 Which winter sport did not originate in Europe?

[1] Ski jump
[2] Ice hockey
[3] Speed skating
[4] Luge
[5] Cross-country skiing

ANSWER TO Q-26

[4] The sextant was invented by John Campbell in 1757.

69%

---

27 The Rhone, France's major river, empties into the:

[1] Adriatic Sea
[2] Bay of Biscay
[3] English Channel
[4] Mediterranean Sea
[5] North Sea

ANSWER TO Q-26

[1] Like most garden vegetables, the others are annuals.

47%

---

27 What term did Benito Mussolini use to refer to the rapport between Italy and Germany?

[1] Vortex
[2] Axis
[3] Reich
[4] Ankh
[5] Matrix

ANSWER TO Q-26

[5] H. Rider Haggard's African adventure novel has been filmed five different times.

59%

---

27 Who sang "I'm So Glad We Had This Time Together" at the end of every show?

[1] Mickey Mouse Club
[2] Donny and Marie Osmond
[3] Mr. Rogers
[4] Carol Burnett
[5] Ed Sullivan

ANSWER TO Q-26

[4] Prolix means wordy and verbose.

24%

---

27 Your gustatory organs are better known as your:

[1] Kidneys
[2] Adrenal glands
[3] Arteries and veins
[4] Erogenous zones
[5] Taste buds

ANSWER TO Q-26

[5] There are 7 cervical, 5 lumbar, 12 dorsal, 5 sacral and 4 coccygeal vertebrae in your back.

36%

4 These music terms are all defined correctly except for:	[1] Lento - slowly [2] Allegro - briskly [3] Forte - softly [4] Tutti - all together [5] Legato - evenly	ANSWER TO Q-3 **[5]** Starting from the top: kingdom, phylum, class, order, family, genus, species. 68%
4 Which of these body parts is not located above the neck?	[1] Stapes [2] Eustachian tubes [3] Coccyx [4] Aqueous humor [5] Gingiva	ANSWER TO Q-3 **[1]** A form of protein, it occurs in blood plasma or serum, milk and in many plant tissues. 81%
4 Which kind of animal has a crop?	[1] Dog [2] Kangaroo [3] Cat [4] Bird [5] Salamander	ANSWER TO Q-3 **[5]** Dried grapes become raisins; dried meat becomes jerky. 79%
4 Where does a Rhodes scholar study?	[1] Rhodes University [2] Cambridge [3] Oxford [4] Harvard [5] Edinburgh	ANSWER TO Q-3 **[5]** Sabah and Sarawak are on the island of Borneo. West Malaysia is made up of the former Malaya. 54%
4 Which famous character kills a wizard to get his fortune in gems?	[1] Aladdin [2] Robin Hood [3] Puss-in-Boots [4] Paul Bunyan [5] Yankee Doodle	ANSWER TO Q-3 **[3]** According to the lyric, "There must have been some magic" in it. 75%

28 India's Gir National Forest is home to the few hundred remaining:	[1] Komodo dragons [2] Black rhinos [3] Asiatic lions [4] Wild mongooses [5] King cobras	ANSWER TO Q-27 **[2]** Ice hockey was first developed in Canada in 1860. 54%
28 Escarole is a broad-leafed member of the ___ family.	[1] Onion [2] Grape [3] Lettuce [4] Orchid [5] Magnolia	ANSWER TO Q-27 **[4]** It divides into the Grand and the Petite Rhone, which enter the sea near Marseilles. 54%
28 According to scientists, an eon is one ___ years long.	[1] Thousand [2] Million [3] Billion [4] Trillion [5] Hundred thousand	ANSWER TO Q-27 **[2]** The Axis Powers later came to include Japan. 46%
28 What is a bombax?	[1] Monkey [2] Snake [3] Tree [4] Cactus [5] Lily	ANSWER TO Q-27 **[4]** They were lyrics from the theme song "It's Time to Say Goodbye." 82%
28 Maidenhair, staghorn and bird's nest are all types of:	[1] Mosses [2] Palms [3] Ferns [4] Geraniums [5] Cacti	ANSWER TO Q-27 **[5]** These numerous sensory nerve endings are located on the tongue and roof of the mouth. 69%

3 Animals are classified in seven ranks, starting with kingdom. What comes next?	[1] Genus [2] Family [3] Species [4] Order [5] Phylum	ANSWER TO Q-2 **[3]** He stars as a scientist who's able to appear in people's nightmares. 59%
3 Albumin is a substance you can find in:	[1] Egg whites [2] Aspirin [3] Blackboard chalk [4] Formica [5] Ale	ANSWER TO Q-2 **[3]** Septicemia is the medical term for blood poisoning. 59%
3 Prunes are really just dried-out:	[1] Grapes [2] Meat [3] Figs [4] Potatoes [5] Plums	ANSWER TO Q-2 **[5]** Mungo Park explored Africa, not the South or North Pole. 46%
3 Since 1966, Sabah and Sarawak are known as:	[1] Sri Lanka [2] Myanmar [3] Kampuchea [4] Bangladesh [5] East Malaysia	ANSWER TO Q-2 **[1]** This 1968 film starred John Wayne as a gung-ho platoon commander. 69%
3 What gave life to that Christmas cartoon hero, Frosty the Snowman?	[1] A carrot nose [2] Coal eyes [3] An old silk hat [4] Snowstorm [5] Frostia the Snowwoman	ANSWER TO Q-2 **[3]** Hemingway's book about the Spanish Civil War was published in 1943. 69%

29 The expensive natural spice saffron is produced from:	[1] Crocus stigma [2] Evergreen buds [3] Nutmeg shells [4] Lily leaves [5] Tree bark	ANSWER TO Q-28 **[3]** Like their African counterparts, they prefer open areas to the jungles. 42%
29 Which famous song was written by jazz pianist Erroll Garner?	[1] As Time Goes By [2] Misty [3] Ain't Misbehavin' [4] Body And Soul [5] Skylark	ANSWER TO Q-28 **[3]** Escarole and endive are more bitter than other members of that family of plants. 72%
29 Which vaccine was developed by Louis Pasteur?	[1] Polio [2] Smallpox [3] Diphtheria [4] Scarlet fever [5] Rabies	ANSWER TO Q-28 **[3]** Astronomers estimate the age of the universe at 14, give or take 3 eons. 58%
29 What does "vodka" mean in Russian?	[1] Bright star [2] Warm wind [3] Little water [4] Peaceful sleep [5] Quiet woman	ANSWER TO Q-28 **[3]** The thick-trunked deciduous trees are a source of balsa and corkwood. 41%
29 South Africa's Afri-kaners are of Dutch or ____ descent.	[1] Spanish Basque [2] Swiss-German [3] Baltic [4] French Huguenot [5] Austro-Hungarian	ANSWER TO Q-28 **[3]** Ferns are widely distributed around the world, but the majority grow in the tropics. 57%

2 Which "Dream" film starred Dennis Quaid?

[1] The Dream Team
[2] Dreamchild
[3] Dreamscape
[4] Dreamstreet
[5] Dream a Little Dream

ANSWER TO Q-1

[5] Clams breathe through gills; they stay in the current so that water can flow through them.
56%

---

2 All of these are diseases of the lungs except:

[1] Pleurisy
[2] Emphysema
[3] Septicemia
[4] Tuberculosis
[5] Silicosis

ANSWER TO Q-1

[1] Sir Hans Krebs, English biochemist, received a Nobel Prize for his work in 1953.
34%

---

2 All these explorers made polar expeditions except:

[1] Robert Peary
[2] Willem Barents
[3] Robert F. Scott
[4] Roald Amundsen
[5] Mungo Park

ANSWER TO Q-1

[2] The agave is known for its fleshy leaves from which we get alcoholic drinks like tequila.
57%

---

2 Which is the only film about Vietnam to be released during the war?

[1] The Green Berets
[2] Coming Home
[3] Go Tell the Spartans
[4] The Deer Hunter
[5] Apocalypse Now

ANSWER TO Q-1

[1] Early thread was made by pulling fibers from a ball on a stick, the distaff, by women.
42%

---

2 Which American classic was published in the 20th century?

[1] Leaves of Grass
[2] Huckleberry Finn
[3] For Whom the Bell Tolls
[4] Moby Dick
[5] The Scarlet Letter

ANSWER TO Q-1

[2] English versions of classic Italian comic characters, they are a quarrelsome couple.
69%

30 Vladimir and Estragon, two tramps, are the central characters in what classic modern play?	[1] Of Mice and Men [2] Waiting for Godot [3] No Exit [4] Awake and Sing [5] The Lower Depths	ANSWER TO Q-29 **[1]** Saffron is the most expensive spice in the world, used for color and a mild flavor. 58%
30 What is the ECU?	[1] Economic cartel union [2] European currency unit [3] Excess capital unit [4] Equilibrium market [5] Exchange rate	ANSWER TO Q-29 **[2]** One of jazz's great romantics, he is noted for developing an "orchestral" style. 32%
30 "Beyond Good and Evil" & "Thus Spake Zarathustra" are writings of which philosopher?	[1] Hegel [2] Nietzsche [3] Schopenhauer [4] Wagner [5] Descartes	ANSWER TO Q-29 **[5]** He created the vaccine for rabies in 1885 and later developed one for cholera. 58%
30 Which is a piece of woolen cloth?	[1] Skimmer [2] Brogan [3] Chemise [4] Mackinaw [5] Frieze	ANSWER TO Q-29 **[3]** Vodka originated during the 14th century and the name is a diminutive of "voda" (water). 45%
30 Which comedy film does not center around amateur bank robbers?	[1] Quick Change [2] Dog Day Afternoon [3] Three Fugitives [4] The Dream Team [5] Going in Style	ANSWER TO Q-29 **[4]** Huguenots are French Protestants. Together with the Dutch, they constituted the Boers. 51%

1 What do humans have that a clam doesn't?	[1] Mouth [2] Foot [3] Heart [4] Anus [5] Lungs	Turn to the top frame on the next left hand page for the correct answer and the next question.
1 The Krebs cycle, the major source of energy in living organisms, is also called the:	[1] Citric acid cycle [2] Carbohydrate cycle [3] Sugar cycle [4] Glucose cycle [5] Amino cycle	Turn to the second frame on the next left hand page for the correct answer and the next question.
1 All of these plants are primarily known for the properties of their roots except:	[1] Ginseng [2] Agave [3] Ginger [4] Mandrake [5] Cassava	Turn to the middle frame on the next left hand page for the correct answer and the next question.
1 The distaff side of something is the _____ side.	[1] Woman's [2] Seamy [3] Bright [4] Hidden [5] Uncooked	Turn to the fourth frame on the next left hand page for the correct answer and the next question.
1 Who are Punch and Judy?	[1] Fairy tale characters [2] Traditional puppets [3] Talk show hosts [4] Cartoon characters [5] Comedy team	Turn to the bottom frame on the next left hand page for the correct answer and the next question.

ANSWER TO Q-30

[2] The author, Samuel Beckett, was the last of the great modernists.

65%

GAME NUMBER 28   BEGINS ON PAGE 422

ANSWER TO Q-30

[2] Rather than legal tender, an ECU is a unit used as a reserve asset.

69%

GAME NUMBER 46   BEGINS ON PAGE 422

ANSWER TO Q-30

[2] The Nazis used Nietzsche's writings to support doctrines of racial superiority.

58%

GAME NUMBER 64   BEGINS ON PAGE 422

ANSWER TO Q-30

[5] The heavy cloth has a shaggy, uncut nap on one end.

53%

GAME NUMBER 82   BEGINS ON PAGE 422

ANSWER TO Q-30

[4] "The Dream Team" features four patients from a mental hospital who get lost in New York City.

82%

If you have a computer and modem, you can play NTN Trivia 24 hours per day, seven days per week. We're proud to introduce you to our online partners America Online, GEnie and the ImagiNation Network. Compete along with the hospitality network while playing at home. There's even a live chat feature that allows you to talk with other players in real time! Meet some great people and have a blast. Call for info.

The nation's fastest-growing provider of online services. Phone number is: 1–800–827–6364.

Thee most fun you can have with your computer on! Call 1–800–638–9636 for a free trial membership.

IMAGI**NATION!**™

Join the ImagiNation Network by calling 1–800–IMAGIN1 for a free start-up kit and 5 free hours. We're changing the way the world makes friends!

**Call 1–800–755–5459
to find the NTN locations nearest you.**